PUDDINGS AND PASTRY

Foolish Pie (Sad C...

... sugar + 1/3 teaspoo...
... egg white. Beat...
... sugar - beat T st...
... well buttered...
... over. Cool in...
... berries an...
... 2 eggs, small...

... doughnuts
cake yeast
cups ...

... love and all good wishes
for Christmas & New Year
from Rosamond.

...pricot Cream
...apricots   gill cream   small tin unsweet...
                            condensed milk
...z. gelatine powdered. 2 tablespoon water
apricots through sieve. Whip cond: milk &
cream & stir into fruit. Dissolve gel: in
water over gentle heat + stir in well. Put
in mould to set.

apple delight.
4 baking apple   + op sugar. lemon rind
2 egg whites   3 tablespoons water.
...core, slice + stew apples sugar & rind
...emove rind + beat till smooth.
... little apple gelatine

...s pale raisi...
1 cup cream   ...
1 cup walnuts   1 teasp...
Boil all quickly 3/4 of an...

apple fritters
...but apple into thick rings - scoop out c...
...p dip in batter + fry.

Amber Cream
3 eggs   1/4 gill cold water
1/2 z. instantaneous gelatine 2 z. castor sugar
1/2 lemon   1 1/2 gills orange j. 1 gill milk
measure milk + sugar : sep: eggs & beat &
add yolks. stir till thick (double saucepan good)
Dissolve gel: in the water. Stir in and the
orange + lemon juice - Beat whites to froth.
fold in + pour in glass dish & serve.

THE CHAFING-DISH

Nov 7 1925

Fudge (Howard)

— 3/4 cup milk
walnut
...ous cocoa.

...store before

Date Bars

3 eggs unbeaten
1 c. nutmeats
1 c. dates
2 th. shortening
1 c. sugar
1 ta. bak. pwd.
1/4 ta. salt
5 th. flour

Break eggs c fork & ...
sugar. Add melted shortening
in dates & nuts. Add flour
c bak. pwd & salt. Bake in
mod. oven 20-30 mins. Remo...
from tin & when cool cut in
1" wide by 2" long. Roll lightly
in powdered sugar.

To Ice the Cake

...Sift double refined Sugar, then beat Whites of
...fresh, some Sugar & Eggs in a stone Mortar
...without... till it is extream white, perfume it
...get Flower water about ap... of Sugar will
...take cake out of the Oven, take it out of the
...it all over with the Icing & sett in
...Stick Coarse Gold Candy Sweetmeats
...the Fancy on the Top.

Seed Cake

...of fine Flower well dry'd, put in
...with a pound & 1/2 of butter
...then put this till it warm
...half a pint of good Ale
...cast as your oven is hot
...their hoop, when mixed
...3/4 of a pound of
...very quick, an hour
Miss

Almond Cake ✓

28 DeKa 83

8 oz. sugar beat until light w...
6 yolks add 8 oz. ground almond
a little cloves (point of knife)
1/2 rind of lemon. Add the
stiff beaten whites of 6 eggs &
slowly in Spring form w...
cold cut in half & spread...
apricot or other jelly & c...
with chocolate icing

Icing

2 pans German sweet choco...
5 oz. sugar add half glass
let boil until shiny & hot
...in oven, watch...
When cake has...
increase heat...

...fold i...
thre...
big...
sli...
...
in

...Put in...
do not grease pan...
stick firmly. Stir...
if it takes good bro...
If cake does not...
it will fall out wh...
in the fall. Put cake...
not hot enough for...
butter cake; you have to...
If you see cake browni...
Top of pan, open oven...
Do not be afraid - th...
hurt the cake, 2 min. will...
cake closely, don't be a...
door every 3 or 4 min....
raised above top of pan...
finish baking rapidly. Will bak...
Baking too long makes cake tou...
to shrink. Let it stay...
carefully...

There was a...
...king X1X, 6.

Butter
...ar
...n (Prepared)

Juc...
...Jeremiah i...
King IV...
I Samuel...
Genesis...
I Samuel XXX, 12
Genesis XXVIII, II
Isaiah XXIV...
Leviticus X...
King
...to advise

eggs
...salt
...flour

HEIRLOOM BAKING

WITH THE

BRASS SISTERS

HEIRLOOM BAKING

with the

BRASS SISTERS

More than 100 Years of Recipes Discovered
from Family Cookbooks,
Original Journals, Scraps of Paper,
and Grandmother's Kitchen

MARILYNN BRASS & SHEILA BRASS

Photographs by **ANDY RYAN**

BLACK DOG
& LEVENTHAL
PUBLISHERS
NEW YORK

To our mother, Dorothy Katziff Brass,
and our aunt, Ida Tucker Katziff, with love

Copyright © 2006 Marilynn Brass and Sheila Brass
Photographs copyright © 2006 Andy Ryan

Published by
Black Dog & Leventhal Publishers
151 W. 19th Street
New York, NY 10011

Distributed by
Workman Publishing Company
708 Broadway
New York, NY 10003

Manufactured in China

Cover and interior design by Susi Oberhelman
Photographs by Andy Ryan
Food styling by Marilynn Brass and Sheila Brass

ISBN-10: 1-57912-588-3
ISBN-13: 978-1-57912-588-2

Library of Congress Cataloging-in-Publication Data is on file at Black Dog & Leventhal Publishers, Inc.

Contributors to Heirloom Baking

Patti Angelina, Mrs. Charles Barker, Bertha Bohlman, Dorothy Katziff Brass, Harry Brass, Mary Brinkman, Cynthia Broner, Reverend Brown, Charlotte Casuto, Mrs. Chubb, Libby Cockrey, Donna, Mrs. William Eaton, Lannie Edmondson, Evalyn, Mrs. Fleisher, Marion Freeman, Mrs. Hall, Helen, Mattie James, Elinor Inman Jennings, Mrs. Justo, Ida Tucker Katziff, Mrs. Paul Knight, Greta Leonard, Virginia P. Lima, Melania Marasi, Marta, Winnie McCarthy, Mrs. Moore, Mary Moretti, Nell, Liz O'Neill, Mrs. Orcott, Lotty Peck, Penny's Cousin Pearl, Esther Pullman, Elva Ross, Bessie Rothblott, Miss Emma Smith, James "Tulsa" Stuart, Ellen Sullivan, Mrs. Tate, The Church Lady, The Radio Lady, Mary Williams, Mrs. Carl Winchenbach, Louise Zimmerman

FABRIC CREDITS: pages 26-27: Joan Kessler for Concord Fabrics Inc. © Crafted with Pride in U.S.A.; 52-53: Amy Butler for Free Spirit; 76-77: Simply Irresistible by Robyn Pandolph © SSI®; 124-125: © Cranston Print Works; 148-149: The Blended Collection IV by Sharon Yenter for "In the Beginning" Fabrics © 2005; 170-171: Patterns of History, A Kansas City Star Collection, Alice's Leafy Bower 1930-1940; 194-195: © Aunt Grace Scrap Bag 2004, from the collection of Judie Rothermet for Marcus Brothers Textiles, Inc.; 262-263: V.I.P® by Cranston® © Cranston Print Works

CONTENTS

CHAPTER 10

BAKING WITH MAMA   242

CHAPTER 11

FOR THE LOVE
OF CHOCOLATE   262

PREFACE

We are two roundish bespectacled women in our sixties who have a combined total of 110 years' home-baking experience. Sheila was 11 years old when she baked her first cake in the kitchen where we grew up, in Winthrop, Massachusetts. Marilynn's first baking attempt was a pineapple coconut cake, although she does have memories of replicating the filled cookies and Welsh rarebit she learned how to make in her seventh-grade cooking class.

Both of us have always felt comfortable in the kitchen. We learned the basics of baking from our mother, who was a talented home cook and baker. When we could barely reach the kitchen table, we were already turning scraps of dough into miniature braided challah loaves and turnovers, lovingly brushed with an egg glaze to make them shiny.

We remember the smell of sour cream coffee cakes and yeast breads baking in the cast iron and enamel stove in our kitchen. We still cherish the good times we had with our mother when she patiently instructed us, transferring her love of family and the art of baking to her two young daughters. The time she invested in us has made us who we are. We love being in the kitchen; it is there that we feel the most happy and creative and adventuresome.

Some of our fondest memories are of summer Fridays spent with Mama, baking, learning, and

Sheila and Marilynn, Winthrop Beach, 1944, and today

Handwritten recipe for Maple Syrup Cookies, 1930s, and Peach Bavarian, 1920s

nibbling our creations. Music and food went together in our family. With the cooking underway and the aroma of chicken soup and parsnips wafting through the house, Mama often "took a break" by sitting down at the piano to play our favorite songs. Almost sixty years later, we still remember what it was like to lie on the oilcloth-covered glider on the back porch, reading and eating an egg salad sandwich, watching our mother through the window as she put together one of her blueberry pies or frosted her chocolate velvet cake.

In time, we began to collect cooking magazines and cookbooks of our own. First, it was *Gourmet*, the whole run, lovingly gathered. Later, it was the Foods of the World series published by Time-Life. In the late 1960s, both of us collected all twelve volumes of the *Woman's Day Encyclopedia of Cooking*.

More than thirty years ago we discovered manuscript cookbooks—collections of personal recipes compiled by home cooks. Handwritten notes on crumbling scraps of paper or the pages of old, well-worn cookbooks led us to "lost" family recipes. Recipe collections that survived were typically gathered together in small bundles, stitched, tied, stapled, or boxed, and handed down to the next generation. These forgotten bundles of culinary history turn up at yard sales and flea markets, in used bookstores, and on the pantry shelves of friends.

Over the years, we have acquired more than eighty-five such collections of living recipes. From them, we selected 150 recipes of interest, researched them, and tested them in our own kitchens. Compiling and writing *Heirloom Baking with the Brass Sisters* has been a labor of love. We are dedicated to recovering, updating, and—above all—

enjoying the best home baking from America's past. By presenting old recipes simply and with contemporary flair, we are able to help a new generation of cooks (and their families) discover and enjoy the special tastes of the culturally diverse American kitchen. And where better to start than with everyone's favorite part of a meal—the dessert!

You may recognize some of these recipes as similar to ones prepared by your own mothers, grandmothers, and aunts. Women all over the United States and Canada shared many of them. Several of the recipes reflect African-American, Hispanic, Armenian, Italian, Asian, Hungarian, and Austrian traditions. You will notice a strong representation of English, Scottish, and Irish recipes because many of the manuscript cookbooks we've baked from were written by women from New England.

We don't know when we became known as the Brass sisters. Maybe, as we grew older, it became more evident that we look very much alike. It is unusual for a day to go by without someone using the "T" word. Although we are not twins, we do share a similarity of tastes, both culinary and personal. We both love holidays, decorating our apartments with culinary antiques, reading mysteries, and planning parties. Some of our happiest times are spent shopping for food. Marilynn has been known to get excited over a beautiful bunch of radishes, while Sheila is dedicated to discovering the best new bakeries.

You may have passed us in an aisle at the supermarket or at the weekend farmer's market. We are often recognized by our signature denim skirts, clogs, and t-shirts advertising local bakeries or dairies. We shop where you do, and we buy the same products you do. There are no exotic, hard-to-find ingredients in *Heirloom Baking with the Brass Sisters*. We also present the instructions for the recipes in our own language, for this is, after all, a book by home cooks for home cooks.

As we share some of what we've learned, the little tricks of the home kitchen, we also want to reassure you that a cheesecake with a few cracks on the top is not a catastrophe. Cutting and serving the first slice from your homemade pie doesn't signify success or failure. A cake that has a bit of slant can be rescued. Think of us as two new friends sharing the adventure of baking recipes that have lain on shelves gathering dust too long.

We do confess that working on this book brought back some very pleasurable family memories. We couldn't resist putting something of ourselves into these pages of living recipes. We hope *Heirloom Baking with the Brass Sisters* will encourage you to explore and celebrate the culinary legacy of your family and friends. We urge you to bake in your own kitchens and come up with your own variations. Be sure to write down your prized recipes to hand along to others so that they will never be lost!

MARILYNN BRASS AND SHEILA BRASS
Cambridge, Massachusetts, 2006

How to Use This Book

We hope you will enjoy using this book. We have tried to make the recipes easy to understand and the ingredients easy to find. We'd like you to be so inspired by the recipes that you go into your own kitchen and start baking. Nearly all of the ingredients for the recipes in *Heirloom Baking* are those found in most family pantries. You probably won't have to make a stop at your local gourmet shop to stock up on special spices, flours, or extracts. If you do find that some ingredients prove to be elusive, we have included a short list of mail-order suppliers (see Sources on page 284).

Ingredients

BRANDY AND WHISKEY

We bought small amounts of good-quality brandy and whiskey for our recipe testing. We like to use brandy and whiskey to flavor recipes, plump raisins, and season fruitcakes and fruited tea breads.

BUTTER

For the recipes in this book, we used unsalted, or sweet, butter, softened at room temperature. Some recipes call for butter that is refrigerator-firm or melted before it is combined with other ingredients. We used generic store brand butters and found them to perform as well as commercial brands. Do not use salted butter; its moisture content can affect the baking results.

CHOCOLATE AND COCOA

Chocolate was often a luxury ingredient in the kitchens of the women whose recipes we tested. Occasionally, we introduced a gourmet chocolate when testing a recipe and noted a subtle enhancement of flavor, but we also found that using familiar commercial brands of chocolate and cocoa such as Hershey's, Baker's, and Nestlé produced good results. We discovered that by judiciously adding small amounts of bitter chocolate to semisweet chocolate, we could achieve the complexity of flavor we were seeking. We were vigilant about using the correct cocoa, either American-style or Dutch, depending on the rising agents used in the recipe. Store chocolate and cocoa in a cool dry dark place.

Some Suggestions

BEFORE YOU BEGIN:

- Read each recipe several times. Make sure you understand the directions and know what ingredients are needed.
- Adjust the oven racks before turning on the oven.
- Have all ingredients at room temperature, unless otherwise stated.
- Prepare the baking pans and set out racks for cooling.
- Assemble your ingredients and utensils.

BAKER'S TIPS:

- Combine ingredients in the order they are listed.
- After the recipe is in the oven, set a timer.
- Allow baked cakes, pies, and cookies to cool completely, unless otherwise noted.
- Store baked items in appropriate containers or refrigerate.

COFFEE AND TEA

We used instant coffee or espresso powder, decaffeinated or regular, when making coffee or mocha desserts. We used orange pekoe tea to make Cold Tea Gingerbread (page 198) and for plumping raisins.

DAIRY PRODUCTS

The recipes in this book use homogenized milk, not skim milk, and cultured low-fat buttermilk. We used whole-fat ricotta. We do not use reduced-fat cream cheese, farmer cheese, or sour cream. For cream, we used heavy cream or whipping cream, not half-and-half. We used canned sweetened condensed milk and canned evaporated milk.

EGGS

For consistency, we used only U.S. graded large eggs. Unless otherwise noted, the eggs should be at room temperature. Some recipes call for beating the eggs before adding them to the other ingredients. Egg whites should be at room temperature before being beaten. Sometimes, eggs are mixed with part of the other ingredients to temper them so they won't be "cooked" by the temperature of the hot ingredients.

EXTRACTS AND PURE FLAVORED OILS

Vanilla is the most popular flavoring in the recipes we tested. Also popular are lemon and almond extracts. Use only pure extracts. Pure citrus oils, when substituted for extracts, resulted in some very true flavors, and we provide a source for ordering them (see Sources on page 284).

FLOUR AND GRAINS

Use all-purpose bleached flour unless the recipe calls for a specific type, such as cake flour or pastry flour. Some recipes require graham flour or bran, and one recipe, Dixie Dinner Rolls (page 91) uses self-rising flour. We also use both yellow and white cornmeal and matzo cake meal. If you don't have a local supplier for specialty flours, you can order these items by mail (see Sources on page 284). We tested several recipes with well-known commercial brands of flour, but we found that using store brands produced the same results.

Measure flour by scooping a cup of flour and leveling it with a knife. If a recipe calls for "1 cup sifted flour," sift the flour and then measure it. If a recipe calls for "1 cup flour, sifted," measure the flour first and then sift it.

Miniature canister set, 1920s

Fruit, Fresh and Dried

We used the fruit called for in the original recipe whenever possible. Most of the manuscript cookbooks call for raisins, currants, cherries, and candied peels such as orange, lemon, or citron. When we did make substitutions, such as dried for fresh or fresh for dried, we noted it. We use fresh fruit only when it is in season and buy dried fruit in small quantities. Often, we found that plumping dried fruit in orange juice, tea, or brandy before baking added another level of flavor.

Lard

We purchased commercial brand lard for use in recipes that call for lard as all or part of the shortening. Old pastry recipes often call for a combination of lard and butter. We found that some cookies and pie crusts were particularly flaky and tender when made from lard or a combination of lard and butter. We also found that using lard gave baked goods an old-world flavor and texture.

Lemon and Orange Juice and Zest

We use medium-sized lemons and oranges with firm, unblemished skins. Use a Microplane® or a traditional grater to remove the zest or yellow part of the rind, leaving behind the bitter white pith. We roll the fruit on a flat surface to break up the juice pockets first. Then cut the fruit in half and juice it on a reamer; strain the juice to remove any seeds. A lemon weighing 4½ ounces yields approximately 2 teaspoons grated zest and 3 tablespoons lemon juice. An orange weighing 6¼ ounces yields approximately 2 tablespoons grated zest and 4 tablespoons orange juice.

Nuts

Our choice of nuts depended on the original recipe. Walnuts, pecans, peanuts, and almonds were typical in the larders and pantries of the women whose recipes we tested. We introduced hazelnuts, pistachios, pine nuts, and pepitas, but only where we felt they would not greatly affect the original results of the recipe. Buy nuts in small quantities and store them in sealed plastic bags or covered plastic containers in the freezer to preserve their freshness.

Spices

Cinnamon is the most popular spice in our recipes, followed by nutmeg, ginger, cloves, and allspice. For the women who wrote these living recipes, spices were not easily accessible and were often expensive. Some women were creative and mixed small amounts of spices, such as cloves with lemon, to achieve another level of flavor. Buy spices in small quantities and store them in a cool dark place.

Sugar

Use white granulated sugar unless a recipe calls for a specific type, such as light brown sugar, confectioners' sugar, or sanding sugar. We generally do not use dark brown sugar because we think the flavor is too assertive for most of the recipes, but you may prefer it. If you use dark brown sugar, use the same amount. We tried store-brand and commercial-brand sugars and found that both provided successful results. Sweeteners with additional flavors include maple syrup, molasses, honey, and dark corn syrup. Store confectioners' sugar in a sealed plastic bag so that it is easier to measure. Sift it after measuring to remove any lumps.

Vegetable Oil

We use a pure vegetable oil such as peanut oil or corn oil for baking and deep-frying. Always use fresh oil when deep-frying.

Vegetable Shortening

We use solid vegetable shortening for some of the recipes. Buy it in small containers to ensure freshness and store it according to the manufacturer's instructions. Whenever we had a choice with a recipe, we used butter.

Yeast

We used active dry yeast in recipes that called for a raised dough. We used quick-rising yeast only when we found that the recipe benefited from its use. We did not use cake yeast. We proofed our yeast in water that had been warmed to 110°F.

Utensils, Stoves, and Appliances

Baking Pans

Each recipe notes the size, weight, and material of bakeware to use. Standard sizes are the norm. For pies, we use 9-inch ovenproof glass pie pans without handles or ruffles. The baking temperatures in the recipes are the ones we used for testing. Manufacturers of glass baking products often suggest a lower temperature when using their products. We suggest that you follow the instructions that come with any product you use. If you need to buy bakeware, we suggest that you explore all the options, buy brand names, and keep instructions on how to use them in a file folder in a handy place.

BAKING PANS WE FIND USEFUL

9-inch by 13-inch by 1-inch jelly roll
    or half-sheet pan

14-inch by 16-inch metal baking sheets

8-cup Bundt pan

10-cup Bundt pan

9-inch tart pan

8-inch metal springform pan

9-inch metal springform pan

10-inch metal springform pan

7-inch metal round cake pan (x 2)

8-inch metal round cake pan (x 2)

9-inch metal round cake pan (x 2)

8-inch by 8-inch by 2-inch pans for
    bar cookies and brownies

9-inch by 5-inch by 3-inch metal loaf pan

9-inch by 13-inch by 2-inch metal or glass pan

9-inch by 9-inch by 2-inch metal pan

9-inch ovenproof glass pie plate (x 2)

Metal pudding molds

10-inch angel food cake or tube pan

8-cup tube pan

1½-quart ovenproof glass or ceramic
    baking dish

Large metal pan for water bath

8-inch frying pan

Heavy-bottomed frying pan

Heavy-bottomed saucepan

Ovenproof custard cups

Copper iced pudding molds, English, 1860 –1910

MIXERS AND FOOD PROCESSORS

We used a KitchenAid® standing mixer for most of the recipes because one of our goals was to save home bakers as much time as possible. A handheld mixer will work for many of the recipes, as will a wooden spoon or whisk, but will take more time and effort. The texture and result may also vary. We are careful to note recipes that benefit from gentle hand mixing. We used a 7-cup Cuisinart® food processor usually fitted with the metal blade. Using a food processor for mixing pastry or cookie dough or grating carrots and oranges saves time and provides a uniform result.

STOVES AND OVENS

We used a gas stove and oven to test the recipes. Since every appliance is different, we suggest that you honor the idiosyncrasies of your own stove and oven. Use an oven thermometer and turn baking sheets with cookies halfway through the baking time. We usually bake one sheet of cookies at a time, but if you do multiples, switch the baking sheets from rack to rack and turn them front to back halfway through baking, especially if your oven doesn't bake evenly. A microwave oven is also helpful to melt butter and chocolate; be sure to use the lowest setting.

Miniature scale and weights, 1900; miniature brass kettle, 1910; miniature tin kitchen implements, 1890s

BAKING AIDS WE CAN'T LIVE WITHOUT

Standing mixer with paddle, whisk, and dough-hook attachments

Food processor with metal blade and grating blade

Microplanes (to grate zest)

Offset spatulas (to smooth batters and frost cakes and cookies)

Oven thermometer

Candy thermometer to test sugar syrup and oil

Instant-read thermometer to test water temperature

Scale (for weighing ingredients)

Disposable gloves

Disposable piping bags

Strainers (for sifting, removing seeds from juice, and dusting with confectioners' sugar)

Cooling racks in a variety of sizes

Parchment paper

Wax paper

Silicone baking liners

Measuring cups for measuring dry ingredients: $\frac{1}{4}$ cup, $\frac{1}{3}$ cup, $\frac{1}{2}$ cup, 1 cup

Measuring spoons for measuring dry and liquid ingredients: $\frac{1}{8}$ teaspoon, $\frac{1}{4}$ teaspoon, $\frac{1}{2}$ teaspoon, 1 teaspoon, 1 tablespoon

Measuring cups for measuring liquid ingredients: 1 cup, 2 cups

Set of flower-shaped tin tart forms, 1890-1910; copper and tin jelly molds, 1890-1920

The Essence of Heirloom Baking

Heirloom baking is one of the most important connections to our past; it nourishes us and it is a great part of our culinary heritage. Inheriting heirloom recipes is what we enjoy most—next to eating what we bake! It is the excitement of the search and the thrill of discovering these treasures. It is the talking about, the chewing over, the digesting of an old recipe, whether it is passed down to us in oral or written form. It is the art of interpreting the recipe, baking it, how it looks, tastes and smells, preparing it, and finally serving it that gives us such joy.

Food has always been important whenever women gather in community, whether it is a *kaffe klatch*, a housewarming, a family celebration or simply the familiar ritual of friends coming together to share a cup of tea and something sweet. These are the times confidences are exchanged, advice about marriage and children is volunteered, and personal recipes are passed on to relatives and to friends. These occasions when women come together are often when recipes become *living recipes*, to be preserved and treasured for the next generation.

Our own experience of baking and talking about desserts is probably as representative as any other American woman's experience in this diversity of cultures we all share. Food has always been a major part of our lives. Our family, like so many others, had good cooks and bad cooks, all women, and every one of them with her own collection of recipes—many of them written on the backs of envelopes, on paper bags, or in little notebooks. The more ambitious cooks developed an orderly method of filing their jottings in small wooden boxes. We refer to these collections as "manuscript cookbooks."

These manuscript cookbooks hold so many families' stories. Together, they are our American biography. Not all of the recipes from our own family came down to us in tangible form. Many were told like stories by three generations of women. Only by talking about their strudels, yeast breads, and cakes could we begin to understand how important our conservation of these recipes in their own words would be.

These collections tell us so much about the women who compiled them. We learn about the foods they loved, their skills at making a little go a long way, their love of beautiful presentation, and how they nourished their families during hard times. We begin to understand how they communicated with other women by baking and handing down their favorite treats. We know that these women passed on recipes at church socials, antique shows, and at the women's bureau, because their recipes were scrawled on the backs of church donation cards, antique fliers, and scraps of stationery.

Cookbooks and cooking pamphlets, American and English, 1900-1940

Sometimes there are fragile pieces of yellowed newsprint, most of them from reader's exchange columns, containing recipes or household hints, tucked into these collections of handwritten recipes. These, too, are an important contribution to heirloom baking because we learn which recipes appealed to the women whose manuscript cookbooks we attempt to translate, and we see how they, in turn, interpreted the recipes of other women to make them all their own.

Developing a self-image was as important to a woman in the late 1800s as it is today. Since most women did not work outside the home after marriage until the mid-twentieth century, one of the ways a woman could individualize herself was by creating and personalizing a recipe that others would admire and want to duplicate. Because so many women were meticulous in crediting other women for their contributions, we've discovered that a woman could be acknowledged for her

Manuscript cookbook with handwritten recipe for Chess Pie, early 1900s

achievements hundreds and even thousands of miles from where she lived and baked (and now several years later as well!).

Sometimes a woman had to sample a recipe before she added it to her recipe collection, but often she wrote it down without baking it because she just knew it would be good. She had the ability to know what a dish would taste like just from hearing about it. A good home cook would have developed a culinary memory bank so that when a neighbor said that a recipe for Frosted Pan Hermits called for ginger, clove, and nutmeg, she could imagine what that combination of spices would taste like and how a change in ingredients or measurements would affect the actual finished product.

By the 1890s and early 1900s there was a more universal understanding that butter the size of an egg was actually two ounces, and that a gill was equal to four fluid ounces. With the publication of cookbooks, such as *The Boston Cooking School Cookbook* by Fannie Merritt Farmer, standardization of measurements and oven temperatures became a reality. But women still continued to share their recipes and did not hesitate to jot down notes in a printed cookbook using the endpapers for recipes gathered by word-of-mouth. A woman could personalize her book with handwritten notes on how to improve upon her neighbor's ginger snaps or a cousin's banana bread.

In manuscript cookbooks from the 1920s and 1930s there are often shopping lists tucked between the pages. By this time, a woman could do a daily or weekly shopping if she needed ingredients for a special recipe because of improvements in transportation and the universal availability of iceboxes and refrigeration. We also found handwritten menus tucked in between recipes. We know that a woman in Cambridge, Massachusetts expected the minister for dinner on a Saturday early in the 1900s and planned a menu including roast lamb with roast potatoes, mint jelly, peas, and blueberry pie.

We've gained an education in kitchen chemistry by baking from these handwritten recipes. We learned early on how different flour was 150 years ago—its texture and flavor often depended on the location of the mill where it was processed. Understanding a recipe from the 1950s, for example, often hinged upon finding flour similar to the brand a woman used then. Sugar was different, too, until processing and shipping led to standardization early in the twentieth century—from hard cones of loaf sugar, which had to be broken and pulverized, to the joys of confectioners' and superfine sugars today.

Handwritten recipe for Soft Honey Cake, 1970s

Oven temperatures and baking times were not given in most of these heirloom recipes because each wood- or coal-burning stove was consistent in its own special way. A woman had an intimate relationship with her stove. She cleaned it, she polished it, and she stoked it. A hot oven meant one thing to one woman; a quick oven meant something entirely different to another.

In writing *Heirloom Baking with the Brass Sisters*, we have had to ask countless questions and search through hundreds of pages of recipes, letters, and menus. To attempt to understand the implications of these women's lives, we have gone to the primary resource—what they themselves have written. We can't read a recipe for compromise cake or war cake without seeing these women as they really were—the centers of their family—and in the very truest sense, the keepers of the hearth, the bakers of the bread, the ones who kept the cookie jar filled. We have come to know the women who created these manuscript cookbooks as very real people, and members of our extended family of home cooks.

CHAPTER I

We have always had a love affair with breakfast, and it continues to intensify. When eating breakfast at a restaurant, we always find it thrilling to pick up a menu

WAKING UP TO BREAKFAST

with a cheerful "good morning" printed on the front in letters large enough to accommodate our sleep-filled eyes. When we were younger, we were particularly vulnerable to the Yankee breakfasts we enjoyed at our favorite Boston cafeteria. Shrines to choice, these chains provided sticky buns, muffins, pancakes, or waffles, eggs any way we wanted them, and oatmeal with butter and salt or brown sugar. Later we would replicate these real American breakfasts at our own family table, because it's the memory of eating at home that really appeals to us.

In this chapter, we salute the best of home breakfasts with the goal of reproducing everyone's family favorites. Looking through our collections of manuscript cookbooks, we find that the recipes for breakfast are predominantly sweet, and once again, it is the creators and the interpreters of these breakfast treats that continue to make them so interesting.

We found that a lady from New Hampshire faithfully listened to WJAR on her radio through the 1920s and 1930s. We learned that broadcasting from Providence, Rhode Island, Claire Wood dispensed her own brand of kitchen wisdom for twenty-

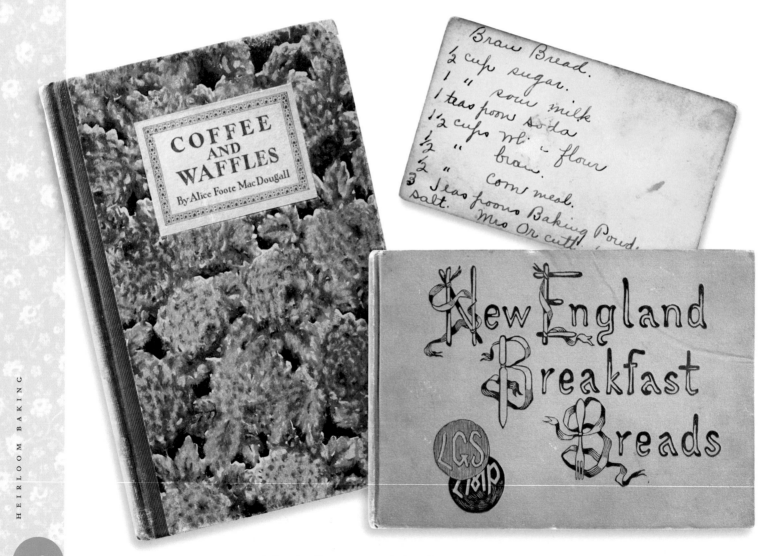

Coffee and Waffles, 1920s; New England Breakfast Breads, 1890; recipe for Bran Bread, 1918

three years, allowing housewives all over New England to jot down rules for cakes, cookies, and breakfast breads. Substituting ingredients, adjusting measurements, and catering to the idiosyncrasies of their own stoves, these listeners took Mrs. Woods' suggestions and made them into their own personal recipes, such as a cake baked with homemade applesauce and plumped golden raisins.

Cranberry-Orange Cream Scones, delicious with either fresh blueberries or dried cranberries, come from the Carter Family in Maine, whose collection spans almost one hundred years. Marion A. Carter started her manuscript cookbook with a nineteenth century recipe for Grandmother's Biscuits. Another family member, Miss M. E. Carter, continued to document the family recipes for steamed puddings, cakes, pies, and preserves through the first half of the twentieth century.

Elinor Jennings warns us not to serve bacon with her crisp delicate Peanut Butter Waffles, while Melania Marasi, a great-grandmother from Cambridge, Massachusetts, who baked for more than eighty years, provides us with the recipe for her special biscotti, generous in size and flavor and amply suitable for dipping in a cup of breakfast coffee. We hope that you will enjoy baking the recipes in this chapter and continue to eat breakfast at home with the family.

APPLESAUCE CAKE

MAKES 14 SLICES

1¾ cups flour

⅛ teaspoon salt

½ teaspoon cloves

1 teaspoon cinnamon

¼ teaspoon nutmeg

1 cup butter

½ cup sugar

½ cup brown sugar

2 teaspoons cold water

1 teaspoon baking soda

1 cup applesauce (use liquid measuring cup)

1 cup raisins plumped in orange juice (see How to Plump Raisins on page 171)

We found this recipe for applesauce cake in a collection of handwritten recipes jotted down in a small notebook given out by the New Hampshire Fire Insurance Company. Because we're purists, we used our own homemade applesauce in this recipe (see "How to Make Applesauce" on page 31) with grand success. However, we also baked the cake with commercial applesauce and found very little difference in texture or flavor.

1. Set the oven rack in the middle position. Preheat the oven to 350°F. Coat a 9-inch by 5-inch by 3-inch metal loaf pan with vegetable spray. Line the bottom and sides of the pan with wax paper and spray again to coat the liner.

2. Sift together flour, salt, cloves, cinnamon, and nutmeg.

3. Cream butter, sugar, and brown sugar in the bowl of a standing mixer fitted with the paddle attachment.

4. Place cold water in a small cup, add baking soda, and stir until dissolved. Pour mixture onto applesauce and stir briskly (the mixture will foam up). Add applesauce to butter mixture and mix thoroughly. Add sifted dry ingredients and mix until well combined. Fold in raisins.

5. Pour the batter into loaf pan. Bake 1 hour 10 minutes, or until a tester inserted into cake comes out dry. Cool on a rack 15 minutes before turning out of pan. Serve warm or at room temperature. Store loosely covered with wax paper at room temperature.

Sweet Tip

This cake is even better the next day. You can serve it with tea or coffee and a side of unsweetened whipped cream.

SWEET TOUCH We like to plump raisins by boiling them in orange juice, but you can skip this step and use raisins that have not been plumped. The orange juice does give an added nuance to the cake.

How to Make Applesauce

Peel and core 3 Granny Smith or other baking apples and cut into wedges. Place the apples and ¼ cup water in a heavy saucepan. Cook over high heat for 4 minutes, or until apples start to boil. Continue cooking on high for another 4 minutes. Stir with a wooden spoon; apples should soften and collapse. Reduce heat to low. Simmer for 4 minutes, or until tender. Let apples cool. Transfer to the bowl of a food processor fitted with the metal blade and process 3 or 4 times until fairly smooth. Be careful not to overprocess or the apples will liquefy.

Tin flour sifter, 1910; aluminum measuring cup, 1930s; green Depression glass juicer, 1930s

HELEN'S COFFEE BANS

MAKES 24 SQUARES

FOR DOUGH

1 cup raisins

2 teaspoons instant coffee

⅔ cup hot water

1½ cups sifted flour

½ teaspoon baking powder

½ teaspoon baking soda

¼ teaspoon salt

⅔ cup butter

1 cup sugar

2 eggs

FOR TOPPING

½ cup sugar

½ teaspoon cinnamon

This original recipe was handwritten, so we're not sure whether Helen meant to call them Coffee Bans or Coffee Buns. Because Helen's recipe doesn't call for yeast, and these are bars rather than rolls, we've decided to stay with Bans. Whatever Helen meant to call them, they are light, delicious, and easy to make.

1. Set the oven rack in the middle position. Preheat the oven to 350°F. Coat a 9-inch by 13-inch pan with vegetable spray. Line the bottom and sides of the pan with foil, shiny side up.
2. Place raisins and instant coffee in a small bowl, add hot water, and stir. Allow raisins to plump at least 5 minutes.
3. Sift together flour, baking powder, baking soda, and salt.
4. Cream butter and sugar in the bowl of a standing mixer fitted with the paddle attachment. With mixer running, add eggs, one at a time. Add liquid coffee, straining out raisins. Add sifted dry ingredients. Fold in raisins by hand.
5. Pour batter into pan and smooth the top with a spatula. Combine sugar and cinnamon in a small bowl and sprinkle over top of batter. Bake 20 minutes, or until a tester inserted into cake comes out dry. Cool on a rack. When cake is completely cool, cut into squares. Store loosely wrapped in wax paper at room temperature.

Sweet Tip

These squares are very delicate. It's best to cut them on the day you bake them as soon as they have cooled. If you wait until the following day, you will find it hard to cut through the raisins.

SWEET TOUCH ♥ Helen recommended that her Coffee Bans be iced. We like them with the cinnamon and sugar on top, but a light glaze is also tasty.

CARROT CREAM CHEESE MUFFINS

This recipe came from a modest collection spanning the 1960s through the 1980s. The woman who wrote these recipes entertained frequently, and her tersely written instructions illustrate the notes of an experienced home cook. Her manuscript cookbook also included the recipes for Dixie Dinner Rolls (page 91) and Cuban Flan (page 120).

1. Set the oven rack in the middle position. Preheat the oven to 350°F. Coat the cups and top surface of a 12-cup muffin pan with vegetable spray.

2. To make the filling: Place cream cheese in a small bowl, add sugar, and mash with a dinner fork until well blended. Cover with plastic wrap and place in the freezer 10 minutes to chill.

3. To make the muffins: Sift together flour, salt, baking powder, and cinnamon.

4. Cream butter and brown sugar in the bowl of a standing mixer fitted with the paddle attachment. With mixer running, add eggs, one a time, beating after each addition. Add orange extract, orange juice, and orange zest. Add sifted dry ingredients and mix well. Fold in carrots, raisins, and walnuts.

5. Place 2 tablespoons batter in each muffin pan cup. Tap pan gently to distribute batter evenly in each cup. Add a generous tablespoon of filling to each cup. Add remaining batter until each cup is full. Spread and smooth batter with the back of a spoon until filling is completely covered. Tap muffin pan again gently. Bake 20 to 22 minutes, or until a tester inserted into muffins comes out clean. Cool on a rack at least 20 minutes. Use the tip of a knife and your fingers to remove muffins from pan (don't tip pan and dump the muffins out). Store cooled muffins loosely wrapped in wax paper in a plastic container in the refrigerator. Warm to room temperature before serving.

FOR FILLING

1 8-oz. package cream cheese, softened in microwave on low for 40 seconds

¼ cup sugar

FOR MUFFINS

1¾ cups flour

½ teaspoon salt

1½ teaspoons baking powder

¾ teaspoon cinnamon

½ cup butter

¾ cup brown sugar

3 eggs, beaten

1 teaspoon orange extract

¼ cup orange juice

1 tablespoon grated orange zest

1¾ cups grated carrots

¾ cup raisins

¾ cup chopped walnuts

Sweet Tips

- Coat a melon baller with vegetable spray and use it to scoop the cream cheese.
- These muffins can be heated in a microwave before serving. They will not be as crisp, but they will be warm.

Pictured on page 29.

ELINOR'S PEANUT BUTTER WAFFLES

This recipe came from Elinor Jennings, who worked with Marilynn at MIT during the 1960s and 1970s. Elinor always said she was not a cook, but that she knew good food. She was particular about how these waffles were made and would lower her voice and gruffly proclaim them "luscious."

1. Prepare and preheat the waffle iron following the manufacturer's instructions.
2. Sift together flour, baking powder, sugar, and salt.
3. Place butter in small glass bowl and microwave 10 seconds on low to soften. Transfer butter and peanut butter to a medium bowl and cream with a wooden spoon. Add eggs and stir to combine. Add sifted dry ingredients alternately with 1½ cups of the milk, stirring just until mixed. If batter seems stiff, add 1 or 2 tablespoons milk.
4. When waffle iron reaches the ideal temperature, pour suggested amount of batter on each section of iron. Bake until waffles are soft and golden brown, not crisp. Serve immediately.

1¾ cups flour

3 teaspoons baking powder

3 tablespoons sugar

¼ teaspoon salt

¼ cup plus 2 tablespoons butter, cut into 6 pieces

6 tablespoons crunchy peanut butter

2 eggs

1½ cups plus 1 or 2 tablespoons milk

SWEET TOUCH ♥ Elinor advised against serving bacon with these waffles because she felt it interfered with their delicate flavor. We serve our waffles with stewed blueberries and yogurt.

CRANBERRY-ORANGE CREAM SCONES

MAKES 12 SCONES

2 cups flour (plus ¼ cup for kneading dough)

1 tablespoon baking powder

½ teaspoon salt

½ teaspoon cinnamon

¼ cup butter

¼ cup sugar

2 eggs

½ cup plus 2 tablespoons heavy cream

1 tablespoon grated orange zest

1 cup dried cranberries, plumped in 4 tablespoons orange juice (see How to Plump Raisins on page 171)

¼ cup sugar

This outstanding recipe comes from a handwritten manuscript cookbook, from the collection of Marion A. Carter and M. E. Carter, that spanned the 1870s through the 1920s. A narrow notebook with a marbled maroon and grey cover, it was filled with tightly written segments on pages spattered with cooking stains. Since there is more than one handwriting in the book, we guess this was a collection compiled by two generations of the Carter family.

1. Set the oven rack in the middle position. Preheat the oven to 425°F. Cover a 14-inch by 16-inch baking sheet with foil, shiny side up. Coat the foil with vegetable spray or use a silicone liner.

2. Sift together flour, baking powder, salt, and cinnamon.

3. Cream butter and sugar in a medium bowl. Combine eggs and ½ cup of the heavy cream and add to butter mixture. Add grated orange zest. Add sifted dry ingredients and stir until a soft dough begins to form. Squeeze orange juice from cranberries and incorporate fruit into dough with your fingers.

4. Place dough on a generously floured surface. Knead gently five times, turning corners of dough toward the center. Pat dough into a ½-inch thick circle. Using a floured knife, cut dough into 12 equal wedges. Using a floured wide spatula, transfer each wedge to baking sheet. Brush wedges with the remaining heavy cream and sprinkle with sugar. Bake 12 to 15 minutes, or until tops of scones are lightly brown and bottoms are golden brown. Place baking sheet on a rack and cool about 10 minutes. Serve scones warm with butter and jam. They are best when eaten the day they are made.

SWEET TOUCH ♥ We made these scones also by substituting a heaping cup of fresh blueberries for the cranberries, and they were wonderful. Sprinkle the blueberries on top of the dough after kneading it twice, and then continue with the instructions.

SUGAR DOUGHNUTS

1 9 2 0 S

MAKES 24 DOUGHNUTS AND 24 HOLES

1 package (2¼ teaspoons) active dry yeast

½ cup water, warmed to 110°F

½ cup plus 1 tablespoon sugar, divided

1 cup butter

2 eggs

3½ cups flour

½ teaspoon nutmeg

½ teaspoon cinnamon

1 teaspoon salt

Vegetable or peanut oil, for frying

Sugar or confectioners' sugar

Our love affair with doughnuts started early when we purchased them dredged in confectioners' sugar from Pearl's Bakery in Winthrop, Massachusetts. Later, we would venture into Boston with our parents to watch the doughnuts at Lord's coming off the line and dropping into their bath of hot fat. We'll never forget the smell of frying dough. We adapted this recipe for yeast dough to recapture the flavor of our youth.

1. Dissolve yeast in warm water. Add 1 tablespoon of the sugar. Set in a warm place to proof, about 10 minutes. Mixture will bubble when yeast is proofed.

2. Cream butter, eggs, and remaining ½ cup sugar in the bowl of a standing mixer fitted with the paddle attachment. Add proofed yeast and mix until combined.

3. Remove paddle attachment and attach dough hook. With mixer running, add 3 cups of the flour, 1 cup at a time, nutmeg, cinnamon, and salt and mix until dough holds together. Add remaining ½ cup flour if dough is too loose. Place dough in an oiled bowl and turn so entire dough is coated with oil. Cover with a towel and refrigerate 4 hours or overnight.

4. Remove dough from refrigerator. Allow dough to rest in a warm place for 30 minutes. Divide dough in half. Place one half between two pieces of lightly floured wax paper or parchment paper. Roll out or pat dough into a ½-inch-thick rectangle. Cut out doughnuts and holes using a doughnut cutter dipped in flour. Transfer cut dough to a parchment-covered baking sheet and allow to rest 15 minutes. Repeat with remaining dough.

5. Line a cooling rack with 3 layers of paper towels. Add 3 inches of oil to a deep flat-bottomed heavy pan or electric fryer. Heat oil

to 375°F. Use a greased spatula to carefully lower dough into hot fat. Fat may foam or bubble. Fry doughnuts in batches of 3 for approximately 1½ minutes on each side until golden brown. Fry doughnut holes in batches of 8 for 1 minute on each side or until golden brown. Place on lined rack to drain, and cover with additional paper towels. Roll doughnuts in granulated sugar while still warm, or dust with confectioners' sugar when slightly cool. Doughnuts are best eaten shortly after frying.

TEN TIPS FOR DEEP-FRYING

1. Always use an electric fryer, following the manufacturers instructions, or a deep flat-bottomed heavy pot on a level surface.
2. Do not use plastic utensils when frying.
3. Use fresh oil every time you fry.
4. Heat oil gradually and in an uncovered pot. The pot should be only half-filled with oil to allow for foaming that may occur when items are lowered into it.
5. Use a thermometer to gauge the temperature of the fat at all times.
6. Keep the temperature of fat constant. Allow time for the temperature to adjust after each batch.
7. Dry items on paper towels before immersing in hot fat.
8. Keep items the same size so they will fry uniformly.
9. Do not crowd items in the pan.
10. Have a bowl of ice water handy for spatters and burns. Never leave the frying area unattended.

LEMON POPPY SEED CAKE

MAKES 16 SLICES

FOR CAKE

2 cups flour

1 teaspoon baking powder

¼ teaspoon salt

1 cup butter

2 cups sugar

2 eggs

1 cup sour cream

¼ cup poppy seeds

3 tablespoons lemon juice

2 teaspoons grated lemon zest

FOR LEMON GLAZE

1 cup confectioners' sugar

2 tablespoons lemon juice

Pinch of salt

This is one of those unassuming recipes that often falls under the heading of "coffee cake," never mind that the batter is rich and looks like whipped cream. There are those who do not hesitate to point out its humble ingredients, but we love this cake and have been making variations on it for years. Chameleon-like, it's presented itself over the years as a Lemon Ginger Cake, Brown Sugar Pecan Cake, and Coconut Cake with Raspberry Butter Cream.

1. Set the oven rack in the middle position. Preheat the oven to 350°F. Coat an 8-cup Bundt pan or an 8-cup tube pan with vegetable spray or butter and dust with flour.

2. To make the cake: Sift together flour, baking powder, and salt.

3. Cream butter and sugar in the bowl of a standing mixer fitted with the paddle attachment. With mixer running, add eggs, one at a time, and sour cream. Add poppy seeds. Fold in sifted dry ingredients in thirds. Add lemon juice and lemon zest and mix well.

4. Pour batter into pan. Bake 50 to 60 minutes, or until cake pulls away from sides of pan and tester inserted into cake comes out clean. Cake may crack on top. Place pan on a rack and cool about 20 minutes. Run a butter knife around edges. Turn out cake onto a rack and allow to cool completely.

5. To make the lemon glaze: Mix together confectioners' sugar, lemon juice, and salt in a small bowl. Slip a sheet of wax paper under rack to catch drips. Use a teaspoon or fork to drizzle glaze over the top of cake. After the glaze has set, store loosely covered with wax paper at room temperature. Cake can be frozen and reheated.

Sweet Tip

If you don't have time to make the lemon glaze, dust the top of the cake lightly with confectioners' sugar instead.

Brown Sugar Rhubarb Cake

MAKES 12 SERVINGS

FOR CAKE

2 cups finely chopped rhubarb

2 cups sifted flour

¼ teaspoon salt

3 teaspoons lemon zest

1½ cups brown sugar

½ cup vegetable oil

1 egg

1 teaspoon baking soda

1 cup buttermilk

1 teaspoon vanilla

3 tablespoons lemon juice

FOR TOPPING

1 cup brown sugar

1 teaspoon cinnamon

Sweet Tip

This cake is best served the day it is baked. One day later, the rhubarb will turn into a layer of jam; the cake will still taste delicious, but the texture will change.

Found written on a lined index card, this little treasure has become part of our personal repertoire. When we first tried to make this recipe, the chopped rhubarb proved to be a challenge. We thought the cake would have a rather tangy taste, but the tart flavor of the rhubarb wasn't distinctive. Then we realized that the role of the rhubarb was to contribute moistness. We added lemon zest and lemon juice to the batter to bring out the true tartness of the rhubarb, and it worked!

1. To make the cake: Place chopped rhubarb in a glass bowl, cover with plastic wrap, and refrigerate overnight. The next day, drain off and discard the liquid. Squeeze rhubarb to extract remaining liquid. Mix together rhubarb, flour, salt, and lemon zest in a bowl.

2. Set the oven rack in the middle position. Preheat the oven to 350°F. Coat a 9-inch by 13-inch glass pan with vegetable spray. Dust pan with flour and tap out the excess.

3. Combine brown sugar, vegetable oil, and egg in the bowl of a standing mixer fitted with the paddle attachment.

4. Dissolve baking soda in buttermilk. Add vanilla and stir. With mixer running, add buttermilk mixture to egg mixture. Add rhubarb mixture and beat in. Turn off mixer. Add lemon juice and stir twice with spatula. Pour batter, which will be very loose, into glass pan.

5. To make the topping: Mix brown sugar and cinnamon in a small bowl. Sprinkle topping on batter, avoiding the edges to prevent sticking at sides of pan. Gently press topping into batter with the palm of your hand. Bake 45 minutes, or until cake bubbles and topping has formed. Cool on a rack. Serve slightly warm or at room temperature. Store loosely wrapped in wax paper in a plastic container in the refrigerator.

SWEET TOUCH   To serve this cake as a dessert, add a scoop of rich vanilla ice cream.

PINEAPPLE WALNUT BREAKFAST BARS

This recipe was a tough one to update because we couldn't taste the pineapple in it. We found that doubling the amount of canned pineapple as well as adding chopped dried pineapple made all the difference. Also, the texture was lightened by the melted butter, and the added fruity crunch from the dried fruit did not coarsen the crumb. The pineapple flavor is rather subtle still, but it makes its presence known.

1½ cups flour, divided

1 teaspoon baking powder

½ teaspoon baking soda

¼ teaspoon salt

2 cups sugar

4 eggs

1 teaspoon vanilla

½ cup butter, melted

½ cup chopped dried pineapple

2 8-oz. cans pineapple chunks, well drained and chopped

1 cup finely chopped walnuts

1. Set the oven rack in the middle position. Preheat the oven to 350°F. Line the bottom and four sides of a 9-inch by 13-inch by 2-inch pan with foil, shiny side up. Coat the foil with vegetable spray.

2. Sift together 1¼ cups of the flour, baking powder, baking soda, and salt.

3. Beat sugar, eggs, and vanilla in the bowl of a standing mixer fitted with the paddle attachment. With mixer running, add sifted dry ingredients. Add butter and mix thoroughly.

4. Combine the remaining ¼ cup flour, dried pineapple, canned pineapple, and walnuts in a medium bowl. Fold into batter. Pour batter into pan. Bake 35 minutes, or until a tester inserted into cake comes out clean. Cool on rack and cut into 2-inch bars. Store loosely wrapped in wax paper at room temperature.

ALL ABOUT RHUBARB

Rhubarb is also called "pie plant" because it's used in so many pies. Select firm stalks that are no more than 1 inch in diameter. Cut the stalks into ½-inch pieces for ease in baking. Peel rhubarb stalks if they appear to be tough or stringy. Because it contains large amounts of fluid, chopped rhubarb should be allowed to drain for at least 30 minutes before using. Remember to use only the stalks of rhubarb—its leaves are toxic and should not be eaten.

Pumpkin Walnut Muffins

One of those unclaimed treasures we found tucked between the pages of an old manuscript cookbook, this recipe, once again, demonstrates the choice of a baked sweet for breakfast. Although early baking was often limited by the selection and availability of ingredients, this muffin illustrates how something simple can still be wonderful.

1. Set the oven rack in the middle position. Preheat the oven to 400°F. Coat the entire top surface and cups of a 12-cup muffin pan and a 6-cup muffin pan with vegetable spray.

2. Sift together flour, baking powder, salt, cinnamon, mace, and ginger in a large bowl.

3. Place sugar in a small bowl. Add egg, vanilla, milk, and heavy cream. Stir gently just until combined. Add egg mixture to sifted dry ingredients and stir. Fold in pumpkin and walnuts. Fold in butter.

4. Fill each muffin cup with batter. (You should have enough for eighteen large muffins.) Add two walnut halves to the top of each cup and sprinkle with brown sugar. Bake 20 to 22 minutes, or until a tester inserted into middle of muffins comes out clean. Cool in pan on a rack 5 minutes before turning out. Serve muffins with butter and jam. Store loosely wrapped in wax paper at room temperature.

2 cups sifted flour

1 tablespoon plus 1 teaspoon baking powder

½ teaspoon salt

1 teaspoon cinnamon

1 teaspoon mace

1 teaspoon ginger

1 cup sugar

1 egg, beaten

2 teaspoons vanilla

½ cup milk

½ cup heavy cream

⅔ cup canned pumpkin

1 cup chopped walnuts

¼ cup butter, melted

36 walnut halves

½ cup dark brown sugar

SWEET TOUCH ♥ We tried a variation of this recipe by folding a cup of dried cherries that we had heated in orange juice (and drained) into the muffin batter. We topped those muffins with brown sugar.

Sweet Tips

- Use a wire whisk or wooden spoon to prepare the muffins. Do not use an electric mixer because the batter should not be overmixed.

- You can use either canned pumpkin or canned squash because either tends to have less moisture than fresh pumpkin or squash. The recipe originally called for squash, but it tastes just as good with pumpkin.

MRS. MARASI'S BISCOTTI

2½ cups flour

1 cup sugar

3 teaspoons baking powder

⅛ teaspoon salt

¼ cup milk

½ cup vegetable oil or peanut oil

2 teaspoons anise extract

3 eggs

MAKES 25 BISCOTTI

Our friend Barbara told Marilynn about a talented baker, Melania Marasi. The phone crackled as Barbara declared, "Mrs. Marasi always has a Scottie in a jar when her family visits." Marilynn found it hard to understand why Mrs. Marasi would keep a dog in a jar. Was she a taxidermist? Another call to Barbara cleared up the mystery. Mrs. Marasi always kept some biscotti in a jar for guests. Of course we asked for the recipe, which turned out to be a wonderful treat with the subtle flavor of anise.

1. Set the oven rack in the middle position. Preheat the oven to 350°F. Cover a 14-inch by 16-inch baking sheet with foil, shiny side up. Coat the foil with vegetable spray or use a silicone liner.
2. Sift together flour, sugar, baking powder, and salt.
3. Combine milk, oil, and anise extract. Add more anise extract if you like a strong anise flavor.
4. Lightly beat eggs in the bowl of a standing mixer fitted with the paddle attachment. With mixer running, add anise liquid. Add sifted dry ingredients. Dough will be loose.
5. Divide dough in half. Using a rubber spatula or oiled hands, shape into 2 flat loaves on baking sheet. Bake 20 to 25 minutes, or until edges are lightly brown and a tester inserted in loaves comes out dry.
6. Cool for 5 minutes. Transfer biscotti from baking sheet to a cutting surface. Using a serrated bread knife, cut diagonal slices ½ inch to ¾ inch thick. Place slices, cut side up, on the same baking sheet and return to 350°F oven for 10 minutes. Remove baking sheet from oven, turn biscotti over, and return to oven to bake an additional 10 minutes. Transfer biscotti to a rack to cool. Store between sheets of wax paper in a covered tin.

Sweet Tip

Save broken or leftover biscotti to make into crumbs for cheesecakes or crumb crusts.

SWEET TOUCH   To make almond biscotti, substitute 1 teaspoon almond extract for the anise and mix ½ cup chopped toasted almonds into the dough.

MRS. ORCOTT'S BRAN BREAD

This recipe came from the collection of Mrs. Orcott, an Ohio woman who was active in the Lakeside Women's Society during the 1950s. An avid home cook, she collected recipes wherever she went, often jotting them on the back of flyers. This recipe is an earlier one from her collection dating from 1918 and could possibly be a war bread. It has the texture of cornbread, but the flavor of a good bran muffin. We think the pepitas bring it into the twenty-first century.

½ cup wheat bran

4 tablespoons honey

½ cup buttermilk

½ cup butter, melted

2 eggs, beaten

1½ cups flour

½ cup cornmeal

3 teaspoons baking powder

1 teaspoon baking soda

1 teaspoon salt

½ cup sugar

¼ cup roasted, salted pepitas (optional)

1. Set the oven rack in the middle position. Preheat the oven to 350°F. Line the bottom and ends of a 9-inch by 5-inch by 3-inch loaf pan with a single strip of wax paper. Coat the pan and wax paper liner with vegetable spray.

2. Place wheat bran, 3 tablespoons honey, buttermilk, butter, and eggs in a large mixing bowl. Gently mix together. Let stand 10 minutes.

3. Place flour, cornmeal, baking powder, baking soda, salt, and sugar in a small bowl. Whisk to combine.

4. Add dry ingredients to wheat bran mixture and stir just until combined. Using a rubber spatula, give batter two quick turns.

5. Place batter in loaf pan. Tap pan twice on counter to level off batter and remove air bubbles. Drizzle remaining tablespoon honey on top of batter and sprinkle with pepitas. Press pepitas gently into batter with the palm of your hand. Bake 45 to 50 minutes, or until a tester inserted into center of loaf comes out clean. Set pan on a rack until completely cool. Remove bread from pan and cut into slices. Store loosely wrapped in wax paper at room temperature.

Sweet Tip

Coat a tablespoon with vegetable spray before measuring the honey.

Winchester Nut Bread

MAKES 14 SLICES

FOR BREAD

½ cup brown sugar

¾ cup hot water

½ cup molasses

¾ cup milk

1 cup flour

2½ teaspoons baking powder

1¼ teaspoons salt

¾ teaspoon baking soda

1 teaspoon nutmeg

2 cups graham flour

¾ cup finely chopped walnuts

FOR NUT TOPPING

2 teaspoons butter, melted

⅓ cup finely chopped walnuts

We love any recipe that has the name of a town or city in it, since we like knowing where our recipes come from. But there are a lot of Winchesters in the United States and Canada so we can't be sure exactly where this nut bread originates. This is a very old recipe, and versions of it may have found their way into several community cookbooks. We found our handwritten version in an old manuscript cookbook, and we like to think of this wonderful coarse-grained bread as a personal adaptation by the woman who wrote it down.

1. Set the oven rack in the middle position. Preheat the oven to 350°F. Line the bottom and ends of a 9-inch by 5-inch by 3-inch loaf pan with a single strip of wax paper. Coat the pan and wax paper liner with vegetable spray.

2. Place brown sugar in a medium bowl. Pour hot water over brown sugar. Add molasses and milk and stir.

3. Sift together flour, baking powder, salt, baking soda, and nutmeg into a large mixing bowl. Whisk in graham flour. Add molasses mixture and mix gently with a wooden spoon or wire whisk. Fold in walnuts.

4. Pour batter into loaf pan. Tap pan twice on counter to level and remove air bubbles. Brush top of batter with melted butter. Sprinkle walnuts on top and press lightly into batter with the palm of your hand. Bake 50 minutes, or until a tester inserted into bread comes out clean. Cool completely in pan on a rack before slicing. Store loosely covered with wax paper at room temperature.

Sweet Tip

This bread should be handled as if it were a muffin batter, which means don't overmix it.

SWEET TOUCH   Serve this bread with sweet butter and orange marmalade.

Dorothy Katziff Brass' Refrigerator Coffee Rolls

FOR DOUGH

1 package (2¼ teaspoons) active dry yeast

½ cup water, warmed to 110°F

1 cup plus 1 tablespoon sugar, divided

4½ cups flour

⅛ teaspoon salt

1 cup butter

3 eggs, beaten

1 cup sour cream

FOR COFFEE ROLL BASES

½ cup brown sugar

¾ cup walnuts, coarsely chopped

½ cup butter

FOR FILLING

½ cup butter, melted

1 cup brown sugar

1 teaspoon cinnamon

2 cups walnuts, coarsely chopped

1 cup raisins or dried cherries

1 egg, beaten

These coffee rolls were the breakfast pastry of choice when we were growing up. Since the dough was made the night before, our mother always baked her coffee rolls the next morning in a flurry of rolling, sprinkling, and shaping. Marilynn remembers recuperating from a winter cold, wrapped in a down comforter, finally able to smell the melting butter and brown sugar of these rolls.

1. To make the dough: Dissolve yeast in warm water. Add 1 tablespoon of the sugar. Set in a warm place to proof, about 10 minutes. Mixture will bubble when yeast is proofed.

2. Sift 4 cups of the flour, remaining 1 cup sugar, and salt into the bowl of a standing mixer fitted with the paddle attachment. Add butter and mix to combine. Add proofed yeast, eggs, and sour cream and mix to combine.

3. Remove paddle attachment and attach dough hook. Knead dough about 5 minutes, adding up to ½ cup flour if needed to make a smooth, silky dough. Place dough in an oiled bowl and turn so entire dough is coated with oil. Cover with a towel and refrigerate overnight.

4. Remove dough from refrigerator. Dough should have risen to top of bowl. Punch down dough and allow to rise in a warm place until doubled in bulk, about 1 hour. Punch down, and divide in half.

5. Set the oven rack in the middle position. Preheat the oven to 350°F. Coat the cups and top surface of two 12-cup muffin pans with vegetable spray.

6. To make the coffee roll bases: Place 1 teaspoon brown sugar, 1 heaping teaspoon chopped walnuts, and 1 teaspoon butter in the bottom of each cup of muffin pan.

7. To add the filling: Roll out half of dough on floured wax paper or parchment paper. Brush surface with melted butter. Mix brown sugar and cinnamon in a small bowl. Cover surface of dough with half of the sugar mixture, 1 cup of the walnuts, and ½ cup of the dried fruit. Use the paper to help lift and roll the dough, jelly-roll style. Cut rolled dough into 12 equal pieces. Place each piece in a muffin pan cup, cut side up. Repeat with remaining dough and filling ingredients.

8. Let rolled dough rise in a warm place 30 minutes. Brush tops with beaten egg. Bake 30 minutes, or until tops are golden brown. Cool in pan on rack 5 minutes and then invert pan over rack. If some of the base remains in bottom of muffin cups, scoop it out with a spoon and place it over inverted coffee rolls. Allow to cool completely. Store coffee rolls in a plastic bag at room temperature.

Sweet Tip

If baking two pans at once, one pan goes on the middle rack and one pan goes on the bottom. Switch and reverse the pans halfway through for even baking.

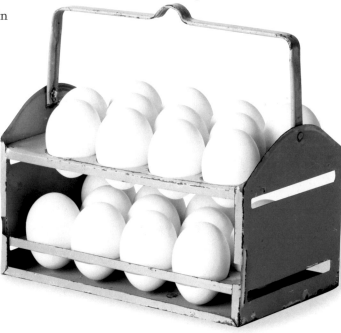

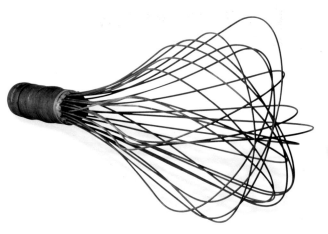

Wire whisk, 1890; metal egg carrier, English, 1920s

We firmly believe that the hands that keep the cookie jar filled are the hands that rule the world. Cookies are the currency with which a home is run. No matter what the

Keeping the Cookie Jar Filled

state of the family, no matter if in times of stress or in times of joy: we know if the cookie jar is filled, everything is all right.

Cookies are very handy treats. You can help yourself to two or three easily with a sleight of hand that we all seem to learn early in life. Since cookies are portable, you can carry them easily. You don't need to bother with a napkin or a fork, although a glass of cold milk would be nice. Some people like them crisp. Others like them soft or chewy. Everyone has a favorite, but to us, cookies have a deeper meaning. They are like small autobiographical worlds, representing the person who baked them. Each one signifies an often fascinating personal story and a life well spent.

Take the story of Libby Cockrey, a woman in her nineties, who has lived in western Massachusetts for most of her life. The telephone operator for the town of Groton for 50 years, she is respected and loved by the residents. She knows everyone and everyone knows her. Her collection of living recipes spans the 1930s to the 1990s; they were "rescued" at a Groton yard sale by our agent, Karen. A talented baker, Libby's Coconut Washboards, Lacy Chocolate Crisps, and Linzer Coconut Bars are outstanding, and she was honored in 2005 by being portrayed in the town's 350th celebration.

Our aunt, Ida Tucker Katziff, who died in 2001 at the age of 93, was an inspiration to us. She was the only member of her large family to go to college. A mother, grandmother, and great-grandmother, she didn't know how to bake before

Handwritten recipe for Hermits, 1920s

she married. For more than 50 years, Ida was the wife of our Uncle Julius, the owner of the only fur-supply company in Boston. She worked with him after her children were grown and took over his role as sales representative to several exclusive fur salons after he died. Her clients still remember the little lady, dressed in a designer coat and gloves, who presented them with boxes of her homemade Poppy Seed Cookies for the holidays.

The cookies we've presented in this chapter are bar cookies, drop cookies, formed cookies, and meringues. We've included cookies flavored with chocolate, maple syrup, ginger, coconut, brandy, and lemon. These recipes use simple easy-to-find ingredients that are readily available in most home pantries. Their flavors are true, and we hope you find the instructions uncomplicated. We might have plumped the raisins in brandy or tea, substituted butter for half of the shortening or lard, but we have stayed pretty close to the originals. We hope these recipes keep your own cookie jar filled to the brim!

Elva Ross' Peanut Cookies

MAKES 48 COOKIES

1¾ cups flour

1 teaspoon salt

1 cup sugar

2 teaspoons baking powder

½ cup butter, melted

1 egg, beaten

¼ cup milk

1 teaspoon lemon juice

1½ cups salted red-skinned peanuts, coarsely chopped and skins on

Sweet Tip

You can also make these cookies with regular salted oil-roasted peanuts.

These cookies are a wonderful blend of sweet and salty because of the coarsely chopped peanuts. The salt and oil in the chopped peanuts give these cookies a more distinct peanut flavor. This recipe was handwritten on a page from a copy of the 1926 edition of *Laboratory Recipes*, prepared for the YWCA in Boston. Elva E. Ross, who attended the YWCA school from 1929 to 1930, owned the copy of the book we found.

1. Set the oven rack in the middle position. Preheat the oven to 375°F. Cover a 14-inch by 16-inch baking sheet with foil, shiny side up. Coat the foil with vegetable spray or use a silicone liner.

2. Sift together flour, salt, sugar, and baking powder into a large bowl. Add butter and egg to sifted dry ingredients and mix well to form a soft dough. Add milk and stir. Add lemon juice and stir. Fold in peanuts.

3. Chill dough in the refrigerator for 1 hour, or until firm enough to handle. Drop by teaspoons onto baking sheets about 2 inches apart. Bake 17 to 18 minutes, or until light brown in color but still soft. Cool on a rack. Cookies will firm up when cool. Store between sheets of parchment paper or wax paper in a covered tin.

Tin cookie cutters, in shape of goose, 1910; in shape of whale, 1960s

AUNT IDA'S POPPY SEED COOKIES

This was our Aunt Ida Tucker Katziff's signature cookie. She baked this cookie for more than sixty years to the delight of four generations of our family, transporting them to parties in covered tins. We baked these cookies and served them at Aunt Ida's memorial gathering after her funeral since this recipe is a part of her legacy. She always stored her poppy seeds in the freezer to keep them fresh.

3 cups flour

2 teaspoons baking powder

½ cup poppy seeds

1 cup peanut oil

1 cup sugar

3 eggs

1 teaspoon vanilla

1. Set the oven rack in the middle position. Preheat the oven to 350°F. Cover a 14-inch by 16-inch baking sheet with foil, shiny side up. Coat the foil with vegetable spray or use a silicone liner.

2. Sift together flour and baking powder, and add poppy seeds.

3. Whisk peanut oil, sugar, eggs, and vanilla in a medium bowl. Add sifted dry ingredients and mix to combine. Chill dough in the refrigerator 1 hour, or until firm enough to handle.

4. With floured hands or wearing disposable gloves, break off teaspoon-size pieces of dough and roll into small balls. Place dough balls on baking sheet about 2 inches apart, or 12 cookies per sheet. Pat into circles with your fingers (rather than rolling or stamping). Bake 10 to 12 minutes, or until lightly browned around edges. Let cookies cool 1 minute on baking sheet on rack and then transfer the cookies to a rack. Cookies will become crisp as they cool. Store between sheets of wax paper in a covered tin or freeze in a tightly sealed plastic bag or container.

Tin cookie cutter in shape of anchor, early 1900s

LIBBY'S COCONUT WASHBOARDS

1 7-oz. package (1⅓ cups)
   sweetened shredded coconut

2 cups flour

¾ teaspoon baking powder

¼ teaspoon nutmeg

⅛ teaspoon salt

¾ cup butter

1 cup brown sugar

1 egg

1 teaspoon vanilla

½ teaspoon almond extract

This recipe was given to us as part of a collection of handwritten recipes belonging to Elizabeth Cockrey of Groton, Massachusetts. Mrs. Cockrey, who is in her nineties, is known as "a very good cook." Her recipes span the 1920s through the 1970s. Be sure to use a dinner fork, not a salad fork, to make the washboards because the tines of the salad fork are too short to do a good job.

1. Set the oven rack in the middle position. Preheat the oven to 375°F. Cover a 14-inch by 16-inch baking sheet with foil, shiny side up. Coat the foil with vegetable spray or use a silicone liner.

2. Place coconut in the bowl of a food processor fitted with a metal blade. Pulse two or three times until coconut flakes are reduced in length. (Be careful not to reduce coconut flakes to coconut dust.)

3. Sift together flour, baking powder, nutmeg, and salt.

4. Place butter and brown sugar in the bowl of a standing mixer fitted with the paddle attachment. Cream gradually until light and fluffy. Add egg, vanilla, and almond extract. Add sifted dry ingredients, blending well. Fold in coconut.

5. Divide dough in half, cover with plastic wrap, and chill in the refrigerator 1 hour, or until firm enough to handle. Place dough on a floured pastry board or floured parchment paper. Spread or pat each piece into a rectangle 8 inches x 12 inches by ³⁄₁₆ inches thick. Cut each piece lengthwise into quarters. Cut these sections into 1-inch pieces.

6. Press a floured dinner fork onto each piece of dough to form a washboard. (Dough will become even thinner when made into washboards.) Place washboards on baking sheet. Bake 8 minutes, or until golden brown. Cool on baking sheet on a rack. Store between sheets of parchment paper or wax paper in a covered tin.

Sweet Tip

It's really important to shorten the shreds of the coconut in a food processor. It's much harder to cut the cookie dough when the flakes are longer.

Pictured on page 2.

LACY OATMEAL COOKIES

These dainty cookies are delicious, and not nearly as heavy as the substantial oatmeal cookies we usually bake. Melted butter makes them light and lacy. We found this recipe typed and pasted at the end of the cookie chapter in a well-worn 1928 copy of The Rumford Complete Cook Book by Lily Haxworth Wallace. This book was produced by the Department of Home Economics of the Rumford Company, which distributed Rumford Baking Powder.

1. Set the oven rack in the middle position. Preheat the oven to 350°F. Cover a 14-inch by 16-inch baking sheet with foil, shiny side up. Coat the foil with vegetable spray or use a silicone liner.

2. Combine sugar and butter in the bowl of a standing mixer fitted with the paddle attachment. Beat in egg and vanilla. Add oats, flour, salt, and baking powder and mix well. Fold in chocolate chips and pecans.

3. Drop by teaspoons onto baking sheet at least 1½ to 2 inches apart. Bake 13 minutes, or until edges are lightly browned. Place baking sheet on rack to cool. (Do not remove cookies from baking sheet until they are completely cool.) Store cookies between sheets of parchment paper or wax paper in a covered tin.

1 cup sugar

½ cup butter, melted

1 egg

½ teaspoon vanilla

1 cup quick-cooking oats

¼ cup flour

¼ teaspoon salt

¼ teaspoon baking powder

½ cup mini chocolate chips

½ cup finely chopped pecans or other nuts

BAKING WITH OATMEAL

Be sure to choose the right type of oats for baking. The size, shape, and texture of the oat grain may vary because of the amount of processing or rolling. As a rule of thumb, use old-fashioned or quick-cooking oats, not instant oatmeal, for oatmeal cookies. Pinhead oats, also known as Irish, Scottish, or steel-cut oats, should be used for cooked cereals or hearty coarse-grained breads.

Oats may be added to toppings for crisps and crumbles. Their nutty taste enhances the flavor of baked fruit. The coarse texture of oats prevents a topping from soaking up fruit juices and becoming soggy.

Maple Syrup Cookie Sandwiches with Lemon Cream Filling

FOR COOKIES

2 cups flour

½ teaspoon salt

½ teaspoon baking soda

1 cup maple syrup or cane syrup

½ cup butter

1 egg

2 teaspoons maple extract
(optional)

FOR LEMON CREAM FILLING

2 cups confectioners' sugar

⅛ teaspoon salt

½ cup butter

3 teaspoons grated lemon zest

4 teaspoons lemon juice

We were thrilled to find this handwritten recipe for a cookie made with maple syrup. We liked them so much we decided to pair them with a lemon cream filling, creating the gustatory opportunity to take them apart, lick the lemon cream and eat the cookies slowly to make them last. We found that it is easier to use a pastry bag to pipe and fill these cookies to insure that they are uniform in size and shape.

1. Set the oven rack in the middle position. Preheat the oven to 350°F. Cover a 14-inch by 16-inch baking sheet with foil, shiny side up. Coat the foil with vegetable spray or use a silicone liner.

2. To make the cookies: Sift together flour, salt, and baking soda.

3. Mix maple syrup and butter in the bowl of a standing mixer fitted with the paddle attachment. Add egg and mix to combine. Gradually beat in sifted dry ingredients until the batter becomes smooth. Add maple extract.

4. Chill batter in the refrigerator until firm enough to pipe with a pastry bag. Fit pastry bag with a plain Ateco #804 metal tip and fill bag with batter. Pipe cookies onto baking sheet, making each cookie about 1½ inches in diameter and allowing no more than 20 cookies per sheet. Bake 18 minutes, or until golden brown. Place baking sheet on a rack. Let rest 2 minutes, then carefully transfer the cookies from baking sheet to rack. Cookies will crisp up on standing.

5. To make the lemon cream filling: Sift confectioners' sugar and salt into a small bowl. Add butter and combine. Whisk in lemon zest and lemon juice. Fit a pastry bag with an Ateco #806 metal tip and fill with lemon cream. Pipe a generous squiggle of filling on half of cookies. Place remaining cookies on top of filling and press together gently, sandwiching the cream in between. Store cookies between sheets of waxed paper in a covered tin in the refrigerator. Remove from refrigerator no more than 10 minutes before serving. This buttery filling will melt at room temperature.

Sweet Tip

When we first tested this recipe, the cookies had a very subtle maple taste. The maple syrup gives these cookies their delicate texture. We decided they really needed to taste more "maple-y," so we added the maple extract.

Marshmallow Fudge Brownies

MAKES 24 BARS

FOR BROWNIE LAYER

¾ cup flour

¼ teaspoon baking powder

¼ teaspoon salt

¾ cup butter

¾ cup sugar

2 eggs

2 oz. bitter chocolate, melted

1 teaspoon vanilla

½ cup chopped walnuts

FOR MARSHMALLOW LAYER

1 cup marshmallow spread

FOR BROWN SUGAR
CHOCOLATE FROSTING

½ cup brown sugar

¼ cup water

2 oz. bitter chocolate, melted

3 tablespoons butter

1 teaspoon vanilla

¼ teaspoon salt

1½ cups confectioners' sugar,
    sifted

2 tablespoons heavy cream
    (optional)

We found this anonymous recipe written on a 5½-inch by 2½-inch slip of yellowed paper—one of those wonderful, but unclaimed, recipes we often come across. This little gem is actually a tea brownie, cloaked in marshmallow and embellished with a layer of spectacular creamy chocolate frosting.

1. Set the oven rack in the middle position. Preheat the oven to 350°F. Line the bottom and four sides of an 8-inch by 8-inch by 2-inch pan with foil, shiny side up. Coat the foil with butter or vegetable spray.

2. To make the brownies: Sift together flour, baking powder, and salt.

3. Cream butter and sugar in the bowl of a standing mixer fitted with the paddle attachment until fluffy. Add eggs, one at a time. Add chocolate and vanilla. Add sifted dry ingredients in batches, beating after each addition. Fold in walnuts.

4. Pour batter into pan. Bake 20 minutes, or until a tester inserted in center comes out clean. Do not overbake.

5. To make the marshmallow layer: Cover top of brownies with marshmallow spread while still hot from the oven. Spread evenly with an offset spatula. Place on rack and cool completely before frosting.

SWEET TOUCH   We tried a version of the recipe by adding 1 cup of mini marshmallows with the nuts in the brownie base, rather than make the separate middle layer. Although the marshmallows melted into the brownie layer and were almost indiscernible, the brownie layer seemed moister.

6. To make the chocolate frosting: Place brown sugar in a saucepan with a heavy bottom, add water, and whisk to combine. Add chocolate and bring to a boil. Boil 3 minutes, stirring to prevent mixture from sticking to bottom of pot. Remove from heat. Whisk in butter. Add vanilla and salt and whisk again. Add confectioners' sugar and mix thoroughly. Frosting may be thinned with heavy cream if it appears too stiff.

7. Pour frosting over brownie-and-marshmallow base, spreading with an offset spatula. Refrigerate at least 3 hours, or until firm. Cut into bars with a wide serrated knife. Store brownies between sheets of parchment paper or waxed paper in a covered tin in the refrigerator. Remove from refrigerator 10 minutes before serving.

Sweet Tips

- Coat a measuring cup with vegetable spray before measuring the marshmallow spread.
- If you don't have commercial marshmallow spread in your pantry, you can substitute mini marshmallows or whole marshmallows cut into small pieces. The brownie base, hot from the oven, will help to soften the marshmallows.

HOW TO MELT CHOCOLATE

In the microwave: Cut the chocolate into shards with a sharp knife. Place the chocolate in glass bowl. Do not cover. Microwave on low for 30 seconds and check progress. Repeat as needed. Two or three 30-second intervals are usually enough to melt the chocolate. Allow to cool.

On the stove: For this traditional method, place shards of chocolate in the top of a double-boiler over gently simmering water. When the chocolate appears to be melted, remove it from the heat. It is important that no water touches the chocolate.

Libby Cockrey's Chocolate and Vanilla Pinwheel Cookies

MAKES 60 COOKIES

These were one of the first cookies our mother learned to make when she was first married. She often made them as pink and white pinwheels by omitting the chocolate and adding a touch of red food coloring to half of the cookie dough. She usually baked them for birthday parties or bridge luncheons. We found this version among the recipes of Elizabeth Cockrey of Groton, Massachusetts.

2 cups flour

1 teaspoon baking powder

¼ teaspoon salt

⅔ cup butter

1 cup sugar

1 egg

1 teaspoon vanilla

2 oz. bitter chocolate, melted

1. Set the oven rack in the middle position. Preheat oven to 375°F. Cover a 14-inch by 16-inch baking sheet with foil, shiny side up. Coat the foil with vegetable spray or use a silicone liner.

2. Sift together flour, baking powder, and salt.

3. Place butter and sugar in the bowl of a standing mixer fitted with the paddle attachment. Cream until light and fluffy. Add egg and vanilla. Add sifted dry ingredients gradually and beat until combined.

4. Divide dough in half. Blend chocolate into one half of dough. Wrap dough in wax paper and chill both halves of dough 1 hour, or until firm enough to roll.

5. Roll chocolate dough between 2 sheets of wax paper into a 12-inch by 8-inch rectangle. Repeat for vanilla dough. Remove top sheets of wax paper and invert vanilla dough onto chocolate dough. Remove remaining wax paper. Roll both doughs together, jelly-roll style. Wrap in wax paper and refrigerate at least 3 hours (or freeze 1 hour) until firm.

6. Cut dough into ¼-inch-thick slices. Place slices on baking sheet. Bake 12 to 15 minutes, or until edges just begin to brown. Cool on a rack. Store between sheets of wax paper in a covered tin.

Donna's Ginger Snaps

MAKES 48 COOKIES

2 cups flour

2 teaspoons ginger

1 teaspoon nutmeg

1 teaspoon cinnamon

2 teaspoons baking soda

½ teaspoon salt

¾ cup butter

1 cup sugar

1 egg

¼ cup molasses

¼ cup ginger jam or bitter orange marmalade

¾ cup sugar (for rolling cookies)

These crispy cookies are the best ginger snaps we've tasted in a long time. We found this cookie recipe handwritten in a copy of *Laboratory Recipes* owned by Rachel W. Banks. This edition also contained the handwritten recipe for One, Two, Three Open-Faced Blueberry Pie (page 224). Thank you, Donna. You should be proud.

1. Set the oven rack in the middle position. Preheat the oven to 350°F. Cover a 14-inch by 16-inch baking sheet with foil, shiny side up. Coat the foil with vegetable spray or use a silicone liner.

2. Sift together flour, ginger, nutmeg, cinnamon, baking soda, and salt.

3. Cream butter and sugar in the bowl of a standing mixer fitted with the paddle attachment. Add egg. Beat in molasses and jam or marmalade. Add sifted dry ingredients gradually until well blended.

4. Wrap dough in plastic wrap and chill in the refrigerator for 1 hour, or until firm enough to handle. With floured hands or wearing disposable gloves, break off 1½ teaspoons of dough and roll into a ball. Continue until all dough is rolled. Roll balls in sugar and place on baking sheet, spaced at least 1½ inches apart, or 12 cookies per sheet, to allow for spreading during baking. Bake 14 minutes, or until golden brown. Cool on baking sheet on a rack. Cookies will firm up when cool. Store between sheets of parchment paper or wax paper in a covered tin.

SWEET TOUCH We confess. We added the ginger jam or the marmalade because we wanted to add a little more texture and depth to the cookies. If you don't have ginger jam or marmalade in your pantry, the grated zest of an orange will add the extra zing.

Brown Sugar Macaroons

This recipe is one we hold dear because it was the first living recipe we ever tried. We found it handwritten in a 1926 copy of *Laboratory Recipes* by Harriet Folger, prepared for the School of Domestic Science of the Boston YWCA. This copy of the book is the source of several wonderful recipes we've used over the years.

2 egg whites

2 cups brown sugar

2 cups chopped salted pecans

⅛ teaspoon salt (optional; use if pecans are unsalted)

1. Set the oven rack in the middle position. Preheat the oven to 350°F. Cover a 14-inch by 16-inch baking sheet with foil, shiny side up. Coat the foil with vegetable spray or use a silicone liner.

2. Place egg whites in the bowl of a standing mixer fitted with the whisk attachment. Beat to form stiff peaks. Slowly fold in brown sugar and pecans. The egg whites will deflate, causing the mixture to become pastelike. Add salt if needed.

3. Drop walnut-sized pieces of the mixture from a teaspoon onto baking sheet, spaced 1 inch apart. Bake 20 minutes, or until pale brown. Cool on rack. When completely cool, remove from rack. Store between sheets of parchment paper or wax paper in a covered tin.

Sweet Tip

We left the batter for the macaroons in the refrigerator overnight and found that it produced cookies the next day that were just as good. This is a real help if you're too busy to make the whole recipe the day you put them together.

Tin cookie cutters, in multiple shapes, 1920s; in shape of numbers, 1950s

NELL'S WONDERFUL
PEANUT BUTTER COOKIES

MAKES 42 COOKIES

1¼ cups flour

½ teaspoon baking soda

½ teaspoon baking powder

½ cup butter

½ cup brown sugar

½ cup sugar

½ cup smooth peanut butter

1 egg

½ cup broken salted peanuts (not dry-roasted)

½ cup mini chocolate chips

This is a great simple recipe. That's all we can say about it. We used tasty salted oil-roasted peanuts. We found that the salt and the oil were essential to this full-flavored treat. We found this recipe jotted on the back of a bridge tally. Dare we say it's a winner?

1. Set the oven rack in the middle position. Preheat the oven to 350°F. Cover a 14-inch by 16-inch baking sheet with foil, shiny side up. Coat the foil with vegetable spray or use a silicone liner.
2. Sift together flour, baking soda, and baking powder.
3. Cream butter, brown sugar, sugar, and peanut butter in the bowl of a standing mixer fitted with the paddle attachment. Add egg and mix thoroughly. Add sifted dry ingredients. Fold in peanuts and mini chocolate chips.
4. Chill dough in the refrigerator 1 hour, or until it is firm enough to handle. With floured hands or wearing disposable gloves, roll dough into balls about 1 inch in diameter. Place balls on baking sheet 2 inches apart and flatten with the bottom of a glass dipped in flour. Bake 12 minutes, or until golden brown. Cool on rack. Store between sheets of parchment paper or waxed paper in a covered tin.

Sweet Tip

We've found that using salted and oiled peanuts lends a richness to these cookies that dry-roasted peanuts do not. If you have to use unsalted dry-roasted peanuts, be sure to add 1/4 teaspoon salt to recipe.

Brandied Raisin Teacakes

1920s

MAKES 60 COOKIES

3½ cups flour

1½ teaspoons baking soda

2 teaspoons cinnamon

½ teaspoon cloves

1 teaspoon nutmeg

1 teaspoon salt

½ cup butter

½ cup lard

1 cup sugar

2 eggs

1 teaspoon vanilla

1 cup buttermilk

2 cups raisins soaked in brandy (see How to Plump Raisins on page 171)

1 cup confectioners' sugar

This is a very Yankee teacake, but the brandy in the raisins elevates it to a new level. The recipe came from a collection of handwritten recipes, but alas, it has no provenance noted. It was definitely valued by the compiler, a lady with extremely good taste. It is apparent from her collection that she never failed to solicit recipes from her friend's cooks, and she faithfully acknowledged all recipe originators.

1. Set the oven rack in the middle position. Preheat the oven to 375°F. Cover a 14-inch by 16-inch baking sheet with foil, shiny side up. Coat the foil with vegetable spray or use a silicone liner.
2. Sift together flour, baking soda, cinnamon, cloves, nutmeg, and salt.
3. Cream butter, lard, and sugar in a standing mixer fitted with the paddle attachment. Add eggs, one at a time. Mix vanilla with buttermilk. Add sifted dry ingredients, alternating with buttermilk, mixing after each addition until completely combined. Fold in raisins.
4. Chill dough in the refrigerator 1 hour, or until firm enough to handle. Drop by generous tablespoons onto baking sheet. Bake 18 minutes, or until lightly browned. Set baking sheet on rack, let cool 2 minutes, then transfer cookies to rack. Sprinkle confectioners' sugar over warm cookies. Store cookies between sheets of parchment paper or wax paper in a covered tin.

Sweet Tip

We've tried baking these cookies with all butter, and they are wonderful. However, the use of lard gives these flaky tea cakes another dimension. Also, since this recipe makes a lot of Brandied Raisin Tea Cakes, we suggest you keep the cookie dough in the refrigerator between preparing cookie trays so the dough will not become too soft to handle.

CHOCOLATE COCONUT CHEWS

We knew we had to test this recipe. Bundled in with a handful of handwritten recipes, we wanted to try them as soon as we read "chocolate" and "coconut." An almost meringue, but fortified with chocolate and coconut, these cookies take only fifteen minutes to bake. They are really chewy and perfect to take to a party because they aren't fragile.

2 egg whites

½ cup sugar

½ teaspoon vanilla

1 6-oz. package chocolate chips, melted and cooled

1 7-oz. package sweetened shredded coconut

1. Set the oven rack in the middle position. Preheat the oven to 350°F. Cover a 14-inch by 16-inch baking sheet with foil, shiny side up. Coat the foil with vegetable spray or use a silicone liner.
2. Place egg whites in the bowl of a standing mixer fitted with the whisk attachment. Beat until very stiff, gradually adding sugar. Add vanilla. Fold in chocolate chips and coconut. Let sit 5 minutes.
3. Drop by tablespoons onto baking sheet. Bake 15 minutes. Cookies will be soft, but will become firm. Set baking sheet on rack, let cool 2 minutes, then transfer chews to rack to cool completely. Store between sheets of wax paper in a covered tin.

HOW TO PLUMP RAISINS

Raisins are like character actors in recipes. With the right plumping liquid, they can assume all kinds of roles in your baking. For a sophisticated taste, plump raisins in good brandy or port. For an old-world taste, plump raisins in tea. For a new-age organic taste, plump raisins in orange juice. For an uncomplicated taste, but a velvety texture, plump raisins in hot water.

Brandy: Pour a generous amount of brandy over the raisins. Refrigerate overnight or for several days, shaking the container at least once a day.

Tea, orange juice, or water: Bring the liquid to a boil, immerse the raisins, and remove from the heat. Allow at least 30 minutes for raisins to absorb the liquid. If you don't use the raisins the same day you plump them, refrigerate and use within 1 week.

FROSTED PAN HERMITS

As children, when anyone mentioned hermits, we always pictured thin elderly white-bearded men living in caves. As adults, we can't forget the delicious hermits we ate as children; they were crunchy, with a light confectioners' sugar frosting on top and a hint of clove. We found more than a dozen recipes for hermits, but most of them were drop cookies. This one is simple to make and a little unusual because it is baked in one layer in a shallow pan.

1. Set the oven rack in the middle position. Preheat the oven to 350°F. Line a 9-inch by 13-inch x 1-inch jelly roll pan with foil, shiny side up. Coat the foil with butter or vegetable spray.

2. To make the hermits: Sift together 1½ cups of the flour, baking powder, salt, cloves, nutmeg, and cinnamon.

3. Cream butter and brown sugar in the bowl of a standing mixer fitted with the paddle attachment. Add egg. Add sifted dry ingredients alternately with milk. Mix the remaining 2 tablespoons flour with raisins and walnuts and fold into batter.

4. Pour batter onto jelly roll pan and spread with an offset spatula until even. Bake 25 to 30 minutes, or until a tester inserted into middle comes out clean. Turn once during baking. Place pan on rack. Frost while warm.

5. To make the frosting: Sift confectioners' sugar and salt into a bowl. Add butter and whisk until combined. Add vanilla and enough milk to form a thin frosting. Pour frosting gently over warm pan and spread evenly. Allow to set. When completely cool, cut into squares. Store hermits in single layers between sheets of wax paper in a covered tin.

FOR HERMITS

1½ cups plus 2 tablespoons flour, divided

2 teaspoons baking powder

½ teaspoon salt

¼ teaspoon cloves

½ teaspoon nutmeg

½ teaspoon cinnamon

¼ cup plus 2 tablespoons butter

1 cup brown sugar

1 egg

½ cup milk

1 cup raisins

1 cup chopped walnuts

FOR FROSTING

⅔ cup confectioners' sugar

⅛ teaspoon salt

1½ teaspoons butter

1 teaspoon vanilla

2 to 3 teaspoons milk, as needed

Sweet Tip

If the frosting seems lumpy, it will melt when it is applied to the warm hermits. The frosting may crackle on top, too.

Libby's Lacy Chocolate Crisps

MAKES 60 COOKIES

½ cup light corn syrup

⅓ cup butter

½ cup brown sugar

⅛ teaspoon salt

4 oz. semisweet baking chocolate

1 cup flour

⅔ cup sweetened shredded
   coconut

Another spectacular recipe from the collection of Elizabeth Cockrey of Groton, Massachusetts, these cookies rival the most sophisticated European Florentines. Libby, in her early nineties, has started to compile a cookbook, with assistance from her friends, of her favorite recipes. The long-time telephone operator for the Town of Groton, Libby is an accomplished baker.

1. Set the oven rack in the middle position. Preheat oven to 350°F. Prepare a 14-inch by 16-inch baking sheet by greasing it, covering it with foil (shiny side up), or using a silicone liner.

2. Heat corn syrup and butter in a heavy 2-quart saucepan over medium heat, swirling with a wooden spoon until butter is melted. Add brown sugar, salt, and chocolate, and stir. Bring to a boil and remove from heat. Add flour and coconut. Stir until well mixed.

3. Drop mixture by teaspoons onto baking sheet, 2½ inches to 3 inches apart and no more than 12 cookies per sheet. Bake 10 minutes, or until crisps bubble vigorously and develop lacy holes. Let cool 2 minutes on baking sheet, then transfer cookies to a rack and cool completely. Store between sheets of wax paper in a covered tin.

Sweet Tips

- It is important to use semisweet baking chocolate, not chocolate chips, for this recipe because they have less fat.
- If the crisps harden on the cookie sheet, return them briefly to oven.

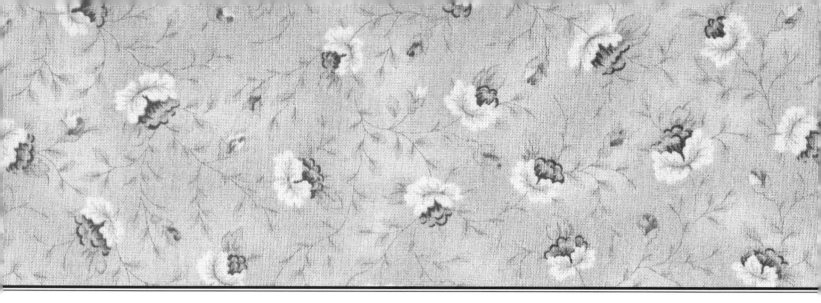

We've always been aware that there was something very special about how you were treated when you went visiting "down South." We always referred to it as

A Southern Lady Pours Tea

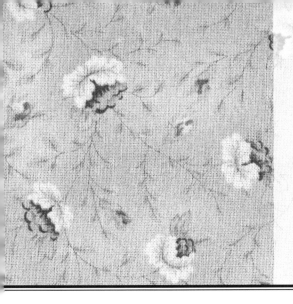

"Southern hospitality." In truth, it probably wasn't that different from the way our own family and friends entertained their guests, but it was fun to consider what it would be like to live on a plantation or visit a southern city like Charleston or Atlanta and eat lots of cornbread, hush puppies, cakes with fluffy frostings, and flaky pies. Part of our imaginary travels included visits to imaginary Southern tearooms,

Cooking pamphlets, American and English, 1915-1920s

rich in tradition and serving cookies, dainty biscuits, and perhaps a slice of Lady Baltimore Cake. Pressed linen and sparkling crystal were always included in our regional daydreams, and the daydreams remained until we actually met someone from the American South.

Elinor Jennings, a true Southern lady, refined and hospitable, was the head of the editorial room at the research and development laboratory at MIT, where Marilynn first worked after graduating from college. Elinor was born in Florida, and she was devoted to the Southern standards with which she had been reared. Although a generation separated them, the two got on famously, chatting between editing projects. Although born to a mother who baked her own biscuits every day, Elinor admitted that she herself was not a cook, but that she had a real appreciation for "good food." Elinor and Marilynn began to take a tea break every afternoon, drinking from real china cups and nibbling home-baked cookies. Elinor gave Marilynn several recipes that had been handed down in her family.

Going over the living recipes that Elinor passed on to Marilynn so many years ago, we found that we were still intrigued by the true meaning of Southern hospitality.

As we began to read our collection of books and pamphlets on entertaining, many of which were written for women living in the American South during the 1920s and 1930s, we began to understand this concept. We found that a successful hostess knew what made her guests feel at ease. Not only did she maintain an open door and provide a laden table, she was expected to promote a tranquil atmosphere in her home. If the lady of the house did not have help, it was acceptable to employ a tiered tea table or any other refinement that made the meal progress smoothly. We learned that certain subjects were not to be brought up at the table, and it was suggested that only current topics be discussed. Guests were always invited to return.

In looking through our collection of manuscript cookbooks, we found several outstanding examples of living recipes such as Chattanooga Chocolate Peanut Butter Bars and Dixie Dinner Rolls created or interpreted by women from the American South. We also included Pecan Wafers, Marion Freeman's Date and Nut Bread, and Mrs. Tate's "Old and Tried" Orange Cake—sweets that a Southern lady who had an appreciation for good food and the comfort of her guests would have baked and served. We hope you will try these recipes when you feel like a taste of Southern hospitality.

Handwritten recipe for Pecan Wafers, 1920s

ELINOR'S LEMON DROP COOKIES WITH LEMON GREMOLATA

MAKES 60 COOKIES

FOR COOKIES

2 cups flour

½ teaspoon baking soda

½ teaspoon salt

½ cup butter

1 cup sugar, plus more for flattening cookies

2 eggs

2 tablespoons grated lemon zest

1 teaspoon vanilla

¼ cup lemon juice

FOR GREMOLATA TOPPING

¼ cup clear sanding sugar

3 tablespoons grated lemon zest

This is a dainty all-natural lemon cookie. The first bite is the most exciting when you taste the sugary lemon crunch of the topping. We think this cookie should be enjoyed with a tall glass of very sweet Southern iced tea. Given to Marilynn by Elinor Jennings, who traveled extensively throughout the American South from the 1930s through the 1950s, Elinor maintained that she had tasted some very good food in her travels.

1. Set the oven rack in the middle position. Preheat the oven to 375°F. Cover a 14-inch by 16-inch baking sheet with foil, shiny side up. Coat the foil with vegetable spray or use a silicone liner.

2. To make the cookies: Sift together flour, baking soda, and salt.

3. Cream butter and sugar in the bowl of a standing mixer fitted with the paddle attachment. Add eggs, lemon zest, and vanilla and beat well. Add flour mixture alternately with lemon juice. Wrap dough in plastic wrap and chill for 2 hours or overnight in the refrigerator.

4. With floured hands or wearing disposable gloves, break off teaspoon-sized pieces of dough and roll into balls. Place balls on baking sheet, spacing them at least 2 inches apart to allow for spreading during baking. Dip the bottom of a drinking glass in warm water and then granulated sugar and press balls flat. Continue until all balls are flattened and have a light coating of sugar.

5. To make the gremolata topping: Mix sanding sugar and lemon zest and sprinkle over cookies. Bake 10 to 12 minutes, or until cookies are slightly browned around the edges. Cool on rack. Store between sheets of wax paper in a covered tin.

Marion Freeman's Date and Nut Bread

This recipe came from the collection of Mrs. George S. Sutton of Penny Farms, Florida. She requested it from Marion Freeman who brought it to a "lunch" given by Mrs. Sutton on Christmas day. We suggest spreading a warm slice with whipped cream cheese. The combination of dense nut-studded sweet bread and tangy cream cheese is one that should not be overlooked.

1 cup dates, chopped

1 tablespoon butter

1 cup boiling water

2 cups flour

1 teaspoon baking powder

1 teaspoon baking soda

½ teaspoon salt

1 cup sugar

1 egg, beaten

1 teaspoon vanilla

1½ cups chopped toasted pecans

1. Set the oven rack in the middle position. Line the bottom and ends of a 9-inch by 5-inch by 3-inch loaf pan with a single strip of wax paper. Coat the pan and wax paper liner with vegetable spray.

2. Combine dates, butter, and boiling water in a small bowl. Let stand 25 minutes, or until at room temperature and most of the liquid is absorbed.

3. Sift together flour, baking powder, baking soda, and salt.

4. Add sugar, egg, and vanilla to date mixture and combine. Add sifted dry ingredients and combine. Fold in pecans.

5. Pour batter into loaf pan. Bake 1 hour, or until top is browned and a tester inserted into bread comes out clean. Place pan on rack and cool at least 20 minutes. Turn out bread onto rack and allow to cool completely. Store covered with a paper towel and wrapped in wax paper at room temperature.

How to Toast Nuts

Preheat the oven to 350°F. Spread the nuts on a foil-wrapped cookie sheet, shiny side up. Toast the nuts for 5 minutes. Remove the cookie sheet from the oven, shake the nuts to expose the other sides and return pan to oven for another 5 minutes. Set baking sheet on rack to cool. We suggest you store any unused nuts in the refrigerator in sealed plastic bags labeled with the name of the nut, the quantity, and the date toasted.

FROZEN CITRUS PIE

MAKES 8 TO 9 PIECES

FOR CRUST

13 graham crackers, 2½ inches by 5 inches each (1 sleeve from a 3-sleeve box)

¼ cup butter, melted

½ confectioners' sugar

FOR FILLING

1½ cups milk, divided

¼ cup light corn syrup

¼ cup cornstarch

1 cup sugar

¼ teaspoon salt

2 teaspoons grated lemon zest

6 egg yolks

½ cup lemon juice or ¼ cup lemon juice and ¼ cup lime juice

2 cups heavy cream, chilled

¼ cup confectioners' sugar

This recipe comes from two sources. The filling is an adaptation of the filling for Mrs. Carl Winchenbach's Banana Cream Pie (page 144), and the crust is a living recipe from the collection of Fran Kelly DaCosta, a well-traveled sophisticate from Watertown, Massachusetts.

1. Set the oven rack in the middle position. Preheat the oven to 375°F. Coat a 9-inch ovenproof glass pie plate with vegetable spray. Set aside a medium metal bowl for the custard and a larger bowl for the ice bath. Have ice cubes handy, but keep frozen until ready to use.

2. To make the crust: Place graham crackers in the bowl of a food processor fitted with a metal blade. Pulse to make crumbs the size of cornmeal (about 1½ cups). Add butter and confectioners' sugar and pulse to combine. Press crumbs on bottom and sides of pie plate. Bake 8 minutes. Set on rack to cool.

3. To make the filling: Combine 1¼ cups of the milk and corn syrup in a heavy saucepan. Cook over medium-low heat, stirring constantly with a wooden spoon until bubbles start to form around the edges, up to 7 minutes. Remove from heat.

4. Whisk cornstarch into remaining ¼ cup milk. Add sugar, salt, and lemon zest and mix thoroughly. Add egg yolks, one at a time, to cornstarch mixture and whisk until well blended. Add a little of the hot milk mixture to egg mixture to temper it and whisk briskly to blend. Whisk remaining hot milk mixture into eggs.

5. Return mixture to saucepan and bring to a simmer over medium heat. Cook about 30 seconds, stirring continuously until mixture begins to thicken. Remove from heat and whisk. Add lemon juice and whisk again. Place custard in metal bowl and set bowl in ice bath. Stir occasionally until custard is chilled.

6. Pour heavy cream into the bowl of a standing mixer fitted with the whisk attachment. Beat until thick. Gradually add confectioners' sugar. Fold 1½ cups of the whipped cream into custard and turn into cooled pie shell. Pipe remaining whipped cream around edge. Place pie in the freezer several hours. Remove pie from freezer 10 minutes before serving. Store leftover pie in freezer.

PINEAPPLE UPSIDE-DOWN CAKE

This is the closest we could come to replicating the Pineapple Upside-Down Cake Elinor Jennings made for Marilynn's birthday in 1971. It was a memorable cake with syrupy candied fruit on top and a macaroon-like crumb. Elinor made her cake in a cast iron frying pan, and it was so heavy she had to ask her husband to turn it onto a rack for her.

½ cup butter, melted

1 cup brown sugar

7 slices canned pineapple, drained, juice reserved

7 candied or maraschino cherries, drained (optional)

1 cup cake flour

1 teaspoon baking powder

½ teaspoon salt

3 eggs, separated

1 cup sugar

1 teaspoon vanilla

1. Set the oven rack in the middle position. Preheat the oven to 350°F. Swirl the melted butter in a 9-inch cake pan, coating the sides, but allowing most of butter to settle on the bottom of pan. Sprinkle brown sugar over bottom of pan.
2. Wipe pineapple slices dry on both sides with a paper towel. Also dry maraschino cherries, if using. Arrange pineapple and cherries in a decorative pattern on bottom of cake pan.
3. Sift together cake flour, baking powder, and salt.
4. Beat egg yolks in a large bowl. Add sugar, vanilla, and 5 tablespoons reserved pineapple juice. Mix well. Add sifted dry ingredients and combine.
5. Place egg whites in the bowl of a standing mixer fitted with the whisk attachment. Beat until moderately stiff, but not dry. Fold egg whites into batter.
6. Pour batter into cake pan. Bake 30 to 35 minutes, or until tester inserted into cake comes out clean. Cool on rack 2 to 3 minutes. Invert cake (it will still be very hot) onto a second cooling rack. If bits of brown sugar or pieces of fruit remain in pan, retrieve and place them on top of cake. Serve warm or at room temperature with whipped cream. Store loosely wrapped in wax paper at room temperature.

SWEET TOUCH   This cake can also be made with canned peach or apricot halves. We used tiny cubes of candied citron with the pineapple and cherries to give the top of the cake a stained-glass effect.

"The Radio Lady's" Pecan Wafers

MAKES 30 COOKIES

1 cup dark brown sugar

6 tablespoons flour

¼ teaspoon baking powder

¼ teaspoon salt

2 eggs, beaten

1 cup chopped pecans

We put these cookies together in about ten minutes while we preheated the oven. Add fifteen minutes for baking, five minutes for cooling, and we had almost instant gratification. This recipe came from "The Radio Lady" who took notes during the 1920s while listening to a cooking show on WJAR radio station. These crispy, light cookies taste of pecans from the Old South.

1. Set the oven rack in the middle position. Preheat the oven to 350°F. Prepare a 14-inch by 16-inch baking sheet by covering it with parchment paper or a silicone liner.
2. Combine brown sugar, flour, baking powder, and salt in a medium bowl. Add eggs and mix well. Fold in pecans.
3. Drop dough by teaspoons 2 inches apart on pans. Bake 15 minutes or until lightly browned. Place baking sheet on a rack and let cool 5 minutes. Transfer cookies to rack and cool completely. Cookies will crisp as they cool.

Nutmeg grater, 1890-1910

Marmalade Cookies

This recipe was printed on a piece of yellowed newspaper found in a manuscript cookbook that spanned the early 1900s to the 1960s. The cookie called for orange marmalade, but you can use any flavor of good commercial marmalade. The cookies have an almost meringuelike taste. They are more like teacakes than cookies because they are soft and delicate and never become crisp. These cookies do not disappoint.

3 cups cake flour
½ teaspoon salt
½ teaspoon baking soda
½ cup butter
1 cup sugar
2 eggs, beaten
1 teaspoon vanilla
¾ cup marmalade

1. Set the oven rack in the middle position. Preheat the oven to 350°F. Cover a 14-inch by 16-inch baking sheet with foil, shiny side up. Coat the foil with vegetable spray or use a silicone liner.

2. Sift together flour, salt, and baking soda.

3. Cream butter and sugar in the bowl of a standing mixer fitted with paddle attachment. Add eggs and vanilla. Add sifted dry ingredients and combine. Add marmalade. Let dough rest 5 to 10 minutes in the refrigerator.

4. Drop dough by teaspoons on baking sheet, about 2 inches apart. (These cookies do not spread.) Bake 15 minutes, turning once after 7 minutes, until cookies are lightly browned. Place baking sheet on a rack and let cool 2 minutes. Transfer cookies to another rack and cool completely. Cookies will become firmer as they cool. Store between sheets of wax paper in a covered tin.

Sweet Tip

This dough will handle more easily if you keep it chilled until ready to bake. Also, keep sheets of unbaked cookies in the refrigerator until they are ready to go into the oven.

OKLAHOMA STRAWBERRY SHORTCAKE

MAKES 8 SHORTCAKES

1 cup flour

2 teaspoons baking powder

¼ cup sugar

⅛ teaspoon salt

¼ cup cold lard, cut in ½-inch cubes

⅓ cup heavy cream

1 egg, beaten

Clear sanding sugar

1½ cups strawberries, washed, hulled, drained, and sliced

8 whole strawberries

1 cup heavy cream, whipped with 2 tablespoons confectioners' sugar

This recipe replicates the shortcake made by James "Tulsa" Stuart, a student from Oklahoma who worked at MIT in the late 1960s. He made this shortcake for an employee gathering. Nearly forty years later, his strawberry shortcake, made exclusively with lard as its shortening, is still unforgettable.

1. Set the oven rack in the middle position. Preheat the oven to 450°F. Cover a 14-inch by 16-inch baking sheet with foil, shiny side up. Coat the foil with vegetable spray or use a silicone liner.

2. Place flour, baking powder, sugar, and salt in the bowl of a food processor fitted with the metal blade. Pulse three times to mix. Add lard and pulse three more times. Add heavy cream and pulse until dough comes together.

3. Place dough on a lightly floured sheet of wax paper or parchment paper. Roll out or pat to a ½-inch thickness. Cut 2½-inch circles using a biscuit cutter dipped in flour. Press cutter straight down and lift up; do not twist cutter in dough, or shortcakes will not rise. Use a spatula to lift and transfer dough to baking sheet. Brush tops with beaten egg and sprinkle with sanding sugar. Gather up scraps and reroll to cut more shortcakes. Shortcakes made from scraps may not be as tender, but they will still be good. Bake 12 minutes, or until lightly browned. Place on a rack to cool.

4. To serve, cut shortcakes in half. Place each bottom half on a plate and cover generously with whipped cream and sliced strawberries. Replace top of shortcake and garnish with more whipped cream and a whole strawberry on the side. Store leftover shortcakes in a sealed plastic bag at room temperature.

BUTTERMILK BISCUITS

MAKES 9 BISCUITS, 2½-INCHES IN DIAMETER

2 cups flour

½ teaspoon baking soda

2 teaspoons baking powder

½ teaspoon salt

6 tablespoons cold butter,
 cut into dice

¾ cup buttermilk

Marilynn made biscuits for what she thought was the first and last time when she was twelve. Although her age may have been tender, her biscuits weren't. Faced with the challenge of writing this book, Marilynn decided it was time to make biscuits again. After consulting several of our collections of living recipes, we found this simple no-nonsense recipe that yielded stellar results. Marilynn has now conquered her fear of biscuits!

1. Set the oven rack in the middle position. Preheat the oven to 450°F. Prepare a 14-inch by 16-inch baking sheet by greasing it or using a silicone liner.

2. Combine flour, baking soda, baking powder, and salt in a large bowl. Work in butter with your fingers (wear disposable gloves, if desired) until butter pieces are the size of small peas. Add buttermilk and work in gently. Knead twice in bowl.

3. Place dough on a floured surface. Knead gently two times. Sprinkle lightly with flour and pat into a circle ½ inch thick. Cut out 2½-inch biscuits using a biscuit cutter dipped in flour. Press cutter straight down and lift up; do not twist cutter in dough, or biscuits will not rise. Transfer biscuits to baking sheet using a wide floured spatula. Gather up scraps, reshape dough, and cut out more biscuits. Biscuits made from scraps may not be as tender, but they will still be good.

4. Bake 12 to 13 minutes, or until lightly browned. Biscuits are best eaten within an hour of baking. Serve with butter and jam.

Sweet Tip

Do not handle biscuit dough too much or the biscuits will be tough. Brush unbaked biscuits with beaten egg to give them a brown color or brush with melted butter to add more flavor.

DIXIE DINNER ROLLS

This recipe was a pleasant surprise. We had never baked with self-rising flour before, and always envisioned southern farmhouse kitchens when we found recipes that called for this type of flour. Less than five minutes to "throw together," and only twelve minutes to bake, these biscuitlike dinner rolls are a great success. Your home will smell like an old-fashioned farmhouse kitchen while these are baking in the oven!

2 cups self-rising flour
½ teaspoon sugar
1 cup milk
¼ cup mayonnaise

1. Set the oven rack in the middle position. Preheat the oven to 450°F. Coat the cups and top surface of a 12-cup muffin pan with vegetable spray.
2. Mix flour, sugar, and milk in a medium bowl. Add mayonnaise and mix until just combined. Fill muffin sections two-thirds full. Bake 12 minutes, or until lightly browned. Remove from oven and cool on rack 10 minutes. Serve while still a little warm with butter or jam.

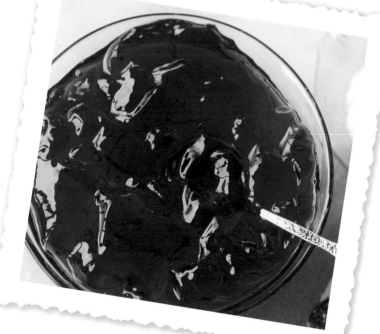

Mrs. Tate's "Old and Tried" Orange Cake

MAKES 10 SLICES

1 8 9 0

We found this recipe as we browsed through a pile of cookbooks we had bought in central Massachusetts. It literally fell into our laps. We were intrigued by the simple little recipe and the reference to "old and tried." This delicate all-natural cake, flavored with the zest and juice of an orange, is very "Southern," and we still wonder how it made it all the way to New England. We'll never know!

1. Set the oven rack in the middle position. Preheat the oven to 350°F. Coat an 8-cup tube pan with vegetable spray or butter. Cut a piece of parchment paper or wax paper to line the bottom of the pan. Insert the liner, coat it with vegetable spray, and dust the pan with flour.

2. To make the cake: Sift together flour, baking powder, and salt.

3. Beat sugar and water in the bowl of a standing mixer fitted with the paddle attachment. Beat in egg yolks, one at a time. Add orange zest and juice. Add sifted dry ingredients and combine until mixture is smooth. Add butter.

4. Place egg whites in the bowl of a standing mixer fitted with the whisk attachment. Beat until stiff. Fold egg whites into batter.

5. Pour batter into tube pan. Bake approximately 45 minutes, or until a tester inserted into cake comes out clean. Cool on rack for 20 minutes before removing from pan. Cake will have pulled away from the sides of the pan.

6. To make the orange glaze: Mix together confectioners' sugar, orange zest, orange juice, and salt to a glaze consistency. Slip a sheet of wax paper under rack to catch drips. Poke tiny holes in top of cake with a cake tester and liberally spoon the glaze over the cake. Let glaze harden before serving. Store under cake dome or loosely wrapped in wax paper at room temperature.

FOR CAKE

2 cups flour

2 teaspoons baking powder

¼ teaspoon salt

2 cups sugar, sifted

½ cup water

5 egg yolks

2 teaspoons grated orange zest

4 tablespoons orange juice

¼ cup butter, melted

4 egg whites

FOR ORANGE GLAZE

1½ cups confectioners' sugar, sifted

2 teaspoons grated orange zest

¼ cup orange juice, as needed

⅛ teaspoon salt

LANNIE'S LORD HAVE MERCY SWEET POTATO PIE

1 9 2 0 S

MAKES 2 PIES, 8 TO 10 SLICES PER PIE

2 unbaked pie shells (see Sheila's Pie Crust on page 110)

2½ lb. raw sweet potatoes (see How to Prepare Sweet Potatoes for Pie, below)

¾ cup butter

1 cup brown sugar

2 cups sugar

3 eggs

½ cup heavy cream

2 teaspoons vanilla

2 teaspoons cinnamon

½ teaspoon cloves

½ teaspoon ginger

1 teaspoon salt

The recipe for this outstanding Sweet Potato Pie was given to us by Yvette Gooding. It is the pie her maternal grandmother, Lannie Waters Edmondson, made for special family gatherings. Mrs. Edmondson, a native of Kinston, North Carolina, taught Yvette how to bake when she was just seven years old. The late Mrs. Edmondson is remembered for having a saying for every occasion and a wonderful sense of humor, too.

1. Set the oven rack in the middle position. Preheat the oven to 375°F.
2. Place prepared sweet potatoes in the bowl of a standing mixer fitted with the paddle attachment. With mixer running on low, add butter. Add brown sugar and sugar. Add eggs, one at a time. Add heavy cream and vanilla. Do not overbeat. Add cinnamon, cloves, ginger, and salt.

HOW TO PREPARE SWEET POTATOES FOR PIE

Preparing the sweet potatoes for Mrs. Edmondson's pie is worth the effort. Select large sweet potatoes, prick them with a fork, and place them on a foiled-covered (shiny side up) metal baking pan that has been coated with vegetable spray. Bake in a 400°F oven for 1 hour.

Place the baking pan on a cooling rack. Carefully cut the hot sweet potatoes in half lengthwise so that they will cool more quickly. When the potatoes are cool enough to handle, scoop out the insides (discard the skins) and place them in the bowl of a food processor fitted with a metal blade. Weigh the sweet potato pulp after scooping it, since the size and weight are hard to discern with your eyes alone. Process until the potatoes are soft and fluffy.

For two pies, you will need 2½ lb. or 40 oz. raw sweet potatoes to make 22 oz. of processed cooked sweet potato—approximately four large potatoes to start. Do not use canned sweet potatoes because freshly baked potatoes still retain some of their fiber.

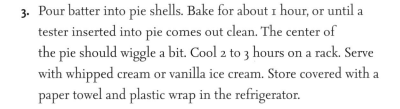

3. Pour batter into pie shells. Bake for about 1 hour, or until a tester inserted into pie comes out clean. The center of the pie should wiggle a bit. Cool 2 to 3 hours on a rack. Serve with whipped cream or vanilla ice cream. Store covered with a paper towel and plastic wrap in the refrigerator.

Sweet Tip

Use only orange sweet potatoes, not white ones, because the texture will be different.

MRS. MOORE'S ANGEL POUND CAKE

1 9 3 0

MAKES 16 SLICES

FOR CAKE

1½ cups sifted flour

½ teaspoon nutmeg

¼ teaspoon salt

1 teaspoon baking powder

½ cup butter, melted and cooled

1 cup sugar

3 eggs

3 tablespoons milk

FOR GLAZE

1½ cups sifted confectioners' sugar

1 tablespoon grated lemon zest

2 tablespoons lemon juice

⅛ teaspoon salt

Sweet Tip

Substitute cinnamon, allspice, or cardamom for the nutmeg. Reduce cardamom to ¼ teaspoon.

This cake has a fine crumb and delicate nutmeg flavor and slices very easily. It is lighter than a pound cake but is not really an angel cake because of the egg yolks and butter. The melted butter gives it the flavor of our old friend, the genoise. Slices of this cake dusted with confectioners' sugar would have been served on a footed milk glass plate. It's great served with a cup of strong tea.

1. Set the oven rack in the middle position. Preheat the oven to 350°F. Butter a 9-inch by 5-inch by 3-inch loaf pan and dust it with flour.

2. To make the cake: Sift together flour, nutmeg, salt, and baking powder.

3. Cream butter and sugar in the bowl of a standing mixer fitted with paddle attachment. Add eggs, one at a time, and beat thoroughly. Add sifted dry ingredients alternately with milk.

4. Pour batter into pan. Bake 35 to 40 minutes, or until tester inserted into cake comes out clean. Cool on rack 20 minutes. Remove cake from pan and set on rack.

5. To make the glaze: Mix together confectioners' sugar, lemon zest, lemon juice, and salt to a pourable consistency. Slip a sheet of wax paper under rack to catch drips. Spoon glaze liberally over cake. Let glaze harden before serving. Store under cake dome or loosely wrapped with wax paper at room temperature.

CHATTANOOGA CHOCOLATE PEANUT BUTTER BARS

MAKES 24 BARS OR 48 TRIANGLES

We found these bars in the collection of a woman we call "The Church Lady." This is a charming southern recipe for a dainty bar cookie, rich with chocolate and peanut butter. Who wouldn't enjoy trying one (or possibly two) with a cup of orange pekoe? The use of peanuts in this bar, albeit as peanut butter, is a very Southern idea.

1. Set the oven rack in the middle position. Preheat the oven to 375°F. Line a 9-inch by 13-inch x 1-inch jelly roll pan with foil, shiny side up. Coat the foil with butter or vegetable spray.
2. To make the bars: Sift together flour, baking powder, and salt.
3. Cream butter and brown sugar in the bowl of a standing mixer fitted with the paddle attachment. Add sour cream, vanilla, and eggs and beat until smooth. Add sifted dry ingredients and combine.
4. Divide batter in half. Add peanut butter to half of batter and chocolate chips to other half; mix in thoroughly. Spread chocolate batter in pan using an offset spatula. (Layer will be very thin.) Gently spread peanut butter batter on top. Bake 18 minutes, or until a tester inserted into middle comes out clean.
5. To make the topping: Remove pan from oven, place on a rack, and sprinkle chocolate chips over the top. Allow 5 minutes for chocolate chips to soften and melt. Spread chocolate with a spatula. Cool on rack 20 minutes more and then refrigerate 1 hour, or until cold and firm. Cut into squares or triangles while cold. Store between sheets of wax paper in a covered tin in the refrigerator.

FOR BARS

1½ cups flour

¾ teaspoon baking powder

¼ teaspoon salt

⅔ cup butter

¾ cup brown sugar

1 cup sour cream

1 teaspoon vanilla

2 eggs

½ cup chunky peanut butter

½ cup semisweet chocolate chips, melted

FOR TOPPING

½ cup semi-sweet chocolate chips

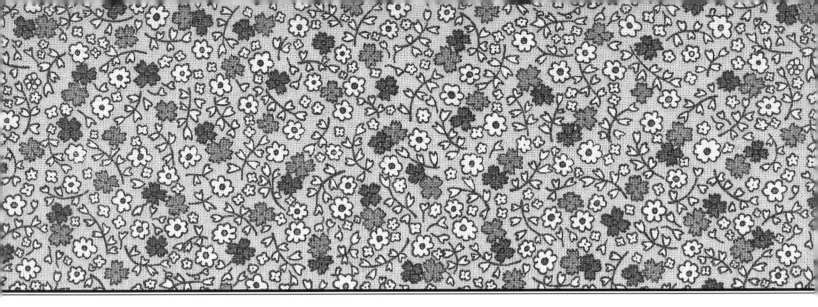

CHAPTER 4

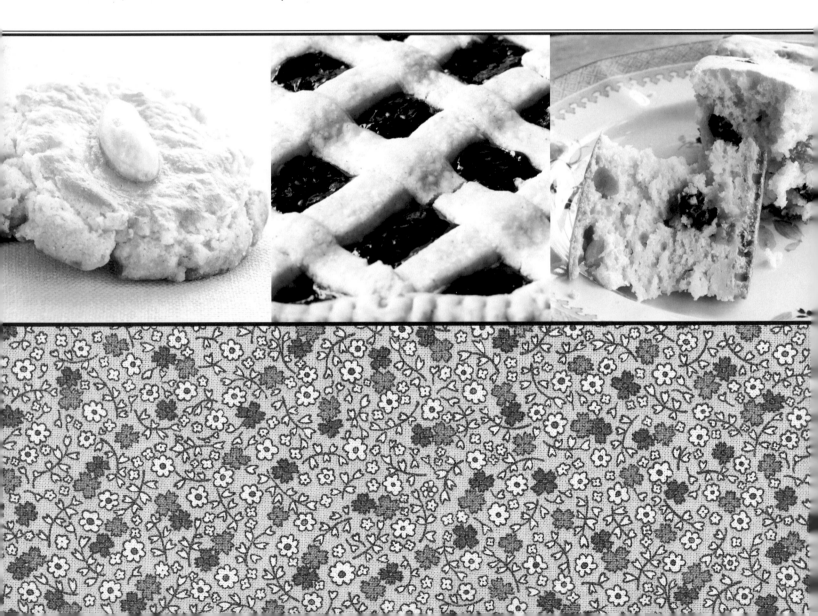

Most of us come from someplace else.
Sometimes we look back from where
we've come, and we deeply miss the place
we've left. Often, we look with hope and

COMING TO AMERICA

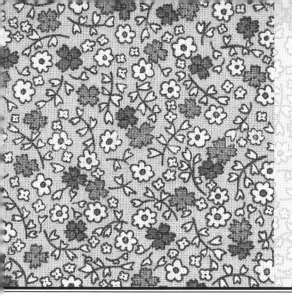

joy to where we're going, and when we
arrive, we know that we've found a new
home. One way to ease that transition
often includes eating familiar foods and
cooking the recipes from our old homeland
in our new homeland. In writing Heirloom
Baking we were fascinated to learn
about the diverse culinary legacy of the
women who compiled the living recipes
in our collection of manuscript cookbooks.

The Art of Making Italian Desserts, 1960s

It is the stories of these adventuresome and courageous newcomers that captivate and delight us.

One Canadian woman's story is especially memorable, that of a young bride who emigrated to Canada by way of Poland. We learned about Bessie Rothblott's Taglich from her great-granddaughter, Michelle Tennen. Bessie, the creator of these delectable jam and nut-filled cookies dipped in boiling honey, was born in a small village and married when she was only fourteen years old. The young couple settled in Toronto where their three children were born and Bessie became known for her generosity, as well as her skillful baking.

Bessie always started her baking at 4:30 in the morning, and her kitchen was filled with the aroma of butter, walnuts, and honey. When she was 75 years old, she decided to take classes to learn how to read English. She followed the adventures of Dick and Jane, while her grandchildren nibbled on her taglich. Bessie lived well into her nineties. Her children and grandchildren still refer to her taglich as "Bubbe's cookies." Because she invited her 16-year-old great granddaughter to watch her make her taglich, the recipe endures. Michelle still carries a copy of this recipe with her because it makes her feel close to Bessie.

Melania Marasi, a well-loved great-grandmother who died at age 103, emigrated from Italy when she was 18. She gave us the recipes for her Butterballs and her biscotti.

Like good home cooks everywhere, Mrs. Marasi made these recipes all her own by the original way in which she baked them. She suggested that her biscotti be eaten "just like a cookie, but dipped in wine, milk, coffee, or tea." When asked how she felt about having her recipes preserved and passed on, Mrs. Marasi replied "wonderful."

The story of Marta's Hazelnut Cake has the excitement and suspense of an international drama. Marta, the baker of this light Hungarian fantasy cake, had walked over the Hungarian border with her husband during the Revolution in 1956. The young couple escaped and stayed with relatives while adjusting to their new life in the United States. A talented woman who was skilled in the cuisine and embroidery of her native Hungary, she and her husband counted their change every night to pay for movie tickets to help them polish their English. Whenever we bake Marta's Hazelnut Cake, we think of Marta and her courage.

We hope you will try some of these memorable recipes. They are precious to those who brought them to their new homes, but they are precious to us all because they allow us to better understand the experience of moving on to a new life while preserving something from the past.

Manuscript cookbook with handwritten recipes, 1870s; Pennsylvania Dutch Cook Book, part of series on American regional cooking

Winnie McCarthy's Irish Bread

MAKES 16 SLICES

3 cups flour

¼ cup sugar

4 teaspoons baking powder

2 cups milk

2 eggs

1 tablespoon vegetable shortening

½ cup raisins

½ cup currants

1 tablespoon butter, melted

We found this recipe handwritten on the endpapers of a well-used copy of the Boston Cooking School Cookbook. Winnie McCarthy was an Irish maid working for a Mrs. Powell, in North Scituate, Massachusetts during the 1920s and 1930s. The owner of the book enjoyed Winnie's bread while visiting with Mrs. Powell, and requested the recipe. This bread is not the traditional crumbly Irish soda bread, but a firmer loaf. Winnie suggests testing for doneness with a silver knife.

1. Set the oven rack in the middle position. Preheat the oven to 350°F. Cut a wax paper liner to fit the bottom of a 9-inch cake pan. Coat the pan with vegetable spray, insert the liner, and spray again to coat the liner.

2. Sift together flour, sugar, and baking powder into the bowl of a standing mixer fitted with the paddle attachment. Add milk gradually, beating to combine. Add eggs, one at a time, and shortening. Fold in raisins and currants.

3. Mix batter twice with folding motion before turning out into pan. Brush top of loaf with melted butter. Bake 55 to 60 minutes, or until top of loaf is crisp and golden brown and a tester inserted into loaf comes out clean. Cool in pan on rack. Store loosely wrapped in wax paper at room temperature.

Sweet Tip

Winnie suggests adding 1 tablespoon of caraway seeds to the batter to give this bread a more authentic Irish taste.

SWEET TOUCH This bread is wonderful toasted and served with butter and orange marmalade.

BESSIE'S TAGLICH (Bubbe's Cookies)

1 9 0 8

MAKES 55 COOKIES

FOR COOKIES

4 cups flour

2 teaspoons baking powder

1 teaspoon salt

⅔ cup vegetable oil

1 cup sugar

4 eggs

FOR FILLING

½ cup golden raisins

½ cup plum jam

½ cup walnut crumbs

½ cup sweetened shredded
  coconut

FOR HONEY DIP

½ cup honey

This is the recipe for Bessie Rothblott's Taglich, a Canadian cookie by way of Poland. These were Bessie's signature cookies. They are a substantial rolled confection filled with golden raisins, plum jam, walnut crumbs, and coconut, baked to a warm brown and then boiled in honey. The slightly sour plum jam balances the sweetness of the coconut and honey.

1. Set the oven rack in the middle position. Preheat the oven to 375°F. Cover a 14-inch by 16-inch baking sheet with foil, shiny side up. Coat the foil with vegetable spray or use a silicone liner.
2. To make the cookies: Sift together flour, baking powder and salt.
3. Place oil and sugar in the bowl of a standing mixer fitted with the paddle attachment. Combine until smooth. Add eggs one at a time and mix thoroughly. Add sifted dry ingredients in thirds. Batter will begin to form dough. Chill dough in the refrigerator 1 hour, or until firm enough to roll out.
4. To make the filling: Combine raisins, jam, walnut crumbs, and coconut in a bowl. Chill in the refrigerator until ready to use.

HOW LONG TO CHILL DOUGH

You may notice that we advise you to chill your dough before rolling out or forming the cookies in this chapter. We've found that several of the doughs we've been working with need at least one hour in the refrigerator before we can work with them. This doesn't mean that you can't chill the dough for longer than one hour or overnight if you don't have time to finish the recipe. Some doughs, like the yeast dough for Dorothy Katziff Brass' Refrigerator Coffee Rolls, need to be refrigerated overnight.

KNOW YOUR OVEN

After reading the handwritten recipes in our collection of manuscript cookbooks, we found that there was no mention of how to cope with differing oven temperatures or baking times. The recipe would simply ask for a hot or quick or slow oven. Some very old sources even suggested that you place flour or a piece of paper in your stove to judge the level of heat by how quickly the flour or paper browned. Some brave souls even mentioned placing a hand into the oven and quickly removing it to judge the temperature. We don't recommend doing any of these!!

Instead, we ask you to get to know your oven. In order to remove the guesswork from your oven, we suggest you invest in an accurate oven thermometer. If you find that it takes a longer or shorter time for a cookie or pie or cake to brown or to test done when you bake in your own oven, go by your own guidelines. If you need to turn a sheet of cookies or brownies halfway through the baking process to be sure of even browning, do so. If you find the temperature that we suggest is too high or too low to produce the desired finished result in your oven, adjust the recipe accordingly. Remember, you and your stove have an intimate relationship, and no one knows it better than you do.

5. Roll out chilled dough on floured wax paper or parchment paper to a thickness slightly less than ³⁄₁₆ inch. Cut 2³⁄₄-inch circles using a cookie cutter or biscuit cutter.

6. Place ½ teaspoon filling horizontally in the center of each dough circle. With floured hands, roll up dough circles toward you, making neat little packages. Using the palm of your hand, roll each package toward you two or three times until it resembles something between a rugelach and a mini egg roll. Place on baking sheet. Bake 23 to 25 minutes, or until warm brown in color. Place baking sheet on a rack to cool.

7. To make the honey dip: Coat a cooling rack with vegetable spray and set it on top of a foil-covered baking sheet. Place honey in a heavy metal saucepan, bring to a boil over medium heat, and reduce heat so honey is at a low boil. Dip taglich, two at a time, into honey. Lift out with long-handled tongs and place on cooling rack. Allow to cool. Store loosely covered with wax paper in a covered tin.

Marta's Hazelnut Cake

MAKES 8 SLICES

FOR CAKE

1 cup hazelnuts

¾ cup sugar, divided

6 eggs, separated, plus 1 whole egg

½ teaspoon salt

1 teaspoon vanilla

½ cup bread crumbs, divided

FOR FROSTING AND FILLING

3 cups confectioners' sugar

1 cup butter

2 tablespoons instant espresso powder, dissolved in 2 tablespoons hot water

4 tablespoons Dutch cocoa

Pinch of salt

4 to 6 tablespoons water

2 tablespoons cognac

½ cup whole hazelnuts, toasted

We tried baking this cake from the modest notes Sheila had taken in the early 1960s. After doing some research, we found that this cake is actually a variation of the Austrian Nusstorte, a light flourless cake made from eggs and ground hazelnuts. The frosting and filling are made from cocoa, espresso powder, and unsalted butter mixed with confectioners' sugar. The cognac used to moisten the layers and the eggs in the batter make this a delicious Hungarian sweet.

1. Set the oven rack in the middle position. Preheat the oven to 375°F. Set aside an ungreased 9-inch springform pan.

2. To make the cake: Place hazelnuts and ¼ cup of the sugar in the bowl of a food processor fitted with the metal blade. Pulse two times, or until nuts are finely ground. Do not overprocess.

3. Place 6 egg yolks, 1 whole egg, salt, and vanilla in a bowl of a standing mixer fitted with the paddle attachment. Beat until thick and lemon-colored. Fold in hazelnut mixture. Set aside 1 tablespoon bread crumbs and fold in the rest.

4. Place 6 egg whites in another bowl of standing mixer fitted with the whisk attachment. Beat until whites form stiff peaks. Gradually add remaining ½ cup sugar and continue beating until sugar is dissolved. Add a quarter of egg whites to batter and combine. Sprinkle remaining tablespoon of bread crumbs into batter. Fold in remaining egg whites.

5. Place batter in pan. Bake 30 minutes, or until top is lightly brown. Cake will seem dry. Place on rack to cool.

6. To make the frosting and filling: Combine confectioners' sugar, butter, espresso mixture, cocoa, and salt in a bowl of standing mixer fitted with the paddle attachment. Add water as needed to achieve a spreadable consistency. Split completely cooled cake in half with long serrated knife. Sprinkle bottom layer with cognac. Spread generously with frosting. Replace top layer of cake and frost top and sides. Place whole hazelnuts around edge of cake.

Libby's Coconut Linzer Bars

Written on a lined index card, this recipe for a bar cookie made with raspberry jam and coconut is an easy way to enjoy the linzer experience. We, like so many other home cooks, have baked traditional linzer cookie sandwiches, cut from a dough made with ground hazelnuts and filled with raspberry jam.

1. Set the oven rack in the middle position. Preheat the oven to 425°F. Line the bottom and four sides of an 8-inch by 8-inch by 2-inch pan with foil, shiny side up. Coat the foil with butter or vegetable spray.

2. Place coconut in the bowl of a food processor fitted with a metal blade. Pulse two or three times until coconut flakes are reduced in length. Set coconut aside. (Be careful not to reduce coconut flakes to coconut dust.)

3. Place flour, salt, and butter in the bowl of a food processor fitted with the metal blade. Process until butter is the size of small peas, Add cold water, 1 tablespoon at a time. Pulse two more times. Particles should cling together. Remove dough from bowl of food processor and form into ball. Pat dough into bottom of pan with fingers until bottom is evenly covered. Bake 20 minutes, or until lightly browned. Place pan on rack and cool. Reduce oven temperature to 375°F.

4. Beat eggs in the bowl of a standing mixer fitted with the paddle attachment. Gradually add sugar and continue beating until mixture is thick and light in color. Fold in coconut.

5. Spread jam over cooled pastry to within ¼ inch of edges. Carefully spread coconut mixture over preserves. Return pan to oven and bake 25 minutes, or until coconut is golden brown. Place pan on rack and cool completely. Cut into bars. Store between sheets of wax paper in a covered tin.

1 8-oz. package unsweetened shredded coconut

1¼ cups flour

½ teaspoon salt

½ cup cold butter, cut into ½-inch dice

2 tablespoons cold water

2 eggs

½ cup sugar

¾ cup seedless raspberry jam or apricot jam

HUNGARIAN CRISSCROSS COOKIES

This is our second encounter with Hungarian Crisscross Cookies. The first ones we tasted and baked in the 1970s were adapted from a handwritten recipe from the Midwest, which we later misplaced. We were overjoyed to find this second recipe, which was written on a lined index card. The jewel-like jam filling peeking from the geometrically consistent pastry strips makes a great presentation.

1. Set the oven rack in the middle position. Heat the oven to 350°F. Line the bottom and sides of a 9-inch by 13-inch x 1-inch jelly roll pan with foil, shiny side up. Coat the foil with butter or vegetable spray.

2. To make the cookies: Place flour, sugar, baking powder, salt, cloves, and cinnamon in the bowl of a food processor fitted with a metal blade. Pulse two or three times until combined. Add butter and combine until mixture is crumbly. Add lemon zest, lemon juice, and ice water. Process just until the dough comes together. Gather dough and scraps, form into ball, and wrap in sheet of wax paper. Chill dough 1 hour, or until firm.

3. To add the filling: Divide dough into thirds. Return one third to refrigerator. Pat two thirds into pan, making sure dough reaches into edges and corners. Spread jam evenly over dough with an offset spatula.

4. Turn out remaining dough onto floured wax paper. Pat to make a rectangle ¼ inch thick. Cut into ½-inch-wide strips along length of rectangle. Carefully lift strips and place them diagonally over layer of jam. Place additional strips in the opposite direction, for a lattice effect. You may have to patch strips of dough (it will still look beautiful after baking). Use remaining strips to form borders around edges of pan.

5. Bake 35 to 40 minutes, or until crust is golden brown and jam is bubbling slightly. Remove from oven and place on rack to cool. Lightly sprinkle confectioners' sugar over top while still warm. Sugar will be absorbed by filling but will remain on crust. When completely cool, remove pastry from foil and cut into squares. Store between sheets of wax paper in a covered tin.

FOR COOKIES

2½ cups flour

⅓ cup sugar

1 teaspoon baking powder

½ teaspoon salt

¼ teaspoon cloves

½ teaspoon cinnamon

1 cup cold butter, cut into ½-inch pieces

1 teaspoon grated lemon zest

4 teaspoons lemon juice

2 tablespoons ice water

¼ cup confectioners' sugar

FOR FILLING

1 cup to 1¾ cups apricot, raspberry, or plum jam, at room temperature

Sweet Tips

- We used a half jelly roll pan. We found that one of our shallow pans had ¾-inch sides and one had 1-inch sides. Both pans are suitable for this recipe.
- We used an 18-inch ruler with a metal edge to measure and cut the strips of dough. You can also use a sharp knife.

SHEILA'S PIE CRUST

2½ cups flour

⅓ cup sugar

¼ teaspoon salt

1 cup cold butter, cut into ½-inch dice

¼ cup ice water

1 egg, beaten (optional; for double-crust pie)

MAKES DOUGH FOR 1 DOUBLE-CRUST 9-INCH PIE, 2 SINGLE-CRUST 9-INCH PIES, OR TWO 8-INCH OR 9-INCH TARTS

We've used this easy-to-make crust for most of the pies in this book because our recipe is very much like the ones we found browsing through our collection of manuscript cookbooks. One woman's recipe in particular, that from Bertha Bohlman, is almost identical. With her artistic background, Sheila is particularly creative in making decorative edges for her pies.

TO MAKE PASTRY

1. Place flour, sugar, and salt in the bowl of a food processor fitted with a metal blade. Pulse three times to mix. Add butter and pulse until crumbly. Add water. Pulse until mixture comes together.
2. Remove dough from bowl of processor, divide in half, and shape each half into a disk. Unless your kitchen is very warm, you don't have to chill dough before rolling out.

TO MAKE A DOUBLE-CRUST PIE

1. Coat a 9-inch ovenproof glass pie plate with vegetable spray.
2. Roll out each disk of dough between 2 sheets of floured wax paper or parchment paper until 2 inches wider than diameter across top of pie plate.
3. Fold one rolled disk in half and then in quarters. Place folded dough into bottom quarter of pie plate. Carefully unfold dough and let it relax into pie plate. Trim excess dough from rim. Chill bottom crust while preparing filling.
4. Brush edges of bottom crust with beaten egg. Fill pie and flip second crust over top of pie. Trim excess dough around rim of pie, leaving just enough to make crimped edge. Press edges of crust together gently with fingers. Crimp edge with the prongs of a salad fork or a pie crimper. Cut six 1-inch decorative slits in center of top crust to allow steam to escape. Brush top crust and edges with beaten egg. Bake as directed in recipe.

TO MAKE A SINGLE-CRUST PIE:

1. Coat a 9-inch ovenproof glass pie plate with vegetable spray.

2. Roll out one disk of dough between 2 sheets of floured wax paper or parchment paper until 2 inches wider than diameter across top of pie plate.

3. Fold rolled disk in half and then in quarters. Place folded dough into bottom quarter of pie plate. Carefully unfold dough and let it relax into pie plate. Trim excess dough around rim, leaving enough to form a decorative edge.

4. Chill crust while preparing filling. Fill and bake pie as directed in recipe.

TO PREBAKE A PIE SHELL

1. Place the oven rack in the middle position. Preheat the oven to 400°F. Follow steps 1–3 above to make a single-crust pie shell.

2. Prick the dough with fork. Cut a piece of foil slightly larger than the pie shell and coat it with vegetable spray. Place the foil, greased side down, in the pie shell, fitting it loosely into bottom and sides. Fill the foil with uncooked rice or beans to prevent the crust from bubbling during baking. Bake 18 minutes.

3. Remove the foil and rice or bean filling carefully. Prick any existing bubbles in the dough. Return the shell to the oven and continue baking, checking every 5 minutes for browning. If the edge of the crust appears to be browning too quickly, cover loosely with foil. Remove the pie from the oven when the shell is golden brown. Cool the crust on a rack before adding the pie filling, unless otherwise directed. The rice or beans can be cooled, placed in a sealed plastic bag, and reused several times to prebake pie shells.

PISTACHIO CRESCENTS

1 9 5 0 S

MAKES 70 COOKIES

FOR DOUGH

2½ cups flour

¼ teaspoon salt

1 cup butter

¾ cup sugar

1½ teaspoons vanilla

1 cup pistachios, toasted
  and ground

FOR TOPPING

1½ cups confectioners' sugar, sifted

Sweet Tip

Use the same dough to make
Pistachio Thumbprint Cookies.
Roll the dough into a ball, place
it on the baking sheet, and
make a thumbprint impression
in the center of the cookie. Place
a toasted pistachio in the
depression. Each baking sheet
will hold 24 cookies. Bake as
for crescents, let cool 3 minutes,
and transfer to a rack. Sift
confectioners' sugar over the top.
Store as for Pistachio Crescents.

Variations of this recipe keep popping up, and we've seen versions using chopped almonds and chopped walnuts, too. We prefer chopped pistachios because we love the slight green color of the nuts and their very Middle Eastern flavor. The veil of confectioners' sugar adds a bit of glamour to their appearance.

1. Set the oven rack in the middle position. Preheat the oven to 350°F. Cover a 14-inch by 16-inch baking sheet with foil, shiny side up. Coat the foil with vegetable spray or use a silicone liner.

2. To make the dough: Sift together flour and salt. Cream butter and sugar in the bowl of a standing mixer fitted with the paddle attachment. Add vanilla and pistachios and combine. Add sifted dry ingredients gradually until dough begins to form. Gather up dough from bowl and knead gently to combine. Continue if dough is workable; if it is too soft to handle, chill in the refrigerator until it is manageable.

3. With floured hands or wearing disposable gloves, break off about 1 teaspoon of dough. Roll dough between your hands to form a 1½-inch-long rope. Shape rope into a crescent and place on baking sheet. Repeat with remaining dough, spacing crescents 1½ inches apart and allowing 30 per sheet (crescents do not spread). Bake 17 minutes, or until lightly brown. Place baking sheet on a rack and cool 2 to 3 minutes.

4. To add the topping: Remove cookies from baking sheet (they may still be hot), dredge in confectioners' sugar, and set on rack until completely cool. Slip a sheet of wax paper under rack. Sift confectioners' sugar generously over cookies. Allow 10 minutes for sugar to set. Store between sheets of wax paper in a covered tin.

Auntie Dot's Dutch Apple Cake

MAKES 10 SLICES

FOR CAKE

2 cups flour

1 tablespoon plus 1 teaspoon
   baking powder

¼ teaspoon salt

½ cup vegetable shortening

½ cup sugar

2 eggs

1 tablespoon vanilla

¾ cup milk

FOR TOPPING

2 tablespoons sugar

1 teaspoon cinnamon

3 apples, peeled and sliced
   ¼-inch thick

1½ tablespoons butter,
   cut into dice

This was the cake that our mother put together when relatives and friends unexpectedly crossed our threshold. It was quick to make because the ingredients could be found easily in our pantry. It baked in 40 minutes, and the apples made the cake moist, almost like a Danish. A slice of Auntie Dot's Dutch Apple Cake is wonderful in the fall with a cup of strong black coffee.

1. Set the oven rack in the middle position. Preheat the oven to 375°F. Cut a wax paper liner to fit the bottom of a 9-inch cake pan. Coat the pan and liner with vegetable spray and dust with flour.

2. To make the cake: Sift together flour, baking powder, and salt into a mixing bowl.

3. Cream shortening and sugar in the bowl of a standing mixer fitted with the paddle attachment. Add eggs and vanilla. Add sifted dry ingredients alternately with milk, mixing well after each addition. Pour batter into pan and spread evenly.

4. To make the topping: Mix sugar and cinnamon in bowl. Arrange apple slices in 2 circles on top of batter. Press apples into batter and sprinkle with cinnamon sugar. Dot with butter.

5. Bake approximately 40 minutes, or until tester inserted into cake comes out clean. Cool on rack. Serve cake slightly warm with vanilla ice cream or whipped cream. Store covered with a paper towel and wrapped in wax paper in the refrigerator.

Sweet Tips

- This is a very moist cake; it is best served the day it is made.
- This cake can be frozen once it has completely cooled.

CANADIAN SUGAR PIE
(Tarte au Sucre)

We found this recipe handwritten on an index card filed among main dishes and salads. We believe it has ties to our neighbors to the north, with origins in France. Although it's simple and quick, this is a serious pie. We love the caramelized sugar taste of this tart, which is so representative of Canadian sweets.

Unbaked 9½-inch tart shell (see
    Sheila's Pie Crust on page 110)

1½ cups brown sugar

2 tablespoons flour

⅛ teaspoon salt

1 teaspoon vanilla

⅓ cup heavy cream

1. Set the oven rack in the middle position. Preheat the oven to 350°F.

2. Use your hands (wear disposable gloves) to combine brown sugar, flour, and salt in a mixing bowl. Pick out and discard any hard particles of brown sugar. Sprinkle mixture evenly over bottom of tart shell.

3. Add vanilla to heavy cream and pour over mixture, spreading lightly with an offset spatula. Bake approximately 35 minutes, or until pastry is golden brown and filling is dark and bubbling. Cool on a rack. Serve either slightly warm or at room temperature with whipped cream. This tart is best when eaten the day it is baked. Store leftover pie loosely covered with a paper towel and wax paper in the refrigerator.

TIPS ON BAKING PIES

Although there has been some debate about whether or not to bake pies on the bottom rack of the oven, we have found that using the middle rack didn't affect the quality of the pies we tested, and it was easier to take pies in and out of the oven.

To solve the problem of pie edges that brown more quickly than the centers, we cover our pies loosely with a piece of foil halfway through the baking process. Placing a ring of foil to fit around the edges of the pie as it bakes can be helpful, too. Commercial edge protectors are also available.

For a shiny top crust, brush on an egg wash before baking. For an opaque brown color, brush on cream.

COMING TO AMERICA

CHINESE ALMOND COOKIES

We searched and searched for this recipe among the many boxes of loose recipes we've been saving for the past forty years. We found it unexpectedly, a small slip of paper with a few handwritten lines, and the yellowed scrap proved as reliable as when we first tried this recipe many years ago. This is representative of the flaky cookies served as dessert at many of the restaurants in U.S. Chinatowns during the 1950s and 1960s.

1. Set the oven rack in the middle position. Preheat the oven to 375°F. Cover a 14-inch by 16-inch baking pan with foil, shiny side up. Coat the foil with vegetable spray or use a silicone liner.

2. To make the cookies: Mix flour, sugar, baking powder, and salt in the bowl of a food processor fitted with the metal blade. Add lard and combine. Sprinkle almond extract over mixture. Add egg and process briefly until all the ingredients are blended and dough starts to form. Pull together dough and chill in the refrigerator for 1 hour, or until firm enough to handle.

3. To add the topping: With floured hands or wearing disposable gloves, roll dough into balls 1¼ inches in diameter. Place balls on baking sheet and flatten with the palm of your hand. Brush tops with beaten egg and place almond in center. Bake 12 minutes, turning baking sheet once after 6 minutes if your oven tends to overbrown. Cool on rack. Store cookies between sheets of parchment paper or wax paper in a covered tin.

FOR COOKIES

3 cups flour

1 cup sugar

1 teaspoon baking powder

½ teaspoon salt

1 cup cold lard, cut into small chunks

1 teaspoon almond extract

1 egg, beaten

FOR TOPPING

1 egg, beaten

48 blanched whole almonds, untoasted

SWEET TOUCH   This cookie can be made with butter, but the original lard produces a cookie with a more substantial texture and flavor.

MEXICAN DEVIL'S FOOD CAKE WITH BUTTER-FRIED PINE NUTS

MAKES 16 SLICES

FOR CAKE

½ lb. zucchini

1½ cups plus 2 tablespoons butter, divided

1¼ cups pine nuts

2½ cups sifted flour

1½ cups cocoa

2½ teaspoons baking powder

1½ teaspoons baking soda

1 teaspoon salt

1½ teaspoons cinnamon

2 cups sugar

4 eggs

2 teaspoons vanilla

½ cup milk

FOR CHOCOLATE GLAZE

¾ cup confectioners' sugar

¼ cup cocoa

⅛ teaspoon salt

1 teaspoon vanilla

2 tablespoons water

This recipe, with its combination of cocoa, cinnamon, and vanilla reminds us of the Mexican hot chocolate that is so popular these days. We decided to add the pine nuts to reinforce the south-of-the-border theme. Browning the pine nuts in a small amount of butter adds to the rich taste of the cake.

1. Set the oven rack in the middle position. Preheat the oven to 350°F. Coat a 10-cup Bundt pan with vegetable spray and dust with flour.

2. To make the cake: Wash zucchini and cut off ends. Grate unpeeled zucchini into a bowl. Let rest 10 minutes, to allow excess moisture to ooze out.

3. Heat 2 tablespoons of the butter in a small frying pan over medium heat. Add pine nuts, stir to coat with butter, and fry, stirring continuously, until buttery and lightly browned, 3 to 4 minutes. Do not let pine nuts darken or they will be bitter. Set aside ¼ cup of the browned pine nuts for topping the glazed cake.

4. Drain zucchini in sieve. Measure 2 cups zucchini, leaving drained liquid in bottom of bowl. Do not squeeze zucchini.

5. Sift together flour, cocoa, baking powder, baking soda, salt, and cinnamon.

6. Place remaining 1½ cups butter and sugar in the bowl of a standing mixer fitted with the paddle attachment. Cream until light and fluffy. Beat in eggs. Mix in zucchini (using the mixer will break up the zucchini and provide a smoother texture). Add vanilla to milk. Add dry ingredients alternately with milk. Fold in 1 cup of the pine nuts.

7. Pour batter into pan. Bake 55 minutes, or until tester inserted into cake comes out dry. Cool on a rack 20 minutes. Invert cake onto second rack. Turn right side up and allow to cool completely.

8. To make the chocolate glaze: Sift together confectioners' sugar, cocoa, and salt. Add vanilla and mix. Add water as needed to form a thin glaze. Slip a sheet of wax paper under rack to catch drips. Drizzle glaze from a teaspoon or fork on top and down sides of cake. Place remaining fried pine nuts on top of cake. Let glaze set before cutting cake. Serve with Mrs. Mattie James' Jamaica Caramel Ice Cream (page 122) or whipped cream. Store under cake dome or loosely wrapped in wax paper at room temperature.

CUBAN FLAN

MAKES 8 SERVINGS

½ cup sugar

1 cup condensed milk

1 cup evaporated milk

3 eggs

1 teaspoon salt

3 oz. cream cheese, warmed in
   microwave for 30 seconds
   on low

1 teaspoon vanilla

We found this recipe in a modest little manuscript cookbook from the 1970s. Although this recipe is a little newer than the others we've selected for this book, we found it intriguing because it seemed so glamorous with its glistening sauce of caramel. The condensed milk gives the flan a very south-of-the-border flavor, while the cream cheese contributes extra richness.

Sweet Tip

If flan does not come out easily, place it in warm water before inverting. Do not use a butter knife to test flan, since it will leave a mark.

1. Set the oven rack in the middle position. Preheat the oven to 350°F. Set aside a 7½-inch round metal cake pan for baking and a larger metal pan and rack for the water bath.

2. Distribute sugar evenly on the bottom of a heavy metal frying pan. Place pan over medium to low heat, swirling sugar in pan until it begins to liquefy and caramelize to a rich golden color, about 15 minutes. Remove pan from heat periodically when swirling sugar to prevent sugar from burning. Do not stir caramel. Carefully pour liquid caramel into cake pan. Using pot holders, tilt pan to coat bottom and sides with caramel.

3. Place condensed milk, evaporated milk, eggs, salt, cream cheese, and vanilla in the bowl of a food processor fitted with a metal blade. Process until smooth. Pour custard into caramel-lined pan.

4. Place pan on rack in large metal pan to make water bath. Pour hot water from a glass measuring cup into outer pan until water level rises halfway up sides of pan containing flan. Place carefully in oven. Bake 50 to 55 minutes, or until surface of flan is firm. Do not allow water to evaporate from the water bath.

5. Remove pan carefully from oven and water bath. Cool on a rack at least 4 hours. Go around edge of pan with a butter knife to loosen flan and invert onto 10–inch plate. Caramel will form sauce when flan is inverted. Store in the refrigerator until ready to serve. Leftover flan should be loosely covered with wax paper and refrigerated.

Mrs. Hall's French Cream Puffs

MAKES 14 TO 16 CREAM PUFFS

1 8 7 5

This is a chou paste or beaten dough used for baking cream puffs and éclairs. It's a simple way to make an elegant dessert. This recipe comes from the same manuscript cookbook that contained the recipe for Mrs. Mattie James' Jamaica Caramel Ice Cream featured on page 122. These ladies were very inventive and adventuresome, and their dessert parties must have been something!

⅔ cup water

6 tablespoons cold butter, cut into ½-inch dice

3 tablespoons sugar

¼ teaspoon salt

1 cup flour

3 eggs, beaten

1. Set the oven rack in the middle of the oven. Preheat the oven to 400°F. Cover a 14-inch by 16-inch baking sheet with foil, shiny side up, or a silicone liner. Do not grease the foil.

2. Combine water, butter, sugar, and salt in a saucepan. Bring to a boil over medium-low heat, stirring with wooden spoon. Remove pan from heat, add flour, and stir briskly until mixture comes together. Return to heat and stir 1 minute.

3. Remove pan from heat. Beat in eggs, one at a time, until batter is silky. Place batter in bowl, cover with plastic wrap, and chill 1 hour in the refrigerator.

4. Transfer batter to a 1-quart zip-close freezer bag and seal closed. Snip diagonally across one lower corner. Pipe mounds of batter 2 inches in diameter onto baking sheet. Press down any peaks in center of mound with a dampened finger.

5. Bake 10 minutes. Reduce temperature to 350°F and bake an additional 20 minutes, or until golden brown. Place on rack to cool. Make a small slit with knife on sides of cream puffs to allow steam to escape. When cool, cut in half. Add filling just before serving. Store unfilled cream puffs loosely wrapped in wax paper in the refrigerator.

SWEET TOUCH These cream puffs are wonderful filled with Mrs. Mattie James' Jamaica Caramel Ice Cream (page 122) and topped with Mrs. Paul Knight's Bittersweet Chocolate Sauce (page 227). They're best eaten the same day they're baked.

Mrs. Mattie James' Jamaica Caramel Ice Cream

MAKES 1 QUART ICE CREAM

FOR CARAMEL SAUCE

½ cup sugar

2 tablespoons water

2 teaspoons light corn syrup

2 tablespoons butter

½ cup heavy cream

Pinch of salt

FOR CUSTARD

6 eggs

2 cups milk

1 cup heavy cream

1 cup sugar

¼ teaspoon salt

1 teaspoon vanilla

This was one of the earliest recipes we tested. It's a rich creamy old-fashioned dessert that reminds us of summer outings and birthday parties. Originally referred to as Mrs. Lyman James' Jamaica Caramel Ice Cream, we were thrilled to find attached to other recipes Mrs. James' first name, which is Mattie.

1. To make the caramel sauce: Combine sugar, water, and corn syrup in a heavy saucepan over high heat. Bring to a boil, stirring with a wooden spoon.

2. Dip a pastry brush in water and wash down insides of pan to prevent crystals from forming. Reduce heat to medium high. Do not stir. Continue boiling until mixture turns golden brown (not dark brown), about 6 minutes.

3. Remove pan from heat. Swirl sauce gently in pan twice. Add butter and stir slowly until melted. Add heavy cream (sauce may foam up) and stir again. (If the caramel seizes—doesn't join with cream—place pan on medium heat and stir with wooden spoon until smooth, about 1 minute.) Add salt. Pour caramel sauce into a glass container and chill in refrigerator. Sauce will thicken on standing. This is a soft caramel sauce and will pour without being reheated.

4. To make the custard: Beat eggs in the bowl of a standing mixer fitted with the paddle attachment. Cook milk, heavy cream, sugar, salt, and vanilla in a heavy-bottomed saucepan over medium heat, stirring continuously until bubbles form around the edges. Remove from heat. Add mixture to eggs in thirds, beating after each addition.

5. Pour custard back into saucepan. Cook over medium heat, stirring with wooden spoon until your finger leaves a mark when drawn

through custard on back of spoon. Remove from heat and strain into a clean bowl. Place plastic wrap on surface of custard and chill in the refrigerator at least 1 hour, or until cold. Combine with chilled caramel sauce.

6. Freeze custard in an ice cream maker, following the manufacturer's instructions. When ice cream is frozen, spoon into a container, cover, and place in freezer for 1 hour to let flavors marry. Serve plain or with Hot Fudge Sauce (page 269).

Cardboard ice cream container, 1930s; ice cream scoop, 1905–1920s

C H A P T E R 5

We are always happy to find a manuscript cookbook, and when we happened across a binder of handwritten recipes from the 1920s through the 1940s at a local yard

The Minister Comes to Dinner

sale, we were excited to add it to our collection. It wasn't just the recipes in the binder for some of the best American desserts that intrigued us. It was the menus we discovered scrawled on scraps of paper tucked between the pages. When we read the menus that had been planned for the minister coming to dinner, we realized that we had found the recipes of an inspired home cook. We learned that on one night in the 1930s, the minister had enjoyed a meal of roast lamb with mint jelly, roast potatoes, peas, and blueberry pie at his hostess's home. Simple, elegant. and homey, the meal represented how seriously this home cook had assumed the role of twentieth-century hostess.

In reading through the collection, we were pleased to find that the hostess also kept her shopping lists, so we now know just which foods she purchased on a daily basis, and which she purchased for special occasions. Although her pantry included brands that might not be familiar to some of today's cooks, such as Blue Ribbon Mayonnaise and Reliable Flour, it was reassuring to find that she bought fresh pineapple and cantaloupe, the best the season had to offer. Whatever she presented at her table was the very best she could find and afford.

Soon we started looking through our other living recipes for dishes that would have been served to that very special guest—the minister or religious leader of the community.

Handwritten recipes for Bible or Scripture Cake, 1890s, and a lemon dessert, 1930s

Cooking pamphlet, American, early 1900s

These signature dishes are ones the successful hostess would have chosen not only to showcase her skill in the kitchen, but also to please the most discriminating of diners.

A woman from Mansfield Ohio, whom we came to refer to as "The Church Lady" because she was active in her Methodist church, provided us with recipes for Christian Service Cookies and Black Pepper Hush Puppies. Well-traveled, she attended many church meetings all over the midwestern and southern regions of the country, collecting recipes wherever she went. And from a German-Jewish aristocrat living in Philadelphia at the turn of the twentieth century comes Mrs. Fleisher's Almond Cake, which is really a torte flavored with clove and lemon and glazed with bittersweet chocolate.

On a faded index card we found Reverend Brown's Cake, spicy and rich with its icing of caramel and golden raisins. A woman whose husband sold poultry feed in Waldoboro, Maine, provided us with the best Banana Cream Pie we've ever tasted, while the manuscript cookbook of Marion Carter tells us how to make the memorable Steamed Chocolate Pudding.

Just as these hostesses baked the best of everything, we hope you too will enjoy baking Mama's Blueberry Pie, Lost and Found Honey Cake, Chocolate Bread and Butter Pudding, and all of the other special recipes in this chapter.

Chocolate Bread and Butter Pudding with Plum Jam

MAKES 20 SERVINGS

FOR CHOCOLATE FUDGE SAUCE

1 cup heavy cream

9 oz. bittersweet chocolate, chopped

1 oz. bitter chocolate, chopped

¼ cup butter

1 teaspoon vanilla

⅛ teaspoon salt

FOR BREAD LAYERS

14 to 16 ½-inch slices brioche or white bread, trimmed of crusts and cut in half

6 tablespoons butter, melted

FOR CUSTARD

2 cups milk

1 cup heavy cream

6 eggs, beaten

1 teaspoon vanilla

¼ teaspoon salt

1 cup sugar

9 oz. bittersweet chocolate, chopped and melted

1 oz. bitter chocolate, chopped and melted

¾ cup plum jam

This pudding may seem like baby food, but it's really the basis for Queen of Puddings, and one of the most elegant of puddings we've ever tasted. It seemed that every other manuscript cookbook we read had a recipe for Queen of Puddings with its layer of jam and crown of meringue. We decided to forego the meringue but to spread the brioche with both butter and chocolate fudge sauce and add two kinds of chocolate to the custard.

1. Set the oven rack in the middle position. Preheat the oven to 350°F. Coat a 9-inch by 13-inch ovenproof glass baking dish with vegetable spray. Set aside a larger metal baking pan and rack for the water bath.

2. To make chocolate fudge sauce: Heat heavy cream in a heavy saucepan over medium heat, stirring with a wooden spoon until little bubbles form around the edges. Remove from heat. Add bittersweet chocolate and bitter chocolate, allow to sit 3 minutes, and stir to combine. Add butter, vanilla, and salt and stir again. Sauce should be thick but spreadable. Set fudge sauce aside. (If fudge sauce hardens before you combine it with brioche and custard, warm in glass bowl in microwave for 30 seconds on low.)

3. To prepare the bread: Brush brioche slices on one side with melted butter.

4. To make the custard: Combine milk, heavy cream, eggs, vanilla, salt, and sugar in a large bowl. Combine bittersweet chocolate and bitter chocolate in a small bowl. Add ½ cup of the custard to chocolate and whisk briskly. Add chocolate mixture to large bowl of custard and whisk again.

5. Place ½ cup of the custard on bottom of baking dish. Tilt and swirl dish until bottom is completely covered. Layer 6 slices of brioche on top of custard, butter side down. Spread half of chocolate fudge sauce thickly over brioche with offset spatula. Pour half of remaining custard over chocolate. Layer on remaining brioche,

butter side down, and chocolate fudge sauce. Spread jam over chocolate sauce. Add remaining custard and smooth with spatula.

6. Use a knife to cut 8 slits through layered pudding. Cover top of pudding with plastic wrap and press down gently with your palm. Let stand 15 minutes. Remove plastic wrap.

7. Place baking dish on rack in large metal pan. Pour hot water from a glass measuring cup into outer pan until water level rises halfway up sides of baking dish. Place carefully in oven. Bake 1 hour to 1 hour 15 minutes. Do not let the water evaporate from water bath. Check after 30 minutes, and cover pudding loosely with foil. Remove foil from pudding after another 40 minutes and leave in oven 5 minutes uncovered to finish baking. Pudding is done when tester inserted into pudding comes out clean. Pudding will look solidified, and bread will pull away from sides of dish.

8. Carefully remove baking dish from oven and water bath. Allow to cool on rack at least 30 minutes. Serve pudding warm or at room temperature with sweetened whipped cream or vanilla ice cream. When completely cooled, store covered with a paper towel and plastic wrap in the refrigerator.

Sweet Tip

We love extra bittersweet chocolate, so we used it in this recipe. We suggest that you use a combination of semisweet and bitter chocolate to achieve a sweeter pudding. Seedless raspberry jam can be used instead of plum jam.

Tin iced pudding molds, American, 1890s -1920s

Mrs. Fleisher's Almond Cake

MAKES 8 TO 10 SLICES

FOR CAKE

8 oz. (1½ cups) whole almonds

1 cup sugar, divided

6 eggs, separated

1 teaspoon grated lemon zest

Pinch of ground cloves

FOR FILLING

¾ cup apricot jam

FOR CHOCOLATE GLAZE

½ cup plus 2 tablespoons sugar

½ cup water

4 oz. bittersweet chocolate, chopped

We discovered this recipe in the manuscript cookbook of Mrs. Fleisher of Philadelphia, Pennsylvania. She wrote the recipe on the back of an invitation to introduce Miss Edna Weil to society. The party was scheduled for Saturday, January 19, 1907. Because of the quality of the paper used for the invitation, the recipe has been preserved.

1. Set the oven rack in the middle position. Preheat the oven to 350°F. Coat a 9-inch springform pan with vegetable spray. Cut a parchment paper or wax paper liner to fit the bottom of the pan. Insert the liner and spray again. Dust pan with flour and tap out the excess.

2. To make the cake: Place almonds and ½ cup of the sugar in the bowl of a food processor fitted with the metal blade. Grind until texture is fine.

3. Place egg whites in the bowl of a standing mixer fitted with the whisk attachment. Beat until stiff but not dry.

4. Place egg yolks and remaining ½ cup sugar in the bowl of a standing mixer fitted with the paddle attachment. Beat until light and fluffy. Add lemon zest and cloves. Add almond mixture. Pour one fourth of beaten egg whites into almond batter and mix to lighten. Gently but thoroughly fold in remaining egg whites.

5. Pour mixture into springform pan. Smooth top gently with an offset spatula. Bake 35 to 45 minutes, or until a tester inserted in center of cake comes out clean. Cool on rack 15 minutes. Run a butter knife gently around edges and remove sides of pan. Allow to cool another 30 minutes. Invert cake onto another rack, remove bottom of pan and paper liner, and invert back onto first rack. Allow to cool completely.

6. To make the filling: Warm apricot jam in a saucepan over low heat. Transfer jam to the bowl of a mini food processor fitted with a metal blade, or put through a mesh strainer. Process until smooth.

7. To make the chocolate glaze: Combine sugar and water in a heavy saucepan over medium heat and bring to a boil. Remove from heat. Add chocolate, stirring constantly until chocolate is melted. Return pan to medium heat and continue stirring until mixture returns to a boil, thickens, and becomes shiny, about 3 minutes. Cool 10 minutes. The glaze will thicken further upon cooling.

8. Split cake into 2 horizontal layers using a serrated knife. Place
   bottom layer on a cake round. Place four strips of wax paper or
   parchment paper under edges of cake to protect plate. Spread
   filling on bottom cake layer with an offset spatula. Set top cake
   layer in position. Pour glaze over top of cake and allow to run
   down the sides. If the sides are not adequately covered, spread
   glaze with offset spatula. Let glaze set. Place cake, uncovered, in the
   refrigerator. About 15 minutes before serving, carefully remove
   strips of wax paper and bring to room temperature. Store loosely
   wrapped in wax paper in the refrigerator.

RICH POPPY SEED CAKE

1 9 4 0 S

MAKES 14 SLICES

2½ cups flour

1 teaspoon baking soda

1 teaspoon salt

1 cup poppy seeds

⅓ cup honey

¼ cup water

1 cup butter

1½ cups sugar

4 eggs, separated

1 teaspoon vanilla

1 cup sour cream

Confectioners' sugar

This cake is one of those wonderful mysteries we came across while browsing through our manuscript cookbooks—it was just a list of ingredients and some sketchy instructions. We were happy to have at least an oven temperature and a suggested baking time. It sounded so good, we had to try it regardless of its lack of information, and it's a good thing we did—this cake is rich and delicious!

1. Set the oven rack in the middle position. Preheat the oven to 350°F. Coat an 8-cup Bundt pan with vegetable spray and dust with flour. Tap pan to remove excess flour.

2. Sift together flour, baking powder, and salt.

3. Heat poppy seeds, honey, and water in a saucepan over medium heat until bubbles form around the edges. Remove from heat.

4. Cream butter and sugar in the bowl of a standing mixer fitted with the paddle attachment. Add egg yolks, vanilla, and sour cream. Add poppy seed mixture. Add sifted dry ingredients and combine.

5. Place egg whites in the bowl of a standing mixer fitted with the whisk attachment. Beat until foamy. Do not beat until stiff. Fold egg whites into batter.

6. Gently pour batter into Bundt pan. Bake 45 to 50 minutes, or until a tester inserted into cake comes out clean. (Cake may require an extra 5 to 10 minutes depending on your oven.) Cool on a rack to room temperature. Invert onto another rack and then invert onto a plate. Dust lightly with confectioners' sugar and serve with lightly whipped sour cream. Store under cake dome or loosely covered with wax paper at room temperature.

CHRISTIAN SERVICE COOKIES

We found this cookie recipe written in a faded spidery hand on an index card from the New York Conference of the Woman's Society of Christian Service. This simple, unassuming cookie surprised us with its rich undertone of honey. It's a recipe from "The Church Lady" of Mansfield, Ohio, the much-traveled lady who collected recipes wherever she visited.

1. Set the oven rack in the middle position. Preheat the oven to 350°F. Cover a 14-inch by 16-inch baking pan with foil, shiny side up. Coat the foil with vegetable spray or use a silicone liner.

2. To make the cookies: Sift together flour, baking powder, cinnamon, and nutmeg.

3. Cream butter and sugar in the bowl of a standing mixer fitted with the paddle attachment. Add egg and combine. Add honey and combine. Add sifted dry ingredients and mix to form dough. Chill in the refrigerator 1 hour, or until firm enough to roll.

4. To add the topping: Roll dough into 1-inch balls. Place balls on baking sheet 1½ inches apart. Flatten cookie balls with bottom of glass dipped in sanding sugar. After all the cookies have been flattened, sprinkle remaining sugar over cookies. Bake 12 minutes, or until cookies are lightly browned. Place pan on rack for 1 minute. Transfer to another rack. Store between sheets of waxed paper in a covered tin.

FOR COOKIES

2½ cups flour

1 teaspoon baking powder

½ teaspoon cinnamon

¼ teaspoon nutmeg

¾ cup butter

1 cup sugar

1 egg

¼ cup honey

FOR TOPPING

½ cup clear sanding sugar

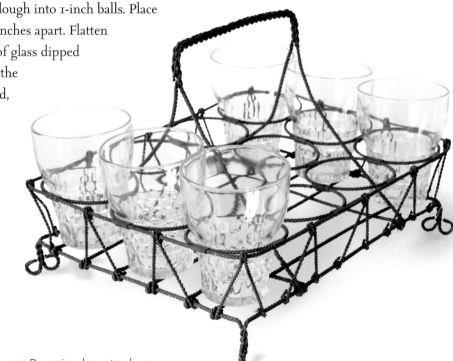

Wire glass carrier, French, 1890-1910; green Depression glass water glasses, 1930s

Reverend Brown's Cake

We don't know who Reverend Brown was, but he lent his name to this cake. Handwritten on a yellowed index card, this recipe from the late nineteenth century is representative of the type of baking done when the minister came to dinner. We don't know if Reverend Brown made this cake himself or whether he inspired the baker. It's a simple festive cake, and we suggest you bake and serve it when someone special comes to dinner.

1. Set the oven rack in the middle position. Preheat the oven to 350°F. Coat a 9-inch springform pan with vegetable spray. Cut a parchment paper or wax paper liner to fit the bottom of pan. Coat the liner with vegetable spray and dust the entire pan with flour. Tap the pan to remove the excess flour.

2. To make the cake: Sift together flour, baking soda, salt, cinnamon, allspice, nutmeg, and cloves.

3. Cream butter and brown sugar in the bowl of a standing mixer fitted with the paddle attachment. Add eggs, one at a time. Add sifted dry ingredients alternately with buttermilk and beat to combine.

4. Pour batter into springform pan. Bake 55 to 60 minutes, or until edges of cake pull away from pan and tester inserted into cake comes out clean. Cool on rack to room temperature.

5. To add the topping: Warm Soft Caramel Sauce in the microwave on low for 30 seconds. Pour over cooled cake and smooth top and sides with offset spatula. Sprinkle raisins on top of cake. Store under cake dome or loosely covered with wax paper at room temperature.

FOR CAKE

2 cups flour

1 teaspoon baking soda

¼ teaspoon salt

½ teaspoon cinnamon

½ teaspoon allspice

½ teaspoon nutmeg

¼ teaspoon cloves

½ cup butter

2 cups brown sugar

3 eggs

1 cup buttermilk or ½ cup buttermilk and ½ cup heavy cream

FOR TOPPING

1½ cups Soft Caramel Sauce (page 193)

⅓ cup golden raisins

LEMON CAKE PUDDING PIE

MAKES 6 SERVINGS

FOR CAKE PUDDING PIE

1 cup sugar

3 tablespoons cake flour

⅛ teaspoon salt

1 cup milk

2 eggs, separated

2 teaspoons grated lemon zest

3 tablespoons lemon juice

FOR TOPPING

¼ cup clear sanding sugar

2 teaspoons grated lemon zest

We found this living recipe written in fine handwriting on a thin slip of paper. While you're probably familiar with this soufflé-like lemon dessert in all its permutations, we think we've carried it to the next level with this version. The layer of sanding sugar and grated lemon rind fuses to present a crème brûlée–style crust. You'll need to break the crust with a spoon to enjoy the molten lemon custard beneath.

1. Set the oven rack in the middle position. Preheat the oven to 325°F. Liberally butter 6 glass or china custard cups (or coat with vegetable spray). For the water bath, set aside a metal baking pan large enough to hold the cups without touching the sides of the pan.

2. To make the cake pudding pie: Sift together sugar, flour, and salt into a bowl. Add milk and egg yolks and combine. Add lemon zest and lemon juice. Beat egg whites in a separate bowl until stiff and fold into batter.

3. To add the topping: Place custard cups in large metal pan. Divide batter among the custard cups. Combine sanding sugar and lemon zest in a small bowl and sprinkle over batter.

4. Pour hot water from a glass measuring cup into outer pan until water level rises halfway up sides of custard cups. Place carefully in oven. Bake 30 to 35 minutes, or until the tops are golden brown and a tester inserted into custard comes out dry. *Do not let the water evaporate from the water bath.*

5. Remove water bath from oven. Place custard cups on a rack and cool about 5 minutes. Serve warm on plate with puff of sweetened whipped cream on the side. This dessert is also good chilled. Store uncovered in the refrigerator.

GRAPE-NUT PUFF PUDDING

This soufflé-like puff pudding is very seductive. As you spoon the warm comforting puff onto a plate, you suddenly realize that from a humble breakfast grain, a star is born. This puff is wonderful when the weather is challenging and is equally tasty hot or cold.

¼ cup butter

1 teaspoon grated lemon zest

1 cup sugar

3 egg yolks, beaten

2 tablespoons lemon juice

2 tablespoons flour

¼ cup grape-nuts

1 cup milk

3 egg whites

1. Set the oven rack in the middle position. Preheat the oven to 350°F. Grease a 1½-quart ovenproof glass baking dish with butter or vegetable spray. Set aside a larger metal pan and rack for the water bath.

2. Cream butter and lemon zest in the bowl of a standing mixer fitted with the paddle attachment. Add sugar gradually. Add egg yolks and lemon juice. Add flour, grape-nuts, and milk and mix thoroughly.

3. Place egg whites in the bowl of a standing mixer fitted with the whisk attachment. Beat until they form stiff peaks. Fold egg whites into batter. Pour batter into baking dish.

4. Place baking dish on rack in large metal pan. Pour hot water from a glass measuring cup into outer pan until water level rises halfway up sides of baking dish. Place carefully in oven. Bake uncovered 50 minutes to 1 hour, or until tester inserted into pudding comes out clean. *Do not let the water evaporate from water bath.* Serve warm or at room temperature with whipped cream. Puff is best served the day it is made. Store leftover puff covered with a paper towel and plastic wrap in the refrigerator.

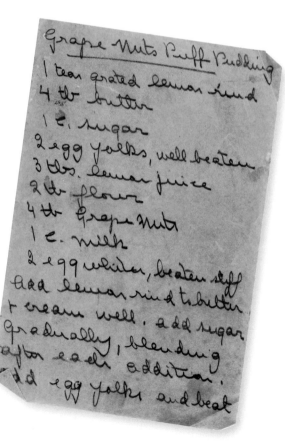

Handwritten recipe for Grape-Nuts Puff Pudding, 1920s

137

CHEDDAR CHEESE AND DILL BISCUITS

1 cup flour

2 teaspoons baking powder

¼ teaspoon salt

1 teaspoon fresh dill

2 tablespoons cold butter, cut into ½-inch cubes

2 tablespoons cold lard, cut into ½-inch cubes

¾ cup freshly grated cheddar cheese (can grate in food processor)

⅓ cup milk

1 egg, beaten

The recipe for these biscuits was tucked into a manuscript cookbook from the 1930s and 1940s. Since rationing was going on in the 1940s, this home cook might have used more lard than butter in the recipe. We like using a combination of both because it lends a rich texture to the biscuits. These are both sophisticated and elegant. Serve them with lots of butter.

1. Set the oven rack in the middle position. Preheat the oven to 450°F. Cover a 14-inch by 16-inch baking pan with foil, shiny side up. Coat the foil with vegetable spray or use a silicone liner.

2. Place flour, baking powder, salt, and dill in the bowl of a food processor fitted with a metal blade. Pulse three times to mix. Add butter, lard, and cheese and pulse three times. Add milk and pulse until dough comes together.

3. Place dough on a lightly floured wax paper or parchment paper. Roll out to ½-inch thickness. Dip a round 2-inch or 3-inch biscuit cutter in flour and cut circles of dough. Press cutter straight down and lift up; do not twist cutter in dough, or biscuits will not rise. Use a spatula to lift and transfer dough to baking sheet. Gather up scraps and reroll to cut more biscuits. Biscuits made from rerolled scraps may not be as tender, but they will still be good.

4. Brush biscuits with beaten egg. Bake 12 minutes for large biscuits, 10 minutes for small biscuits. Place on rack to cool. Serve while still warm. Store leftover biscuits loosely covered with wax paper in a container in the refrigerator. Reheat before serving.

Sweet Tips

- Do not handle the dough too much or the biscuits will be tough.
- Brushing unbaked biscuits with beaten egg gives them a brown color.

Black Pepper Hush Puppies

MAKES 20 HUSH PUPPIES

2 cups flour

2 teaspoons baking powder

½ teaspoon salt

1 teaspoon coarsely ground
   black pepper

2 teaspoons sugar

1 cup milk

2 eggs, beaten

Vegetable oil or peanut oil,
   for frying

Coarse salt (optional)

This recipe for hush puppies was found among the recipes of a lady who was very active in her Ohio church. "The Church Lady" traveled frequently attending church gatherings and convocations. From her handwritten notes, we learned that she discovered this recipe for hush puppies while staying at Epworth–By-The-Sea, on St. Simon Island, Georgia. This recipe differs from most other hush puppy recipes because it uses flour rather than cornmeal.

1. Cover a cooling rack with 3 layers of paper towels.
2. Mix flour, baking powder, salt, pepper, and sugar in a bowl. Add milk and eggs to sifted dry ingredients and combine thoroughly.
3. Heat oil to 360°F in deep flat-bottomed heavy pan or in electric fryer.
4. Coat a tablespoon with vegetable spray and dip into batter. Slide batter carefully into hot fat. Fat may bubble up. Fry hush puppies in batches of 3 (to keep oil temperature from dipping). Turn once after 4 minutes and fry another 3 minutes, or until evenly brown on both sides. Place on prepared rack, cover with additional paper towels, and allow to drain. Serve immediately or keep warm in a 200°F oven until ready to eat. Sprinkle with coarse salt if you want a salty treat.

Green Depression glass and tin measuring cup beater, 1930s; tin egg beater, early 1900s

BANANA DESSERT CROQUETTES

This unusual recipe came from the manuscript cookbook of Marion Carter and M. E. Carter. These are more like fritters, but the Carters called them "croquettes." Presentation was very important to the two ladies, who advised us to "cut the ends off of bananas" so that these deep-fried treats would really look like croquettes. Dusted with confectioners' sugar, these tasty little morsels are best when eaten hot.

2 cups flour

2 teaspoons baking powder

½ teaspoon salt

2 tablespoons sugar

2 eggs

1 cup milk

1½ cups bread crumbs, divided

8 medium bananas, ends trimmed, cut in fourths

Vegetable oil or peanut oil, for frying

Confectioners' sugar (for sprinkling)

1. Cover a cooling rack with 3 layers of paper towels.
2. Sift together flour, baking powder, salt, and sugar into a bowl. Add eggs to milk and beat. Pour milk-egg mixture over sifted dry ingredients and combine thoroughly.
3. Line a baking sheet with wax paper. Sprinkle ¾ cup of the bread crumbs across the surface. Dip bananas in batter, place on crumbs, and cover with remaining crumbs. Gently roll bananas until they are completely coated. Let sit 10 minutes.
4. Heat 2 inches of oil to 360°F in deep flat-bottomed heavy pan or in electric fryer. Use a slotted spoon to transfer bananas, one at a time, into hot fat. Fry croquettes in batches of 5 or 6 (to keep oil temperature from dipping), turning once until both sides are golden brown, 1 minute on each side. Place on prepared rack, cover with additional paper towels, and allow to drain. Remove top layer of towels. Shake a strainer filled with confectioners' sugar over croquettes, turning them so both sides are covered. Serve immediately or keep warm in a 200°F oven until ready to eat.

Tin egg beater, 1886

LOST AND FOUND HONEY CAKE

This is the cake Marilynn baked during the early 1970s. She doesn't remember where this recipe came from, but she does remember that the tiny blue index card it was written on was lost for more than twenty years. When we found the card tucked between some papers that had been packed away, we wondered if the cake was as good as we remembered. It was! This is a light buttery honey-kissed cake, wonderful with butter pecan ice cream.

2 cups sifted cake flour

1 teaspoon baking powder

¼ teaspoon salt

½ teaspoon ginger

½ teaspoon nutmeg

½ cup butter

1 cup mild honey

1 egg, beaten

½ cup buttermilk

1. Set the oven rack in the middle position. Preheat the oven to 375°F. Coat an 8-cup Bundt pan with vegetable spray. Dust pan with flour and tap out the excess.

2. Sift together flour, baking powder, salt, ginger, and nutmeg.

3. Place butter and honey in the bowl of a standing mixer fitted with the paddle attachment. Cream until fluffy. Add egg and combine. Add buttermilk and combine. Add sifted dry ingredients gradually and mix to combine.

4. Pour batter into Bundt pan. Bake 35 to 40 minutes, or until tester inserted into cake comes out clean. Cool on rack. Remove from pan after 20 minutes. Serve warm or at room temperature with ice cream or whipped cream or dusted with confectioners' sugar. Store loosely covered with wax paper at room temperature.

Sweet Tip

This cake can also be baked in a standard 9-inch by 5-inch by 3-inch loaf pan. Prepare the pan by lining the bottom and two narrow ends of the pan with a strip of wax paper. Coat the pan and liner with vegetable spray. Bake 30 to 35 minutes, or until tester inserted in the loaf comes out dry.

MRS. CARL WINCHENBACH'S BANANA CREAM PIE

MAKES 8 TO 9 SLICES

9-inch pie shell, baked and cooled
   (see Sheila's Pie Crust on
   page 110)

2 cups milk, divided

¼ cup light corn syrup

¼ cup cornstarch

½ cup sugar

¼ teaspoon salt

3 egg yolks

1 teaspoon vanilla

3 to 4 ripe bananas, sliced

We think you should forget all you know about traditional banana cream pie and start over with this recipe. We found it in a manuscript cookbook rescued from the town dump in Maine. Mrs. Winchenbach lived in Waldoboro, Maine. Her recipe is simple, creamy, and delicious, and with its halo of lightly sweetened whipped cream, it is gorgeous, too. There are no sliced bananas on top, but a wealth of the sweet-smelling fruit is buried in the layers under the custard.

1. Heat 1¾ cups of the milk and corn syrup in a heavy saucepan over medium-low heat, stirring with a wooden spoon until bubbles start to form around the edges, up to 7 minutes. Remove from heat.

2. Whisk together remaining ¼ cup milk and cornstarch in a bowl, Add sugar and salt and mix thoroughly. Add egg yolks, one at a time, and whisk until well blended. Add a little of the hot milk mixture to the egg mixture to temper it, continuing to whisk briskly. Whisk remaining hot milk into eggs.

3. Return combined egg-milk mixture to saucepan. Bring to a simmer over medium heat and cook, stirring continuously, about 30 seconds, or until mixture begins to thicken (this will happen very quickly). Remove from heat, whisk briefly, add vanilla, and whisk again.

4. Spread a small amount of custard on bottom of pie shell using an offset spatula. Place a layer of sliced bananas on custard. Spread half of remaining custard over bananas. Add remaining bananas and custard in layers. Cool to room temperature and refrigerate until ready to serve. Decorate pie with lightly sweetened whipped cream before serving. Store loosely wrapped in wax paper in a plastic container in the refrigerator.

Sweet Tip

Banana Cream Pie can be made up to one day ahead.

MAMA'S BLUEBERRY PIE

This is another one of our family recipes that we had to reconstruct from memory. Mama never used cornstarch, tapioca, or cinnamon in her blueberry pies; just the juice and zest from a lemon and a little sugar so the true taste of the blueberries would be enhanced by the heat of the oven.

FOR CRUST

Pastry for double-crust pie, divided in half and chilled (see Sheila's Pie Crust on page 110)

1 egg, beaten

FOR FILLING

4 cups blueberries

½ cup sugar

¼ cup flour

⅛ teaspoon salt

2 teaspoons grated lemon zest

3 tablespoons lemon juice

1½ tablespoons butter, cut into dice

1. Set the oven rack in the middle position. Preheat the oven to 400°F. Coat a 9-inch ovenproof glass pie plate with vegetable spray. Line a 14-inch by 16-inch baking sheet with foil, shiny side up, and coat with vegetable spray.

2. To prepare the crust: Roll out pastry dough. Fit half of dough into bottom of pie plate and trim off excess. Chill in the refrigerator. (For detailed instructions, see "To make a double-crust pie," steps 2 and 3.)

3. To make the filling: Dry blueberries thoroughly on a baking sheet lined with 2 thicknesses of paper towel.

4. Combine blueberries, sugar, flour, salt, lemon zest, and lemon juice in a bowl.

5. Add blueberry mixture to pie shell. Dot with butter. Add top crust, seal and crimp edges, and cut decorative slits. Brush top crust and edges with beaten egg. (For detailed instructions, see "To make a double-crust pie," step 4.)

6. Place pie on baking sheet. Bake 20 minutes and check crust for browning. If crust is browning too quickly, cover loosely with foil. Bake another 25 to 30 minutes, or until top crust is evenly browned and juices begin to bubble. Cool pie on rack at least 2 hours before serving. Store loosely covered with wax paper at room temperature.

STEAMED CHOCOLATE PUDDING

MAKES 10 SERVINGS

1½ cups flour

½ cup cocoa

1 tablespoon plus 1 teaspoon
  baking powder

½ cup brown sugar

½ teaspoon salt

¼ cup butter, melted

1 egg, beaten

2 tablespoons molasses

1½ teaspoons vanilla

1 cup milk

1½ cups mini chocolate chips

Hot water for steaming

This recipe is based on one from the manuscript cookbook of Marion Carter and M. E. Carter. Although the Carters' pudding calls for raisins and currants as well as grated chocolate, we have omitted them here. Also, we simplified things by using chocolate chips and steaming the pudding for one hour. This makes a very impressive presentation for dessert.

1. Liberally butter sides and bottom of a 1½-quart covered tin pudding mold. Prepare a buttered parchment sheet to fit the top of the mold. Cut a hole in parchment to fit over center spoke. Select a covered pot large enough to accommodate the pudding mold with a 2-inch clearance around sides. Set a metal rack inside the pot.

2. Mix flour, cocoa, baking powder, brown sugar, and salt in a large bowl. Add butter and stir. Combine egg, molasses, vanilla, and milk. Pour into batter and stir to combine. Fold in chocolate chips.

3. Pour batter into pudding mold, making sure that it is no more than two thirds full. Place buttered parchment round on top of mold and add cover. (If mold has no cover, fold 2 sheets of foil over open top and tie securely with kitchen string.)

4. Set filled mold on rack in deep heavy pot. Add water until one-third of mold is covered. Remove mold. Cover pot and bring water to a boil. Turn off heat, lift pot cover, and carefully place filled mold on rack. Cover pot. Adjust heat so that water simmers; do not not let water come to boil. Steam pudding 1 hour, checking periodically to make sure that water level remains stable. Do not let the water boil out because a tightly covered mold could explode.

5. Turn off heat. Remove pudding mold carefully from steamer and place on cooling rack. Carefully remove cover (or foil) and parchment from top of mold. Pudding should have risen to top of mold. Allow to cool 10 minutes. Pudding should still be warm and should release easily when mold is inverted. Serve while warm in slices with unsweetened whipped cream. Leftover pudding should be loosely wrapped in wax paper and stored in the refrigerator.

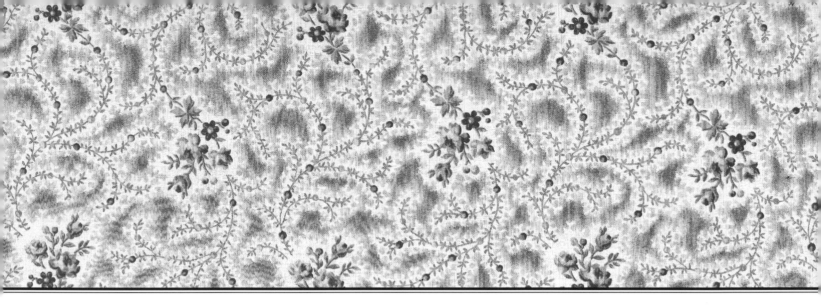

CHAPTER 6

Like so many other women in the 1940s and 1950s, our mother and aunts often gathered with their friends to play cards, solve family problems, and share

Bridge with the Girls

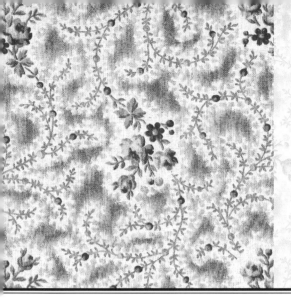

favorite desserts. Many of the wonderful recipes for the sweets in this chapter come from these gatherings.

Bridge clubs flourished in the days before and during World War II. It was a fun and inexpensive way for women to continue the earlier traditions of gathering to share joy and sorrow and, most importantly, to work. Food was always central to those gatherings; whether women were cooking

Cookbook and pamphlets, 1920-1930s

the harvest meals or putting up jams and relishes, they were always sharing kitchen wisdom and recipes.

Early in the twentieth century, labor-saving appliances, advances in transportation, and the availability of prepared foods gave women more leisure time. Their gatherings became increasingly social. Bridge with the girls became such a phenomenon in American social life in the middle of the last century that chocolate-covered nuts and raisins are still known as "bridge mix." "Bridge" became the prefix of choice. We still refer to "bridge" tables, chairs, and rolls.

Our mother and her friends, like so many other women around the country, were the recipients of this legacy of community, refreshments, and good works. Many fundraisers for local charities were launched when she and her friends gathered in each other's homes where their favorite desserts—recipes such as Sour Cream Spice Cake, Mandelbrot with Cherries and Walnuts, and Chocolate Fudge Pie—were proudly presented. It was clear that although bridge playing was fun, it was really only an excuse to chat, serve their favorite recipes, and share old family secrets. That is why, in our collection of manuscript cookbooks, we find so many recipes from all over the country handwritten on the backs of bridge tallies.

Sometimes a hostess was one of the rare few that declined to share her baking secrets—either openly or, more often, by being politely vague about the composition of a particular treat. This often resulted in a round of phone calls the next morning among the evening's guests, who hotly debated possible ingredients and amounts. So intense were these quests, that some women still remember their attempts to capture the most elusive recipes, or their chagrin at not being credited for their own contributions. A friend from Ohio still voices her pride in developing a recipe for kumquats stuffed with a cheese and nut mixture for a community cookbook and remembers her fear that credit would go to someone else.

Although these stories could be called the bitter side of sweet talk, most of the competition was good fun, and resulted in the best recipes, such as Louise Zimmerman's Cookies Without a Name and Graham Cracker Fudge, being widely shared. In the end, almost all of these women bonded over bridge and something sweet. We've heard of clubs that stayed together for three generations, bickering, sweet-talking, and supporting one another until the members were well into their nineties. The recipes in this chapter are for some of the sweets, remembered or found, that were served when women enjoyed "bridge with the girls."

Heirloom recipes for Chocolate Fudge Pie, 1930s; Mrs. Chubb's Nut Cake, 1920s

BUTTERSCOTCH BARS WITH BROWN SUGAR MERINGUE TOPPING

MAKES 40 BARS

FOR BARS

2 cups pecan pieces

1½ cups flour

1½ teaspoons baking powder

⅛ teaspoon salt

1 cup brown sugar

½ cup cold butter, cut into dice

2 egg yolks

1 teaspoon vanilla

FOR TOPPING

2 egg whites

1 cup brown sugar

This is a delicious sweet bar. It's like two cookies in one, a bar cookie and a brown sugar meringue. This Butterscotch Bar was very popular with midwestern ladies and their bridge clubs during the 1930s and 1940s. Variations are still being exchanged at twenty-first century bridge parties.

1. Set the oven rack in the middle position. Preheat the oven to 350°F. Line the bottom and sides of a 9-inch by 13-inch by 2-inch pan with foil, shiny side up, and coat with vegetable spray. Line a 14-inch by 16-inch baking sheet with foil.

2. To make the bars: Place pecan pieces on baking sheet. Toast in oven 7 to 10 minutes, stirring a few times for even browning. Do not allow pecan pieces to burn. Cool to room temperature.

3. Combine flour, baking powder, salt, and brown sugar in the bowl of a food processor fitted with a metal blade. Add butter. Process until butter is the size of small peas. Add egg yolks and vanilla and pulse three or four times until the mixture has the consistency of sandy clumps.

4. Pat mixture into pan and level off by pressing with a small offset spatula. Press pecans into mixture.

5. To make topping: Place egg whites in the bowl of a standing mixer fitted with the whisk attachment. Beat until whites hold a peak when the whisk is lifted. Add brown sugar and beat at highest speed about 4 minutes. Spread meringue over pecan layer. Bake 25 minutes, or until a tester inserted into bars comes out clean. The meringue will crack slightly, but this will not significantly affect the appearance. Let cool on rack completely and cut into squares. Store between sheets of wax paper in a covered tin.

Daddy's Bangor Brownies

MAKES 48 SQUARES

1½ cups flour, sifted

1 teaspoon salt

¾ cup butter

1 cup brown sugar

2 cups sugar

6 eggs

6 oz. bitter chocolate, melted and
   cooled

2 teaspoons vanilla

¾ cup milk

2 cups chopped walnuts

There really was a Daddy: ours, Harry Brass, a hospital pharmacist, who loved anything chocolate. How Daddy got involved with these brownies we will never know. They are more cakey than fudgy, but we think they're wonderful, and our mother baked them often for her bridge parties.

1. Set the oven rack in the middle position. Preheat the oven to 350°F. Line the bottom and sides of a 9-inch by 13-inch by 2-inch pan with foil, shiny side up, and coat with vegetable spray.

2. Sift together flour and salt.

3. Place butter, brown sugar, and sugar in the bowl of a standing mixer fitted with the paddle attachment. Cream together until fluffy. Add eggs, one at a time. Add chocolate. Add vanilla to milk. Add sifted dry ingredients alternately with milk, beating after each addition. Fold in walnuts.

4. Pour batter into pan. Bake 30 to 35 minutes, or until tester inserted 1 inch from edge comes out dry. (Tester inserted in center should come out with moist crumbs.) Cool to room temperature and refrigerate until cold. Cut into squares or triangles. Store between sheets of wax paper in a covered tin.

Factory chocolate mold used by Walter Baker & Co., Inc., Dorchester, Massachusetts, 1900-1950s

GRAHAM CRACKER FUDGE

We found this recipe in a manuscript cookbook from the North Shore of Massachusetts. This fudge tastes as if it were made with milk chocolate. The comment written on the actual recipe is "This fudge has an interesting texture and is not a too sweet confection." We suggest placing squares in fluted white paper cups when serving.

1. Line an 8-inch by 8-inch by 2-inch pan with foil. Butter the bottom and sides of pan generously.

2. Combine chocolate, sugar, evaporated milk, salt, and vanilla in a large saucepan. Cook slowly over medium heat, stirring constantly with a wooden spoon, until mixture begins to boil. Boil 5 minutes, stirring continuously.

3. Remove pan from heat. Fold in butter and marshmallows. Allow to cool 25 minutes. Fold in graham cracker crumbs and walnuts. Pour into foil-lined pan. Let stand until cool and set. Cut into pieces. Store between sheets of wax paper in a covered tin.

4 oz. bitter chocolate, chopped

2 cups sugar

1 cup evaporated milk

¼ teaspoon salt

1 teaspoon vanilla

1 tablespoon butter

2 cups miniature marshmallows

2 cups graham cracker crumbs

1 cup walnuts, toasted and coarsely chopped

Manual tin chocolate grater, early 1900s

Chocolate Fudge Pie

MAKES 8 SLICES

½ cup flour

⅛ teaspoon salt

½ cup butter, melted

1 cup sugar

2 eggs

1 oz. bitter chocolate, melted
and cooled

1 teaspoon vanilla

We had to include this recipe in this chapter because we found it written on the back of a bridge tally. We were amused to see the columns labeled "We" and "They." After tasting this pie, we're sure that "We" and "They" must have liked it. Simple, fudgy, and great with vanilla ice cream, this is a pie that makes its own crust. A homey little dessert, it's easy to make, and seductively chocolate.

1. Set the oven rack in the middle position. Preheat the oven to 325°F. Cut a wax paper or parchment paper liner to fit the bottom of a 9-inch ovenproof glass pie plate. Coat the plate with vegetable spray, insert the liner, and spray again to coat the liner.

2. Sift together flour and salt.

3. Cream butter and sugar in the bowl of a standing mixer fitted with the paddle attachment. Add eggs, one at time, and beat until thoroughly mixed. Add sifted dry ingredients. Add chocolate and vanilla and combine.

4. Pour batter into pie plate. Bake approximately 30 minutes, or until tester inserted into center of pie comes out clean. Pie will have cracks on top. Cool pie on rack. (Pie may collapse slightly while cooling.) Serve slightly warm or at room temperature with vanilla or chocolate ice cream. Store loosely covered with wax paper in the refrigerator.

SWEET TOUCH   Having a piece of this pie with a scoop of ice cream is like having a brownie à la mode. We also suggest serving a slice of Chocolate Fudge Pie on a pool of Mrs. Paul Knight's Bittersweet Chocolate Sauce (page 227) and topped with whipped cream.

Louise Zimmerman's Cookies Without a Name

MAKES 40 SQUARES

6 oz. semisweet chocolate chips

6 graham crackers broken into small pieces

1 14-oz. can sweetened condensed milk

⅛ teaspoon salt

1½ teaspoons vanilla

1½ cups pecans or walnuts, toasted and coarsely chopped

We never met Louise, but we think she's quite a gal! We love the fact that she wasn't afraid to advise us to "mix this mess together and spread on a greased pan." This is a great recipe for children to make with an adult's supervision.

1. Set the oven rack in the middle position. Preheat the oven to 350°F. Line a 9-inch by 13-inch by 2-inch pan with foil, shiny side up. Coat the foil with vegetable spray.

2. Combine chocolate chips, graham cracker pieces, condensed milk, salt, and vanilla extract in a medium bowl. Do not overmix. Mixture will look rather messy.

3. Spread mixture in pan and scatter pecans or walnuts on top. Bake 20 minutes. Remove from oven. Cool on rack 20 minutes and then chill in the refrigerator 20 minutes. Cut into squares with a sharp knife. Store between sheets of waxed paper in a covered tin.

Rolling pin for springerle cookies, American, 1870s

CHARLOTTE CUSATO'S DATE AND COCONUT COOKIES

Although these cookies resemble the Pistachio Crescent Cookie (page 94), looks can be deceiving. Never judge a cookie by its coating. These little darlings have more substance because of the toasted pecans, coconut, and dates. What makes these cookies even more unusual is that the cinnamon is in the confectioner's sugar in which they are rolled, not the cookie dough. Charlotte divulged her cookie recipe to friends in September of 1957.

2 cups flour

1 teaspoon baking soda

½ teaspoon salt

½ cup butter

1 cup sugar

½ cup brown sugar

2 eggs, beaten

2 teaspoons vanilla

4 tablespoons buttermilk

1 cup chopped toasted pecans

1 cup chopped dates

1 cup unsweetened shredded coconut

1½ cups confectioners' sugar

½ teaspoon cinnamon

1. Set the oven rack in the middle position. Preheat the oven to 375°F. Cover a 14-inch by 16-inch baking sheet with foil, shiny side up. Coat the foil with vegetable spray or use a silicone liner.

2. Sift together flour, baking soda, and salt.

3. Cream butter, sugar, and brown sugar in the bowl of a standing mixer fitted with the paddle attachment. Add eggs and mix thoroughly. Add vanilla to buttermilk. Add sifted dry ingredients alternately with buttermilk, beating after each addition. Fold in pecans, dates, and coconut.

4. Drop from teaspoon onto baking sheet. Bake 12 minutes, or until lightly browned. Cool on rack about 5 minutes. Mix confectioners' sugar and cinnamon in a small bowl. Roll warm cookies in cinnamon sugar and shake in a sieve to remove excess. Store between sheets of wax paper in a covered tin.

Cast-iron mold for shaping springerle cookies, American, early 1880s

MRS. CHUBB'S NUT CAKE

MAKES 16 SLICES

This recipe came from the manuscript cookbook of an artist living in Cambridge, Massachusetts. She did not specify what type of nut to use in the cake, but the lemon-clove flavoring and toasted almonds make it resonate. This a rich dense cake with a crisp macaroon-like topping. The almonds used for the topping brown and meld with the sanding sugar during baking.

1. Set the oven rack in the middle position. Preheat the oven to 350°F. Cut a parchment paper or wax paper liner to fit the bottom of a 10-inch tube pan. Coat the pan with vegetable spray. Insert the liner, spray again, and dust with flour.

2. To make the cake: Place toasted almonds and 2 tablespoons of the sugar in the bowl of a food processor fitted with a metal blade. Pulse until texture resembles coarse meal.

3. Sift together flour, baking powder, salt, nutmeg, and cloves.

4. Cream butter and remaining ⅞ cup sugar in the bowl of a standing mixer fitted with the paddle attachment. Add egg yolks, 2 at a time. Add lemon zest, lemon juice, lemon oil, and vanilla and mix to combine. Add sifted dry ingredients alternately with milk, mixing after each addition until completely blended. Fold in almond mixture.

5. Place egg whites in another bowl of standing mixer fitted with the whisk attachment. Beat until egg whites hold a firm peak. Fold egg whites into batter.

6. To add the topping: Place batter in tube pan. Sprinkle almonds and sanding sugar on top of batter. Bake 50 to 55 minutes, or until tester inserted into cake comes out dry. Cool on rack completely before turning out of pan. Store loosely wrapped in wax paper at room temperature.

FOR CAKE

- **1 cup toasted whole almonds**
- **1 cup sugar, divided**
- **2 cups flour**
- **1 teaspoon baking powder**
- **1 teaspoon salt**
- **¼ teaspoon nutmeg**
- **⅛ teaspoon cloves**
- **1 cup butter**
- **4 eggs, separated**
- **3 teaspoons grated lemon zest**
- **4 tablespoons lemon juice**
- **½ teaspoon lemon oil or lemon extract**
- **2 teaspoons vanilla**
- **¾ cup milk**

FOR TOPPING

- **3 tablespoons untoasted slivered almonds**
- **3 tablespoons clear sanding sugar**

MANDELBROT WITH CHERRIES AND WALNUTS

1 9 3 0 S

MAKES 24 TO 30 COOKIES

3 eggs, beaten

1 cup plus 1 tablespoon sugar

1 cup peanut oil or vegetable oil

1¾ cups matzo cake meal plus extra for shaping dough

Pinch of salt

2 teaspoons vanilla

1 cup walnuts, chopped

½ cup maraschino cherries, dried on paper towel and chopped

½ teaspoon cinnamon

Sweet Tips

- Do not roll cylinders in too much cinnamon sugar because the sugar could caramelize and burn at the edges.

- Mandelbrot will crisp up as it cools. For an even crisper cookie, extend the final baking time.

This could be a tricky recipe if we let it, but chilling the dough makes all the difference between a shapeless mass and a light biscotti-like cookie. Mandelbrot originally meant almond bread, but this recipe uses maraschino cherries and walnuts instead. The walnuts give the twice-baked slices an extra level of flavor and more substance. You could try this with dried cherries and almonds if you're a purist. We also like them with chopped bittersweet chocolate.

1. Set the oven rack in the middle position. Preheat the oven to 375°F. Cover a 14-inch by 16-inch baking sheet with foil, shiny side up. Coat the foil with vegetable spray or use a silicone liner.

2. Place eggs, 1 cup of the sugar, and oil in a mixing bowl. Whisk to combine. Add matzo cake meal, salt, and vanilla and mix. Fold in walnuts and cherries. Cover bowl with plastic wrap and place in the refrigerator 30 minutes, or until dough is firm enough to shape. If dough is still loose after chilling, add a little more cake meal.

3. Divide dough in half. Working on wax paper or plastic wrap, form each piece into a cylinder about 3-inches wide. Combine cinnamon and remaining tablespoon sugar in a small bowl. Sprinkle half of cinnamon sugar onto work surface and roll cylinders in it until lightly coated. Place dough cylinders on baking sheet. To prevent burning, dough must not touch ends of baking sheet. Bake 35 minutes, or until lightly browned. Place on rack and cool 10 minutes. Do not turn off oven.

4. Transfer mandelbrot from baking sheet to a cutting surface. Using a serrated bread knife, cut diagonal slices ½ inch thick while bread is still warm. Place slices, cut side up, on the same baking sheet and sprinkle with remaining cinnamon sugar. Return to oven for an additional 10 minutes, turning once after 5 minutes. Place on rack to cool completely. Store between sheets of wax paper in a covered tin.

Chopped Apple Cake with Sticky Toffee Topping

1 9 3 0 S

MAKES 16 SQUARES

This anonymous recipe seemed better and better to us as we read it, especially when we realized that the innocuous topping so casually presented on the creased piece of paper turned out to be a voluptuous sticky toffee adornment. It's hard to believe that the sweet-talker who jotted down this recipe tells us to skip the topping if we wish. We would never do that!

FOR CAKE

2 cups sifted flour

1 teaspoon baking soda

¼ teaspoon salt

1 teaspoon cinnamon

2 cups sugar

½ cup butter

2 eggs

1 teaspoon vanilla

4 cups raw apples, peeled, cored, and chopped by hand

1 cup walnuts, finely chopped

FOR TOFFEE TOPPING

½ cup butter

1½ cups dark brown sugar

⅛ teaspoon salt

1 cup heavy cream

1. Set the oven rack in the middle position. Preheat the oven to 350°F. Line the bottom and sides of a 9-inch by 13-inch by 2-inch pan with foil, shiny side up, and coat with vegetable spray.

2. To make the cake: Sift together flour, baking soda, salt, and cinnamon.

3. Sift sugar into bowl of standing mixer fitted with the paddle attachment. Add butter and cream together. Add eggs, one at a time, beating well after each addition. Add vanilla. Add apples alternately with sifted dry ingredients, beating after each addition. Fold in walnuts.

4. Pour batter into pan. Bake 1 hour, or until cake pulls away from sides of pan and tester inserted into cake comes out clean. Cool on rack 25 minutes, or until just warm.

5. To make the toffee topping: Melt butter in a heavy metal saucepan over low heat. Add brown sugar and salt and whisk until blended. Add heavy cream, increase heat to medium, and stir with a wooden spoon until mixture comes to a boil. Boil 5 minutes, stirring constantly. Remove from heat. Mixture will thicken as it rests.

6. Make several slits in warm cake with a butter knife. Pour sauce over cake. Let rest until topping sets, about 15 minutes. Serve with vanilla ice cream or unsweetened whipped cream. Store loosely covered with wax paper at room temperature.

Sweet Tip

We suggest you chop the apples for this recipe by hand. A food processor will chop the pieces too small and may liquefy them. Unlike minced or processed apples, hand-chopped apples won't fall apart when beaten into the batter.

SOUR CREAM SPICE CAKE

This spice cake was the favorite of The Harmony Club, the select group of women from the Sisterhood at Temple Tiferith Abraham who made up our mother's bridge group. The twelve women met frequently to play bridge, lend each other support, and go on educational field trips. Unfortunately, The Harmony Club later broke up because the members couldn't get along!

1. Set the oven rack in the middle position. Preheat the oven to 350°F. Line the bottom and ends of a 9-inch by 5-inch by 3-inch loaf pan with a single strip of wax paper. Coat the pan and wax paper liner with vegetable spray. Dust pan with flour and tap out the excess.

2. Sift together 1¾ cups of the flour, cinnamon, nutmeg, cloves, allspice, and baking soda. Toss remaining ¼ cup flour with raisins.

3. Place butter and sugar in the bowl of a standing mixer fitted with the paddle attachment. Cream until soft and fluffy. Add egg and vanilla and mix well. Add sifted dry ingredients alternately with sour cream. Fold in raisins.

4. Pour batter into loaf pan. Bake approximately 1 hour, or until tester inserted into center of cake comes out clean. Cool on a rack 20 minutes before removing from pan. Store loosely covered with wax paper in the refrigerator.

2 cups flour, divided

1 teaspoon cinnamon

1 teaspoon nutmeg

1 teaspoon cloves

1 teaspoon allspice

1 teaspoon baking soda

1 cup raisins

½ cup butter

1 cup sugar

1 egg

1 teaspoon vanilla

1 cup sour cream

Sweet Tips

- This cake is tasty with a little warm apricot or cherry jam. Some have been known to eat it toasted and spread with butter.
- This cake slices well whether it's chilled or at room temperature.

Marion Carter's Blueberry Lemon Bread Pudding

MAKES 16 SERVINGS

FOR BLUEBERRY LAYERS

3 cups blueberries

2 tablespoons flour

FOR BREAD LAYERS

14 to 16 ½-inch-thick slices brioche, trimmed of crusts and cut in half

½ cup plus 2 tablespoons butter, melted

FOR CUSTARD

2 cups milk

1 cup heavy cream

¼ teaspoon salt

1 teaspoon nutmeg

1⅓ cups sugar

2 teaspoons grated lemon zest

¾ teaspoon lemon extract

1 teaspoon vanilla

6 eggs, beaten

FOR TOPPING

2 tablespoons butter, melted

⅓ cup sugar

Sweet Tip

We use brioche, but you can use a firm bread such as pain de mie, challah, or even croissants.

From the manuscript cookbook of Marion A. Carter, this is just one of the many desserts this lady from Maine baked and recorded. We've updated it with brioche and heavy cream, but essentially it is the same recipe Marion made around the turn of the twentieth century.

1. Set the oven rack in the middle position. Preheat the oven to 350°F. Coat a 9-inch by 13-inch ovenproof glass baking dish with vegetable spray. Set aside a larger metal pan and rack for the water bath.
2. To prepare blueberries: Toss blueberries with flour and shake in sieve to remove excess flour.
3. To prepare bread: Brush brioche slices with melted butter.
4. To make custard: Combine 1 cup of the milk, heavy cream, salt, nutmeg, sugar, lemon zest, lemon extract, and vanilla in a large bowl. Add eggs and beat to combine.
5. Layer 6 slices of buttered brioche in baking dish. Fill in spaces with extra brioche. Pour half of custard over brioche and sprinkle with half of blueberries. Add remaining brioche, custard, and blueberries in layers.
6. To add topping: Use a knife to cut 8 slits through pudding. Cover top of pudding with plastic wrap and press down gently. Let stand 15 minutes, or until custard has moistened brioche layers. Remove plastic wrap. Brush with melted butter and sprinkle with sugar.
7. Place baking dish on rack in large metal pan. Pour hot water from a glass measuring cup into outer pan until water level rises halfway up sides of baking dish. Cover with foil. Place carefully in oven. Bake 30 minutes, checking water level periodically and replenishing if needed. Do not let the water bath evaporate. Remove foil and bake another 45 minutes, or until pudding is bubbling, topping has caramelized, and a tester inserted into pudding comes out clean.
8. Carefully remove baking dish from water bath and oven. Allow to cool on rack 1 hour. Serve warm or at room temperature. Store covered with a paper towel and plastic wrap in the refrigerator.

Mah Jong Candy

MAKES 40 DISKS

FOR CANDY

3 cups sugar

¼ cup brown sugar

2 oz. bitter chocolate, melted

1 cup almonds, toasted and finely chopped

FOR DECORATIVE TOPPING

1 cup confectioners' sugar

⅛ teaspoon salt

1 to 2 teaspoons water, as needed

¼ cup clear sanding sugar

We were intrigued by the name of this candy. We have pleasant memories of our mother's friends playing Mah Jong with little game pieces topped with mysterious oriental symbols. Mah Jong Candy did not disappoint. Toffeelike chocolate wafers studded with crisp bits of almond and decorated with those exotic Mah Jong symbols, this is candy for someone with a very sweet tooth.

1. Line two or three 14-inch by 16-inch baking sheets with parchment. Butter the parchment.

2. To make the candy: Combine sugar and brown sugar in a heavy frying pan over medium heat and melt slowly, stirring with wooden spoon, 10 to 20 minutes. When mixture comes to a boil, add chocolate and continue stirring. Watch carefully that the mixture does not burn. *Keep a bowl of ice water nearby in case of hot sugar spatters.*

3. Continue cooking until temperature of mixture reaches 260°F on a candy thermometer, or hard ball stage (mixture will form a hard ball when dropped in a cup of water), 5 to 10 minutes. Stir in almonds.

4. Coat both sides of the bowls of 2 teaspoons with vegetable spray. Drop mixture by teaspoons in quarter-sized disks onto parchment-lined baking sheets. As soon as one sheet of parchment is full, transfer it to a rack to cool. Continue until mixture is used up.

5. To make the decorative topping. Combine confectioners' sugar, salt, and water as needed to form an opaque white topping. Dip a toothpick in white topping and draw Mah Jong symbols on the tops of candy disks. Sprinkle with sanding sugar. Allow to dry and then use a pastry brush to remove excess sugar. The sugar that adheres to topping will form an iridescent sparkling design. Store between sheets of wax paper in a covered tin.

Forget-Me-Not Cookies

No one should snub this little recipe. We've tried it several times, and are always thrilled when we open the oven door at breakfast and see these lovely meringue cookies ready to eat. We can't resist sampling them with our morning coffee. So easy to make, they're perfect for those times when it's your turn to bring something sweet to the office, your child's school, or a gathering of bridge club members. This anonymous living recipe was found tucked between the pages of a much-used cookbook.

2 egg whites

½ cup sugar

⅛ teaspoon salt

1 cup semisweet chocolate chips

1 cup finely chopped walnuts

½ teaspoon vanilla

1. Set the oven rack in the middle position. Preheat the oven to 350°F. Line two 14-inch by 16-inch baking sheets with parchment paper or a silicone liner.

2. Place egg whites in the bowl of a standing mixer fitted with a whisk attachment. Whip until foamy. Gradually add sugar and beat until stiff but not dry. Fold in salt, chocolate chips, walnuts, and vanilla.

3. Drop by teaspoons onto baking sheet. Place in preheated oven. Close door *and turn off oven*. Do not open oven door. Keep cookies in oven 6 hours or overnight until cool. Peel cookies carefully from parchment paper or silicone liner. They will be fragile but chewy. Store between sheets of wax paper in a covered tin.

Wire egg holder, American, 1880s

CHAPTER 7

We love holidays and like to think they bring out the very best in people and in cooking. During holiday gatherings, it is not unusual to have an identity parade of

HOLIDAYS WITH FAMILY & FRIENDS

the cakes, pies, cookies, and breads that people are best known for. The nicest thing we can say when holidays bring us together is, "It wouldn't be Easter without your custard rice pudding," or "It wouldn't be Passover without your doughnut rolls." At Thanksgiving and Christmas, as we grow older, and the generations change, more of the conversation focuses on sweet-talking and the people and years that have passed.

Christmas Pudding

1½ lbs Raisins
½ — Currants
½ — Mixed Peel
¾ — Bread crumbs
¾ — Suet
4 Eggs
3 Tablespoonfuls sugar
3 do do flour
½ oz bitter Almonds
½ oz sweet do
1 wineglass of Brandy
Press the pudding into a well buttered mould, boil 5 or 6 hours first day and 2 hours day of serving.
E. S. M—

A light Lemon Pudding.

¼ lb Bread crumbs
¼ " Flour
" Butter
spoonful Baking Powder

Recipe for Christmas Pudding and Lemon Pudding, 1880s –1890s

We realize that desserts and pastries usually play a supporting role at these gatherings. It's the turkey, the ham, or the roast that have the starring roles. But really, what would these get-togethers be without Persimmon Pudding with its crown of glistening fruit and nuts, or the substantial flavors of Pumpkin Cheesecake Bread Pudding, or Holiday Apple Custard Pie filled with fragrant baked fruit?

Most families maintain their own traditions when it comes to holiday dinners and desserts. Our family always honored its own idiosyncratic ritual of not immediately serving sweets with the holiday meal. The coffee perked and the tea steeped as the women of the family put away the remnants of dinner and did the dishes. After letting our stomachs settle, the holiday table was then reborn as a buffet laden with desserts, such as Fluffy White Cake or Pumpkin Pie with Maple Spiced Nuts, or perhaps a big bowl of fruit salad because it was healthy. In time, the memory of how the holidays were celebrated becomes almost as important as the celebration itself.

As the years go by and new members of the family host these holiday gatherings, we find that mothers and grandmothers are sometimes released from their main-dish commitments but are still held responsible for the sweetest part of the meal. More and more time is spent with the generations mingling because the younger members fear that the old recipes and the old stories will someday be lost if they don't pursue a gentle interrogation of their elders.

In looking through our collection of manuscript cookbooks, we found that several versions of recipes for special holiday desserts kept turning up. We found over a dozen recipes for Baked Indian Pudding, and more than a dozen for bread puddings and apple pies. The Holiday Apple Pie is a variation we vow to make frequently, and again, we found that often the sweetest part of the dessert was its story. We hope you will enjoy baking Aunt Ida's Cheese Turnovers, Apple Walnut Strudel, or Baked Indian Pudding with Maple Spiced Nuts, but we also hope you make and bake your own holiday memories.

Baking pamphlet, 1930s

Baked Indian Pudding with Maple Spiced Nuts

1730s–1960s

MAKES 8 SERVINGS

This is a quintessential New England pudding, and we can't think of a better way to end a meal. The addition of Maple Spiced Nuts brings out the buttery sweet flavor of this slow-baked dessert.

FOR INDIAN PUDDING

¼ cup sugar

½ teaspoon salt

1 teaspoon cinnamon

¾ teaspoon ginger

¾ teaspoon nutmeg

½ cup yellow cornmeal

1 egg, beaten

½ cup molasses

1 teaspoon vanilla

4 cups milk, divided

4 tablespoons butter, melted

FOR MAPLE SPICED NUTS

½ cup maple syrup

2 tablespoons butter

½ teaspoon salt

¼ teaspoon cinnamon

¼ teaspoon nutmeg

1 cup whole pecans

1. Set the oven rack in the middle position. Preheat the oven to 275°F. Prepare a 1½-quart ovenproof glass baking dish by buttering it or coating it with vegetable spray. Cover a 14-inch by 16-inch baking pan with foil, shiny side up. Coat the foil with vegetable spray or use a silicone liner.

2. To make the Indian pudding: Sift together sugar, salt, cinnamon, ginger, and nutmeg in a bowl. Add cornmeal and stir to combine.

3. Add egg to molasses and stir to combine. Add vanilla.

4. Cook 3 cups of the milk in a heavy bottomed saucepan over medium heat, stirring with wooden spoon, just until scalded and bubbles form around the edges. Remove from heat. Add dry ingredients slowly, stirring with a wooden spoon. Place pan over low heat and continue stirring until mixture begins to thicken. Spoon a small amount of hot pudding mixture into egg mixture to temper it. Add egg mixture to pudding in pan and continue stirring until thick. Remove from heat and stir in butter.

5. Pour pudding into baking dish. Pour remaining cup milk over top, but do not stir in. Bake 2½ to 3 hours, or until pudding has a warm brown crust pulling away from the sides of dish. Pudding will be set but will still wiggle a bit. Place on a rack to cool.

6. To make the maple spiced nuts: Heat maple syrup, butter, salt, cinnamon, nutmeg, and pecans in a heavy frying pan over medium heat, stirring constantly with a wooden spoon until mixture begins to boil. Boil 5 minutes, stirring constantly. Spread nut mixture on baking sheet. Place baking sheet on rack to cool. When completely cool, break into shards.

7. Serve warm with vanilla ice cream and Maple Spiced Nuts. Store pudding covered with plastic wrap and in the refrigerator.

THE CHURCH LADY'S OHIO SPOON BREAD

MAKES 6 GENEROUS SERVINGS   1 9 4 0 S

This living recipe for spoon bread came from the manuscript cookbook of a woman who was active in the First Methodist Church in Mansfield, Ohio from the 1930s through the 1950s. It's an Ohio woman's take on a Southern specialty. This spoon bread is cornbread on top and silky, creamy cornmeal pudding on the inside. More sophisticated than polenta or grits, the spoon bread recipe illustrates how someone who travels can move a recipe over state lines.

1. Set the oven rack in the middle position. Preheat the oven to 375°F. Coat an 8-inch by 8-inch by 2-inch pan with vegetable spray.

2. Place cornmeal in a large bowl, pour boiling water over top, and let stand 3 minutes. Add baking powder, sugar, salt, milk, and heavy cream and whisk briskly. Add egg yolks and mix thoroughly, Add butter.

3. Place egg whites in the bowl of a standing mixer fitted with the whisk attachment. Beat until soft peaks form. Fold egg whites into batter.

4. Pour batter into pan. Bake 10 minutes, reduce heat to 350°F, and bake 27 minutes, or until top is golden brown and a tester inserted into bread comes out clean. Serve warm. Spoon bread is best served the same day it is made. Store any leftover bread in a glass dish covered with paper towels and plastic wrap in the refrigerator.

1 cup cornmeal

2 cups boiling water

2 teaspoons baking powder

1 teaspoon sugar

½ teaspoon salt

½ cup milk

½ cup heavy cream

2 egg yolks, beaten

2 tablespoons butter, melted

2 egg whites

Elinor's Persimmon Pudding

MAKES 12 SLICES

2 ripe persimmons, quartered and
   skins removed

1 cup flour

1 cup sugar

1 teaspoon baking soda

1 teaspoon cinnamon

1 teaspoon salt

½ cup milk

1 cup golden raisins

1 cup chopped walnuts

1 tablespoon butter, melted

Brandied whipped cream
   (optional)

Sweet Tip

After the pudding cools, you can poke holes in the top with a skewer and pour brandy over it, instead of adding brandy to the whipped cream. Although Elinor did not believe in drinking alcoholic beverages herself, we don't think she would have objected if your whipped cream is slightly enhanced with a touch of brandy. We like to also brush the top of the pudding with warmed apricot jam and decorate it in a geometric pattern with candied fruit, almonds, and pecans. We suggest that you brush the decorative fruit and nuts with more of the warm apricot jam.

This was the signature dessert of Elinor Inman Jennings. We waited more than thirty years to try it because we had never baked with persimmons before. It was a revelation! The result is a rich pudding with a firm crumb. Raisins and nuts add to the texture. This extra-sweet dessert does well with a touch of whipped cream.

1. Set the oven rack in the middle position. Preheat the oven to 350°F. Coat the bottom and sides of a 1½-quart ovenproof glass baking dish with butter or vegetable spray. Cut a parchment paper liner to fit the bottom of the pan and coat it with vegetable spray. Set aside a larger metal pan and rack for the water bath.

2. Place persimmons in the bowl of a food processor fitted with a metal blade. Pulse until creamy. Measure 1 cup of persimmon pulp and place in a bowl.

3. Sift together flour, sugar, baking soda, cinnamon, and salt in a medium bowl. Add milk to sifted dry ingredients and mix. Fold in persimmon pulp. Fold in raisins and walnuts. Fold in butter.

4. Place mixture into baking dish. Cover with foil. Place dish on rack in large pan. Pour hot water from a glass measuring cup into outer pan until water level rises halfway up sides of baking dish. Place carefully in oven. Bake 1 hour to 1 hour and 15 minutes. Check water bath occasionally and add more water if needed. Do not let the water evaporate from the water bath. Remove foil after 30 minutes. Pudding is done when tester inserted in center comes out clean.

5. Carefully remove baking dish from oven and water bath. Allow to cool on rack 30 minutes. Serve warm or at room temperature with fruit sauce or whipped cream flavored with brandy. Store leftover pudding loosely covered with wax paper in refrigerator.

Pumpkin Cheesecake Bread Pudding

MAKES 20 SERVINGS

FOR BREAD LAYERS

14 to 16 ½-inch slices brioche or firm white bread, trimmed of crusts and cut in half

1½ cups butter, melted

FOR CUSTARD

2 8-oz. packages cream cheese, at room temperature

1 cup sugar

6 eggs

1 15-oz. can pumpkin

2 cups milk

1 cup heavy cream

1 teaspoon vanilla

¼ teaspoon salt

1 teaspoon allspice

1 teaspoon ginger

1 teaspoon nutmeg

1 teaspoon cinnamon

FOR TOPPING

½ cup brown sugar

2 tablespoons butter, melted

This is an amalgam of several bread pudding recipes found in our collection of manuscript cookbooks. Most of the pudding recipes used stale bread cut into cubes or crumbs by thrifty housewives. We found that using brioche or good-quality bakery white bread was a quick alternative and contributed to the delectable density of the pudding. Serve this at Thanksgiving and make it a family tradition.

1. Set the oven rack in the middle position. Preheat the oven to 350°F. Coat a 9-inch by 13-inch ovenproof glass baking dish with vegetable spray. Set aside a larger metal baking pan and rack for the water bath.

2. To prepare the bread: Brush each slice of brioche on both sides with melted butter.

3. To make the custard: Combine cream cheese and sugar in a bowl and mix until smooth.

4. Combine eggs, pumpkin, milk, heavy cream, vanilla, salt, allspice, ginger, nutmeg, and cinnamon in the bowl of a standing mixer fitted with the paddle attachment. Beat until smooth. Add cream cheese mixture and combine.

5. Pour ½ cup pumpkin custard in bottom of baking dish. Tilt and swirl dish until bottom is completely covered with a thin layer of custard. Layer 6 slices of brioche on top of custard. Pour half of remaining custard over brioche. Add remaining brioche and custard in layers.

6. To add the topping: Use a knife to cut 8 slits through layered pudding. Cover top of pudding with plastic wrap and press down gently with your palm. Let stand 15 minutes. Remove plastic

ALL ABOUT BAKED PUDDINGS

Puddings have traditionally been a way to use leftover foods such as bread, cake crumbs, cookies, and macaroons. In its simplest form, bread pudding is made from sliced, crumbed, or cubed bread that is soaked in a rich-flavored custard and baked. There is an alchemy that occurs when these humble ingredients meld together in the oven.

Victorian and Edwardian meals almost always included a pudding, and the English referred to any sweet dessert as a pudding. Most nineteenth- and twentieth-century cookbooks, whether manuscript or printed, include recipes for puddings, especially bread puddings. The most spectacular bread puddings were filled with candied fruit and topped off with a layer of jam and a layer of meringue. No wonder they're called "Queen of Puddings."

wrap and sprinkle brown sugar over top of pudding. Pour melted butter over sugar.

7. Place baking dish on rack in large metal pan. Pour hot water from a glass measuring cup into outer pan until water level rises halfway up sides of baking dish. Place carefully in oven. Bake 1 hour to 1 hour and 15 minutes, or until top is nicely browned and custard has risen to top of baking dish. Check water bath occasionally and add more water if needed. *Do not let the water evaporate from the water bath.*

8. Carefully remove baking dish from oven and water bath. Allow pudding to cool on rack 1 hour. Serve slightly warm or cold with whipped cream or vanilla ice cream. Store covered with a paper towel and plastic wrap in the refrigerator.

CHOCOLATE APRICOT HAMANTASCHEN

1 9 6 0 s

MAKES 18 TO 25 HAMANTASCHEN, DEPENDING ON SIZE

FOR DOUGH

1⅔ cups flour, plus extra for rolling dough

⅓ cup cocoa

1 teaspoon baking powder

⅓ cup sugar

⅛ teaspoon salt

¾ cup cold butter, cut into large dice

1 egg, beaten

1 teaspoon vanilla

2 tablespoons cold water

FOR APRICOT FILLING

8 oz. dried apricots

1 tablespoon lemon juice

⅓ cup sugar

FOR CHOCOLATE FUDGE FILLING

¼ cup plus 2 tablespoons heavy cream

4 oz. bittersweet or semisweet chocolate, chopped

½ teaspoon vanilla

⅛ teaspoon salt

Hamantaschen are the triangular sweets made to celebrate Purim. We often find ourselves caught in the debate between those who prefer the yeast-raised bunlike Hamantaschen and those who prefer the more delicate Hamantaschen made from cookie dough. We vote for the cookie-dough version. When we found ourselves baking this traditional sweet a few years ago, we decided to try our own variation made with chocolate and apricot jam—we think they're worth trying.

1. Set the oven rack in the middle position. Preheat the oven to 350°F. Cover a 14-inch by 16-inch baking sheet with foil, shiny side up. Coat the foil with vegetable spray or use a silicone liner.

2. To make the dough: Place flour, cocoa, baking powder, sugar, and salt in the bowl of a food processor fitted with a metal blade. Pulse twice to combine. Add butter and process until butter is the size of small peas. Add egg and vanilla and process. Add water and process until dough pulls away from sides of bowl. Turn dough onto plastic wrap and gather into a ball. Wrap and chill until firm enough to roll, at least 1 hour. Dough may be refrigerated up to 3 days.

3. To make the apricot filling: Place apricots in a saucepan and cover with water. Bring to a boil over medium heat. Cover and simmer until apricots form a soft paste, about 15 minutes. Check periodically to see that fruit does not burn, especially toward end of cooking time. Place apricot paste in bowl, add lemon juice and sugar, and allow to cool.

4. To make the chocolate fudge filling: Heat heavy cream in a small saucepan over medium heat to just under a boil. Remove from heat and add chocolate. Let stand a few minutes. Mix gently with a wooden spoon until combined and smooth. Add vanilla and salt and stir. Chill in the refrigerator until firm.

5. Divide dough into fourths and shape into disks. Wrap three disks in plastic and keep refrigerated. Roll out one disk on floured wax paper or parchment paper to a ¼-inch thickness, sprinkling top with flour as needed to prevent sticking.

6. Cut dough into 3-inch or 4-inch circles using a floured biscuit cutter or the floured rim of a glass. Gather up scraps, wrap in plastic, and refrigerate. Dip an offset spatula in flour and slide it under dough circles to loosen them from paper. Place 1 teaspoon chocolate filling in the center of each circle. Add ½ teaspoon apricot filling on top of chocolate. Moisten circle around edges with water. Bring edges of dough up around filling and pinch together to form a tricorn hat shape. Work remaining dough, one disk at a time, in the same way. Combine scraps and reroll to make a few final pieces.

7. Place cookies on baking sheet. Bake 20 minutes, or until firm and crisp. Place on rack to cool. Remove and store between sheets of wax paper in a covered tin. Hamantaschen freeze beautifully.

FLUFFY WHITE CAKE

This was the cake our mother baked for special celebrations and during the holidays. She would divide the white frosted cake in half, and decorate one side in red and green and the other in blue and yellow. Holly and Chanukah candles shared equal placement on the top of the cake. Little did we know our mother was baking the first politically correct cake of the time!

1. Set the oven rack in the middle position. Preheat the oven to 350°F. Coat a 10-inch springform pan with vegetable spray. Cut a parchment paper or wax paper liner to fit the bottom of pan. Insert the liner and spray again. Dust pan with flour and tap out the excess.

2. To make the cake: Add lemon juice to milk and stir. Set aside to sour.

3. Sift together flour, baking powder, and salt.

4. Place butter and sugar in the bowl of a standing mixer fitted with the paddle attachment. Cream together until soft and fluffy. Add eggs, one at a time. Add vanilla to sour milk. Add sifted dry ingredients alternately with sour milk, beating after each addition.

5. Place batter in springform pan. Bake 35 to 45 minutes, or until tester inserted into cake comes out clean. Place on rack and allow to cool 30 minutes. Run a butter knife gently around edges and invert cake onto a second rack. Let cool completely.

6. To make the caramel icing: Combine confectioners' sugar, butter, and Soft Caramel Sauce in the bowl of a standing mixer fitted with the paddle attachment (or place in a small bowl and mix by hand). Thin with water if necessary, 1 teaspoon at a time, to desired spreading consistency. Frost top and sides of cake with an offset spatula. Immediately cover top and sides with sliced almonds. Store under cake dome or loosely wrapped in wax paper at room temperature.

FOR CAKE

- 1 tablespoon lemon juice
- 1 cup milk
- 2¼ cups flour
- 2½ teaspoons baking powder
- 1 teaspoon salt
- ½ cup butter
- 1½ cups sugar, sifted
- 2 eggs
- 1 teaspoon vanilla

FOR CARAMEL ICING

- 3 cups confectioners' sugar
- ½ cup butter
- ½ cup Soft Caramel Sauce (see recipe on page 193)
- 1 cup sliced almonds, toasted

Sweet Tips

- Buttermilk can be substituted for soured milk.
- This batter can also be baked in two 7-inch pans. Line the pans with parchment paper and coat with vegetable spray, dust with flour, and tap out the excess. Bake approximately 35 to 45 minutes.
- The cake layers may be split to make a four-layer cake. Add another cup of confectioners' sugar and water as needed to the icing.

IDA'S CHEESE TURNOVERS

MAKES 36 TURNOVERS

FOR DOUGH

1 package (2¼ teaspoons) active dry yeast

½ cup water, warmed to 110°F

¼ cup plus 1 tablespoon sugar, divided

1 cup butter

1 teaspoon salt

3 eggs

3½ cups flour

FOR FILLING

1 8-oz. package cream cheese

1 8-oz. package farmer cheese

1 egg

1 teaspoon vanilla

2 tablespoons sugar

1 egg, beaten

½ cup butter, melted

These were the turnovers our Auntie Ida always offered us in times of personal crisis, whether professional or romantic. These flaky turnovers with their double cheese filling are both substantial and light at the same time.

1. Set the oven rack in the middle position. Preheat the oven to 350°F. Cover a 14-inch by 16-inch baking sheet with foil, shiny side up. Coat the foil with vegetable spray or use a silicone liner.
2. To make the dough: Dissolve yeast in warm water. Add 1 tablespoon of the sugar. Set in a warm place to proof, about 10 minutes. Mixture will bubble when yeast is proofed.
3. Cream butter, remaining ¼ cup sugar, salt, and eggs in the bowl of a standing mixer fitted with the paddle attachment. Add proofed yeast mixture. Remove paddle attachment and attach dough hook. Add 3 cups of flour, 1 cup at a time, and knead until dough holds together, about 5 minutes. Add remaining ½ cup flour if dough is too loose. Place dough in a buttered bowl and turn so entire dough is coated with butter. Cover with towel and refrigerate 4 hours or overnight.
4. To make the filling: Combine cheeses, egg, vanilla, and sugar in the bowl of a standing mixer fitted with the paddle attachment.
5. Remove dough from refrigerator. Allow dough to sit in a warm place 30 minutes. Divide dough in half. Roll out one half between two pieces of lightly floured wax paper or parchment paper to a ¼-inch thickness. Cut 4-inch circles using a biscuit cutter dipped in flour. Brush each circle with beaten egg. Place 1 tablespoon filling in center, fold over dough, and pinch edges together. Place turnovers on baking sheet. Continue to assemble turnovers, gathering and rerolling scraps, until all dough is used. Set turnovers in a warm place to rise, 20 minutes.
6. Brush tops of turnovers with melted butter. Bake approximately 30 minutes. Remove from oven and cool on rack. Serve warm or at room temperature. Store leftover turnovers loosely wrapped in wax paper in refrigerator. Turnovers can be frozen when cool by wrapping them in wax paper and placing in a sealed freezer bag.

Sweet Tip

For a savory filling, omit the sugar and add a pinch of salt and a small onion, chopped and caramelized in butter.

Custard Rice Pudding

We found this recipe from the 1960s in a small notebook which contained only a dozen recipes, but, oh, what recipes! Featuring Dixie Dinner Rolls (page 91), Carrot Cream Cheese Muffins (page 33), and this down-home pudding, which combines a light and creamy custard base with a more substantial rice and raisin element. Everything old is new again!

1. Set the oven rack in the middle position. Preheat the oven to 325°F. Coat a 9-inch by 13-inch ovenproof glass baking dish with vegetable spray. Set aside a larger metal pan and rack for the water bath.

2. Heat heavy cream and milk in a heavy saucepan over medium heat until scalded. Remove from heat and add rice, stirring with a wooden spoon.

3. Combine eggs, egg yolks, sugar, nutmeg, vanilla, and salt in a large bowl. Add ¼ cup hot rice mixture to eggs, whisking briskly to temper. Whisk in another ½ cup hot rice mixture. Pour egg mixture into rice mixture and whisk to combine. Fold in raisins.

4. Pour mixture into baking dish. Place dish on rack in large pan. Pour hot water from a glass measuring cup into outer pan until water level rises halfway up sides of baking dish. Place carefully in oven. Bake 1½ hours. Check water bath occasionally and add more water if needed. Do not let the water evaporate from the water bath. Pudding is done when top begins to brown and bubble and tester inserted into custard comes out clean.

5. Carefully remove baking dish from oven and water bath. Allow to cool on rack until just barely warm, about 30 minutes. Serve warm with whipped cream. This pudding is also delicious served at room temperature or chilled. Store covered with a paper towel and plastic wrap in the refrigerator.

2 cups heavy cream

2 cups milk

1 cup cooked rice

4 eggs, beaten

2 egg yolks, beaten

1 cup sugar

1 teaspoon nutmeg

2 teaspoons vanilla

1 cup golden raisins

¼ teaspoon salt

Sweet Tip

It may seem like a lot of whisking, but the key to making this custard pudding successfully is to temper the egg mixture (to raise the temperature of one mixture by adding small amounts of the hot mixture to colder mixture) before adding it to the hot creamy mixture. If you add room temperature eggs to the hot cream and milk without tempering them, there is a chance the eggs will cook and form curds.

HOLIDAY APPLE CUSTARD PIE

MAKES 12 SLICES

1 unbaked 9-inch pie shell (see Sheila's Pie Crust on page 110)

4 medium apples, peeled, cored, and cut into thin wedges (enough for two layers)

1 cup sugar

1 teaspoon cinnamon

½ teaspoon salt

1 cup heavy cream

2 eggs

1 teaspoon vanilla

2 tablespoons butter, cut into small dice

We found this recipe written on the back of a private outpatient admitting notification form from Salem Hospital. The recipe was credited to someone named S. Lake. Although it was titled German Apple Pie, we found similar recipes for Swiss Apple Pie and French Apple Pie. We decided to refer to it as Holiday Apple Pie because it's not only simple to make and bakes in less than an hour, but it also presents well. No holiday is complete without a good apple pie.

1. Set the oven rack in the middle position. Preheat the oven to 450°F. Coat a 9-inch ovenproof glass pie plate with vegetable spray.

2. Arrange approximately half of apple slices on bottom of pie crust in an overlapping pattern. Sift together sugar, cinnamon, and salt. Sprinkle half of cinnamon sugar over apples.

3. Pour heavy cream into 2-cup glass measuring cup. Add eggs and vanilla and beat with a fork or small whisk to combine. Pour half of egg mixture over top of pie. Layer remaining apples in pie and sprinkle with remaining cinnamon sugar. Pour remaining cream mixture over top of pie. Dot with butter.

4. Bake 10 minutes, reduce oven temperature to 350°F, and bake 45 minutes more, or until filling bubbles rapidly and edges of crust are nicely browned. Check pie during baking; if crust is browning too quickly, cover loosely with foil. Cool pie on rack at least 2 hours before serving. This pie is best served the day it is baked. Store covered with paper towels and plastic wrap in the refrigerator.

APPLE WALNUT STRUDEL

MAKES 36 SLICES

FOR FILLING

¼ cup plus 2 tablespoons butter

6 Golden Delicious apples, peeled, cored, and cut into wedges

3 tablespoons lemon juice

¼ cup plus 2 tablespoons sugar

¼ teaspoon salt

½ teaspoon cinnamon

2 teaspoons lemon zest

1 cup walnuts, coarsely chopped

16 soda crackers, finely crushed

FOR DOUGH

½ cup butter

4 oz. (½ package) cream cheese

1⅔ cups flour

¼ teaspoon salt

¼ cup cold milk

½ cup butter, melted

Our mother baked Apple Walnut Strudel during the high holiday of Rosh Hashanah. Family and friends would come by during the holiday to drink tea and nibble from the tin of strudel on the kitchen table.

1. Set the oven rack in the middle position. Preheat the oven to 400°F. Cover a 14-inch by 16-inch baking sheet with foil, shiny side up. Coat the foil with vegetable spray or use a silicone liner.

2. To make the filling: Melt butter in large heavy frying pan. Fry apples, turning several times with a wooden spoon, until light golden brown in color. Add lemon juice and sugar and continue cooking, turning frequently, until apples are cooked but still a little firm, about 15 minutes. Do not overcook. Add salt, cinnamon, and lemon zest. Bring apples to a boil and cook until they start to thicken and caramelize, 1 to 2 minutes. Remove from heat.

3. To make the dough: Add butter and cream cheese to the bowl of a standing mixer fitted with the paddle attachment. Cream together until soft and fluffy. Add flour and salt and mix. Add milk to form a soft dough. Wrap dough in plastic wrap and chill in the refrigerator until firm enough to roll, about 1 hour.

4. Divide dough into 4 pieces. Dough should be kept in the refrigerator until needed. Roll out one piece of dough on floured wax paper or parchment paper to a ¹⁄₁₆-inch thickness. Brush with melted butter. Place a quarter of apples at top of dough leaving a 1-inch edge. Sprinkle a quarter of walnuts and soda cracker crumbs on top of apples. Roll strudel lengthwise from top to bottom, jelly-roll style, using paper as aid. Place strudel on baking sheet, seam side down. Repeat to assemble three more strudels.

5. Brush strudels with melted butter. Bake 20 minutes, turn oven down to 350°F, and bake 10 to 12 minutes more, or until crust is golden. Brush once with melted butter during baking. Cool in pan on rack 10 minutes. Cut strudel into 1-inch diagonal slices and continue cooling. Dust with confectioners' sugar just before serving. Store between sheets of wax paper in a covered tin.

PASSOVER DOUGHNUT ROLLS

MAKES 14 ROLLS

These are actually doughnut-shaped rolls. It seems that every Jewish housewife has her own version of these Passover rolls. Filling and tasty, they satisfy the need for a substantial accompaniment to the traditional roast chicken or brisket dinner.

⅔ cup water

⅓ cup vegetable oil

1 tablespoon sugar

¼ teaspoon salt

1 cup matzo meal

3 eggs, beaten

1. Set the oven rack in the middle position. Preheat the oven to 375°F. Coat a 14-inch by 16-inch baking sheet with vegetable spray or use a silicone liner.

2. Combine water, oil, sugar, and salt in a saucepan over medium-low heat. Bring to a boil, stirring with a wooden spoon. Remove pan from heat and add matzo meal, stirring briskly until mixture comes together. Place back on heat and stir 1 minute. Remove from heat. Cool at least 5 minutes. Add eggs and beat in. Set aside until cool enough to handle.

3. Using greased hands, roll dough into egg-sized balls (about 1 tablespoon of dough each). Place dough balls on baking sheet. Dip forefinger in oil and press down on center of each ball, leaving an indentation. Bake 30 to 35 minutes, or until golden brown. Place on rack to cool slightly, but serve rolls while still hot. Store loosely wrapped in wax paper in the refrigerator. To serve leftover rolls, reheat in 350°F oven 5 minutes, or until heated through.

Sweet Tips

- Care should be taken when bringing water, oil, sugar and salt to boil. If done slowly and carefully and on a medium-low heat, mixture should not foam up or spatter.
- Doughnut rolls are best served on the day they are baked.

Pumpkin Pie with Maple Spiced Nuts

MAKES 10 SLICES

1930S

We found this recipe handwritten on a half-sheet of lined paper. The author was somewhat cryptic, and left out any reference to the molasses in the directions, but we were able to translate this living recipe into a delectable pumpkin pie. We were pleasantly surprised to find this to be one of the best pumpkin pies we've ever tasted.

1. Set the oven rack in the middle position. Preheat the oven to 450°F. Coat a 9-inch glass pie plate with vegetable spray.

2. Place pumpkin in a large bowl. Sift brown sugar, cinnamon, ginger, and salt into pumpkin and stir with a wooden spoon. Add eggs, molasses, and butter and stir to combine. Combine water and evaporated milk, add to batter, and stir until well mixed.

3. Pour batter into pie shell. Bake 15 minutes. Lower oven temperature to 350°F and bake 50 minutes. Place pie on rack and allow to cool 2 to 3 hours. Serve with vanilla ice cream and Maple Spiced Nuts. Store covered with a paper towel and plastic wrap in the refrigerator.

Unbaked pie shell, at room temperature (see Sheila's Pie Crust on page 110)

1½ cups canned pumpkin

1 cup brown sugar

1 teaspoon cinnamon

½ teaspoon ginger

½ teaspoon salt

2 eggs, beaten

1 tablespoon molasses

1 tablespoon butter, melted

1 12-oz. can evaporated milk

½ cup water

1 cup Maple Spiced Nuts (page 174)

MAMA'S CHALLAH

MAKES 2 LOAVES

2 packages quick-rising yeast

½ cup water, warmed to 110°F

3 tablespoons sugar, divided

2 eggs

¼ cup vegetable oil

8 cups flour

1 tablespoon salt

2½ cups water, divided

1 cup raisins or dried cherries (optional)

1 tablespoon sesame, poppy, or caraway seeds (optional)

1 egg, beaten

Sweet Tip

We used quick-rising dry yeast in our interpretation of this challah recipe because we wanted to shorten the amount of rising time. We found that our challahs were just as light and tasted just as satisfying as the ones made with regular yeast.

This recipe, more than any other, is what preserving living recipes is all about. This was the rich egg bread our mother braided into loaves and baked every Friday before the Sabbath. It was one of the first recipes we made with our mother at her kitchen table, and no Friday night dinner was ever complete without it.

1. Set the oven rack in the middle position. Preheat the oven to 375°F. For round challah, cut a liner from parchment paper to fit the bottom of a 9-inch round cake pan. Insert the liner and coat with vegetable spray. For braided challah, line a 14-inch by 16-inch baking sheet with parchment paper and coat with vegetable spray.

2. Dissolve yeast in warm water. Add 1 tablespoon of the sugar. Set in a warm place to proof, about 10 minutes. Mixture will bubble when yeast is proofed.

3. Place eggs and oil in a small bowl and beat until combined.

4. Sift together flour, remaining 2 tablespoons sugar, and salt into the bowl of a standing mixer fitted with the paddle attachment. Make well in center of sifted dry ingredients, add proofed yeast, and mix about 10 seconds. Add egg mixture and beat to combine. Slowly add 2 cups of the water. Remove paddle attachment and attach dough hook and knead dough 6 minutes at medium speed. If dough is too dry, add remaining ½ cup water.

4. Oil a large bowl. Place dough in oiled bowl and turn dough so that all surfaces have a film of oil. Cover with a towel. Put in a warm place and allow to rise until double in size, about 1 hour. Punch down dough and divide in half.

5. To make round challah: Knead raisins or cherries into half of dough. On a lightly floured surface, roll dough into rope about 18 inches in length. Connect both ends and pinch together to form a circle. Place in cake pan and allow to rise until double in size, about 30 minutes. Brush with beaten egg.

6. To make braided challah: Divide remaining dough in 3 equal pieces. On a lightly floured surface, roll each piece into a rope

about 16 inches long. Pinch top ends together, braid the ropes tightly, and pinch bottom ends together. Place challah on baking sheet and let rise until double in size. Brush with beaten egg. Sprinkle with seeds.

7. Bake challah loaves 25 minutes, or until golden in color. Remove from pan and cool on a rack to room temperature. Although easy to slice with a serrated knife, tradition suggests that guests tear pieces from challah to eat. Store wrapped in plastic at room temperature.

SOFT CARAMEL SAUCE

MAKES APPROXIMATELY 2 CUPS   1 9 4 0 S

This caramel sauce is light, intensely sweet, and incredibly smooth. It's a thick caramel you could easily stand a spoon in, and it enhances everything it is paired with. Try it over vanilla ice cream or homemade chocolate pudding.

1 cup sugar

¼ cup water

1 tablespoon light corn syrup

¼ cup butter

1 cup heavy cream

⅛ teaspoon salt

1. Combine sugar, water, and light corn syrup in a heavy saucepan over high heat. Bring to a boil, stirring with a wooden spoon.

2. Dip a brush in water and wash down insides of pan. Reduce heat to medium high. Do not stir. Continue boiling until mixture turns golden brown (not dark brown), about 6 minutes.

3. Remove pan from heat. Swirl sauce gently in pan twice. Add butter and stir slowly until melted. Add cream (sauce may foam up) and stir again. (If the caramel seizes—doesn't join with cream—place pan on medium heat and stir with wooden spoon until smooth, about 1 minute.) Add salt. Pour caramel sauce into glass containers. Cool to room temperature and store in refrigerator for up to 2 weeks. Sauce will thicken on standing.

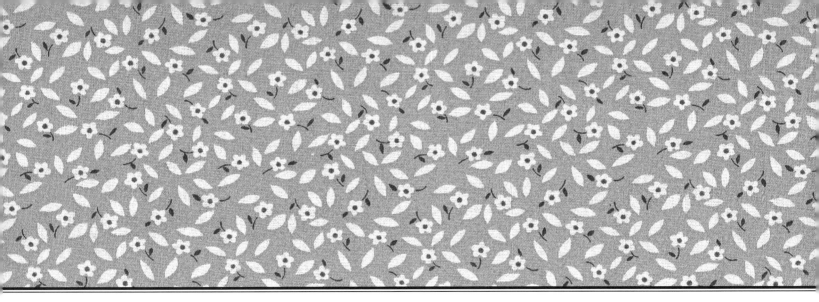

CHAPTER 8

There are moments when we just need

something. Times are tough. Decisions

have to be made. The wind blows

cold and shrill, and snow is mounting on

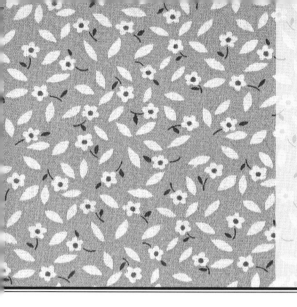

COMFORTING THE FAMILY

the front steps. We want to wrap ourselves

in pleasant memories, eat something

good, and feel confident that what we need

is just around the corner.

    The English call it nursery food—

food they enjoyed as children. We are never

too old to seek out the treats whose

culinary magic still makes us feel good. We

want a cup of tea or coffee and something

sweet and warm to go with it, maybe a

wedge of Classic Bread Pudding, loaded with butter and cream, or a slice of Banana Bread, soft and fragrant. In times of stress, some crave the rich taste of chocolate or simply the cakey texture of a muffin. In this chapter we pay tribute to those foods that smooth the rough edges, make us feel found when we are lost, and let us remember what it feels like to be cared for and loved when hard times come visiting.

In talking with friends about what made their childhood memorable and safe, it is not uncommon for a grown woman or man to become misty-eyed when talking of the nurturing received years before. In describing her mother, one friend remarked, "She was the captain of the ship. Everything was all right when she was in charge."

It is this gift of nurturing love that we frequently come across when reading through our collection of manuscript cookbooks. We acknowledge that it's not just what we eat that's important when we are challenged, but who provides it and who shares it with us. One of a mother's greatest achievements has always been the ability to comfort and sustain her family through cooking the foods that make everyone feel good again. Somehow, solutions seem nearer over a slice of Cold Tea Gingerbread or a piece of spicy Compromise Cake.

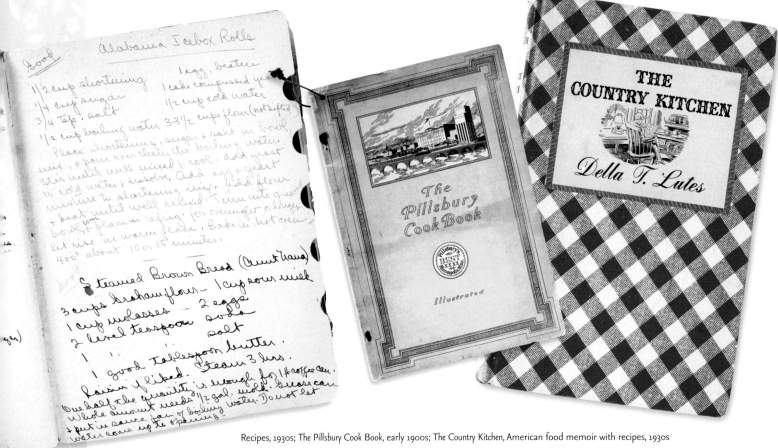

Recipes, 1930s; The Pillsbury Cook Book, early 1900s; The Country Kitchen, American food memoir with recipes, 1930s

We were excited when we found Miss Emma Smith's recipe for War Cake because it illustrated so well the essence of this chapter. It is a recipe that demonstrates the creativity and determination of an American woman to produce a tasty inexpensive quick bread, despite the scarcity of butter, eggs, and milk during World War I. Because Emma Smith was credited for this recipe, we learned that the culinary contributions of an unmarried woman were just as important as those of her married sisters.

Although we may never know just who Jane was, her recipe for Compromise Cake lives on because she sweet-talked with someone at a Massachusetts Women's Bureau. Women's Bureaus were established to meet the social, financial, and educational needs of women and their families. The comfort they offered through advice and aid, as well as providing the opportunity for women to meet and support one another, helped preserve many a family in desperate times.

Sharing your own comforting desserts with family and friends, or better yet, baking them together, is a therapeutic thing to do. It's the companionship of eating, talking, and coming up with solutions that makes us feel better. In times of stress, the kitchen, once again, becomes the center of the home. We hope you will bake the recipes in this chapter when you and those you care about need comfort and love.

Cold Tea Gingerbread

1 9 1 0

MAKES 12 SLICES

1¼ cups plus 2 tablespoons
   sifted flour

1 teaspoon ginger

½ teaspoon cinnamon

¼ teaspoon salt

½ cup butter

½ cup brown sugar

½ cup molasses

½ cup cold tea

1 scant teaspoon baking soda

1 tablespoon hot water

1 egg, beaten

We love baking with tea or coffee. Although we found that almost every collection of manuscript cookbooks we looked at had recipes using ginger, this was the only one asking for cold tea. We were intrigued. Not only does this gingerbread turn out moist and spicy, it also serves to illustrate the thrifty habits of New England cooks—not even cold tea was wasted.

1. Set the oven rack in the middle position. Preheat the oven to 350°F. Line the bottom and ends of a 9-inch by 5-inch by 3-inch loaf pan with a single strip of wax paper or parchment paper. Coat the pan and wax paper liner with vegetable spray.

2. Mix together flour, ginger, cinnamon, and salt.

3. Cream butter and brown sugar in the bowl of a standing mixer fitted with the paddle attachment. Add molasses and combine.

4. Add sifted dry ingredients alternately with cold tea. Dissolve baking soda in hot water and add to batter. Add egg and combine thoroughly.

5. Pour batter into loaf pan. Bake 45 minutes, or until tester inserted into loaf comes out clean. Cool in pan on rack for 20 minutes. Invert pan and place on rack to continue cooling. Serve gingerbread hot with lemon sauce or cold with whipped cream and chopped walnuts. Store loosely covered with wax paper at room temperature.

BANANA BREAD

This handwritten recipe for a thrifty staple uses those overly ripe bananas most of us usually have on hand. Most of the banana breads we've tried use mainly vegetable oil, sugar, and bananas. This recipe calls for melted butter. With our addition of finely chopped walnuts, it has more the flavor and texture of a banana cake.

1. Set the oven rack in the middle position. Preheat the oven to 350°F. Line the bottom and ends of a 9-inch by 5-inch by 3-inch loaf pan with a single strip of wax paper or parchment paper. Coat the pan and paper liner with vegetable spray.
2. Sift together flour, baking soda, salt, and nutmeg.
3. Cream butter, brown sugar, and sugar in the bowl of a standing mixer fitted with the paddle attachment. Add egg and bananas and combine. Add sifted dry ingredients. Fold in nuts.
4. Pour batter into loaf pan. Bake 50 to 55 minutes, or until tester inserted into loaf comes out clean. Cool on rack. Serve with butter and orange marmalade. Store covered with a paper towel and wax paper at room temperature.

1½ cups flour

1 teaspoon baking soda

¼ teaspoon salt

½ teaspoon nutmeg

¼ cup butter, melted

½ cup brown sugar

½ cup sugar

1 egg, beaten

1⅓ cups mashed bananas (about 3 medium bananas)

1½ cups finely chopped walnuts

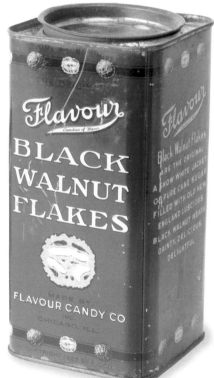

Nut tins, 1930s

WINTHROP BEACH BROWNIES

We never wrote down the ingredients or instructions for this family recipe, but the taste has long been committed to memory. About twenty years ago, Sheila was given a recipe for cream cheese brownies and they tasted similar to the brownies we'd enjoyed when we were young girls. With a few adjustments, we now have our Winthrop Beach Brownies once again.

1. Set the oven rack in the middle position. Preheat the oven to 350°F. Line the bottom and sides of an 8-inch by 8-inch by 2-inch metal pan with foil, shiny side up. Coat with butter or vegetable spray.

2. Combine cream cheese, ⅓ cup of the sugar, 1 egg, and ½ teaspoon of the vanilla in a bowl until smooth. Do not overbeat.

3. Sift together flour, baking powder, and salt.

4. Cream butter and remaining 1 cup sugar in the bowl of a standing mixer fitted with the paddle attachment. Add remaining 2 eggs. Add remaining ½ teaspoon vanilla and chocolate and combine. Add dry ingredients gradually and mix thoroughly.

5. Pour half of chocolate batter into pan and spread evenly with off-set spatula. Add cream cheese mixture to pan and smooth over chocolate base. Top cream cheese layer with remaining chocolate batter. Smooth with spatula. Sprinkle top with sliced almonds. Bake 50 to 55 minutes, or until a tester inserted in center comes out clean. Brownies will rise and fall and may crack. Place pan on rack and cool. Place pan of brownies, covered with sheet of wax paper, in the refrigerator for at least 2 hours or overnight before cutting. Store brownies between sheets of wax paper in a covered tin in the refrigerator.

1 8-oz. package cream cheese

1⅓ cups sugar, divided

3 eggs, divided

1 teaspoon vanilla, divided

¾ cup flour

½ teaspoon baking powder

½ teaspoon salt

½ cup butter

3 oz. bitter chocolate, melted and cooled

½ cup thinly sliced almonds

Sweet Tip

We found that we could turn these into Mocha Cream Cheese Brownies by dissolving 2 tablespoons instant coffee or espresso in 2 tablespoons boiling water. We added the cooled coffee liquid to the cream cheese filling and omitted the vanilla.

Oatmeal Cookies with Dried Cranberries and Toasted Walnuts

1 9 3 0 S

MAKES 48 COOKIES

2 cups flour

¼ teaspoon salt

1 teaspoon baking soda

1 teaspoon cinnamon

1 cup butter

½ cup brown sugar

½ cup sugar

2 eggs

1 teaspoon vanilla

2 cups rolled oats

¼ cup buttermilk

1 cup dried cherries

1 cup walnuts, coarsely chopped

These oatmeal cookies are not the substantial chunky ones you may be used to. They're petite and toasty, and the tartness of the cranberries and richness of the walnuts set off the nutty taste of the oatmeal. These cookies were originally made with raisins, but we couldn't resist substituting dried cranberries, which weren't readily available in the 1930s.

1. Set the oven rack in the middle position. Preheat the oven to 350°F. Cover a 14-inch by 16-inch baking sheet with foil, shiny side up. Coat the foil with vegetable spray or use a silicone liner.
2. Sift together flour, salt, baking soda, and cinnamon in a bowl.
3. Cream butter, brown sugar, and sugar in the bowl of a standing mixer fitted with the paddle attachment until soft and fluffy. Add eggs, one at a time, and vanilla.
4. Add sifted dry ingredients and beat until dough begins to form, about 1 minute. Add oats alternately with buttermilk and mix until completely blended. Fold in cherries and walnuts.
5. Drop by tablespoons onto baking sheet, no more than 12 cookies on a sheet. Flatten cookies with the palm of your hand. Leave 2 inches between cookies because they spread. Bake 15 minutes, turning baking sheet after 7 minutes. Allow to cool thoroughly on baking sheet on rack. Oatmeal cookies will firm up when cool. Store cookies between sheets of wax paper in a covered tin.

Sweet Tips

- Chilling the dough before forming the cookies is very important. Placing baking sheets of unbaked cookies in the refrigerator before baking also adds to the crispness factor.
- We found that using a melon baller made it easier to scoop the dough.

PENNY'S COUSIN PEARL'S BRAN MUFFINS

We found this recipe handwritten in a copy of *Laboratory Recipes*, owned by Rachel W. Banks. We never learned very much about Penny or her cousin Pearl, but these bran muffins are as good as any we've ever tasted. They are generously portioned muffins, with the dark sweet flavor of molasses and the signature candied cherry on top.

1. Set the oven rack in the middle position. Preheat the oven to 400°F. Coat the cups and top surface of a 12-cup muffin pan with vegetable spray.
2. Combine wheat bran, buttermilk, molasses, and egg in a large bowl. Let stand 10 minutes. Add flour, sugar, salt, and baking soda and mix gently. Fold in raisins, being careful not to overstir. Fold in butter.
3. Pour batter into muffin pan. Place candied cherry on top of each muffin. Bake 20 minutes, or until tester inserted in middle comes out clean. Store covered with a paper towel and loosely wrapped in wax paper at room temperature.

¾ cup wheat bran
1 cup buttermilk
1 tablespoon molasses
1 egg, beaten
1¼ cups flour
⅓ cup sugar
½ teaspoon salt
1 teaspoon baking soda
½ cup raisins
¼ cup butter, melted
12 candied cherries

Sweet Tip

If you don't have candied cherries, you can use maraschino cherries. Dry them on a paper towel before placing them on top of the muffins.

Cheese Blintzes

FOR BLINTZES

2 eggs, beaten

¾ cup water

½ cup flour

4 tablespoons butter, melted, plus
   extra for frying

1 teaspoon sugar

Pinch of salt

1 teaspoon vanilla

FOR FILLING

6 oz. farmer cheese or pot cheese

4 oz. (½ package) cream cheese

1 egg, lightly beaten

2 teaspoons sugar

½ teaspoon vanilla

Pinch of salt

Sweet Tip

You can also fill your blintzes
with fresh blueberries mixed with
sugar and a little cinnamon.

We remember our mother making blintzes in the early summer.
The ritual was always the same—the clean white bed sheet on
the kitchen table, the battered little frying pan, and the crumbled
piece of wax paper dipped in melted butter for greasing it. After
each blintz was fried, she'd flip the pan onto the covered table,
lining them up on the sheet. We'd rush to eat the filled blintzes
with sour cream and applesauce.

1. Coat an 8-inch frying pan with vegetable spray. Set aside sheets of
   wax paper or parchment paper to place between blintzes.
2. To make the blintzes: Combine eggs and water in a bowl. Add
   flour, butter, sugar, salt, and vanilla and whisk until smooth. Strain
   batter to remove any lumps.
3. Heat pan on medium-high heat. Pour ¼ cup of batter into pan,
   swirl to cover bottom of pan lightly, and pour excess batter back
   into bowl. Fry until blintz comes away from pan and is opaque in
   color. Loosen edges of blintz with a butter knife and flip with a
   spatula onto wax paper or parchment paper. Place each cooked
   blintz between sheets of wax or parchment paper. Continue to fry
   blintzes, spraying pan before each one, until the batter is used up.
4. To make the filling: Combine farmer cheese, cream cheese,
   eggs, sugar, vanilla, and salt in a bowl. Beat with a wooden spoon
   until combined.
5. Place a blintz on a work surface and spoon some filling onto
   the center. Fold in two opposite edges, overlapping in the middle,
   and then fold in ends, to make a neat package. Repeat for each
   blintz, dividing the filling evenly among them.
6. Melt 1 tablespoon butter in a frying pan or on a greased griddle
   and add blintzes. Fry until golden brown on both sides,
   turning once. Serve at once with sour cream and applesauce.
   Store leftover or unfried blintzes on a plate, loosely wrapped in
   wax paper in the refrigerator.

COMPROMISE CAKE

MAKES 16 2-INCH SQUARES

FOR CAKE

1 cup raisins, finely chopped in food processor

Peel from 1 medium juice orange, finely ground in food processor (about ¾ cup)

¼ cup walnuts, finely ground

2 cups flour, divided

1 teaspoon baking soda

½ teaspoon salt

½ cup butter

½ cup sugar

⅔ cup brown sugar

2 eggs, separated

1 cup buttermilk

FOR ORANGE GLAZE

1½ cups confectioners' sugar

2 tablespoons grated orange zest

¼ cup orange juice

⅛ teaspoon salt

We think this delightful old-fashioned orange-nut cake is from the nineteenth century. We've seen versions in early community cookbooks, but this one is handwritten and credited to "Jane at Woman's Bureau." This living recipe makes reference to "seeded raisins" and instructs us to "put the peel through the food chopper twice." Obviously, at the time, it was still a novelty to be able to buy raisins that didn't have to be put through a raisin seeder or be seeded by hand.

1. Set the oven rack in the middle position. Preheat the oven to 350°F. Coat an 8-inch by 8-inch by 2-inch metal pan with vegetable spray. Cut a liner from wax paper or parchment paper to fit the bottom on the pan. Insert the liner and coat with vegetable spray.

2. To make the cake: Combine raisins, orange zest, walnuts, and 2 tablespoons of the flour in a medium bowl.

3. Sift together remaining 1⅞ cups flour, baking soda, and salt.

4. Cream butter, sugar, and brown sugar in the bowl of a standing mixer fitted with the paddle attachment until soft and fluffy. Add egg yolks, one at a time, beating after each addition. Add sifted dry ingredients alternately with buttermilk. Beat in raisin mixture.

5. Attach clean bowl and whisk to standing mixer. Beat egg whites until they form stiff peaks. Fold into batter.

6. Pour batter into pan. Bake 50 to 55 minutes, or until cake is golden brown and tester inserted into cake comes out clean. Cool on rack at least 20 minutes before turning out of pan. Set cake on rack to cool completely.

7. To make orange glaze: Place confectioners' sugar, orange zest, orange juice, and salt in a small bowl and mix to combine. Slip a sheet of wax paper under rack to catch drips. Spoon glaze liberally over cake. Let glaze harden before cutting and serving. Store under a cake dome or loosely wrapped in wax paper at room temperature.

Sweet Tips

- Halve the orange and juice before pulsing in food processor.
- Add flour to orange peel, raisins, and chopped nuts immediately after processing to prevent clumping.
- Beat the peel, raisins, and nuts into batter with paddle attachment. It will allow for a more even distribution.

MISS EMMA SMITH'S WAR CAKE

This recipe is a war cake, born out of necessity, since it includes no eggs, butter, or milk. It's also an example of a recipe giving the marital status of the originator. Miss Smith's contemporary, Mrs. William Eaton, apparently added the two teaspoons of cocoa to the recipe. Also noted by Miss Smith, "This cake is better at the end of a week or even longer. It ripens as does all fruitcakes."

3 cups flour, sifted

2 cups plus 1 teaspoon hot water, divided

2 cups brown sugar

2 tablespoons lard (or butter)

1 cup raisins

1 teaspoon salt

1 teaspoon cinnamon

½ teaspoon cloves

½ teaspoon nutmeg

2 teaspoons cocoa

1 teaspoon baking soda

1. Set the oven rack in the middle position. Preheat the oven to 300°F. Line the bottom and ends of a 9-inch by 5-inch by 3-inch loaf pan with a single strip of wax paper. Coat the pan and wax paper liner with vegetable spray.

2. Add flour to the bowl of a standing mixer fitted with the paddle attachment.

3. Add 2 cups of the hot water, brown sugar, lard, raisins, salt, cinnamon, cloves, nutmeg, and cocoa to a large heavy-bottomed saucepan. Cook over medium heat, stirring with a wooden spoon, until mixture begins to bubble. Boil 5 minutes, stirring constantly. Remove from heat and cool thoroughly. Dissolve baking soda in remaining 1 teaspoon hot water and add to syrup. Allow to cool.

4. Add mixture to flour and beat until thoroughly blended. Place in loaf pan. Bake 45 minutes, or until a tester inserted into cake comes out clean. Cool on rack for 15 minutes before removing from pan. Cake should be eaten at room temperature. Store leftover cake covered with a paper towel and wax paper in the refrigerator.

MARION CARTER'S STEAMED BLUEBERRY PUDDING

1 8 9 5

MAKES 10 SERVINGS

1½ cups blueberries

2 cups flour, divided

4 teaspoons baking powder

½ cup sugar

½ teaspoon salt

1½ teaspoons cinnamon

¼ cup butter, melted

2 teaspoons grated lemon zest

¼ teaspoon lemon oil or lemon extract

1 egg, beaten

2 tablespoons molasses

1 cup milk

Hot water for steaming

This recipe comes from the manuscript cookbook of Marion Carter, from Maine. This pudding should be made with fresh blueberries for the best results. Don't be intimidated by our warning of an exploding pudding mold. Just be sure that the water doesn't run out during steaming and that you lift the cover off the steaming pot carefully when you check it.

1. Liberally butter sides and bottom of a 1½-quart covered tin pudding mold. Prepare a buttered parchment sheet to fit the top of the mold. Cut a hole in parchment to fit over center spoke. Select a covered pot large enough to accommodate the pudding mold with a 2-inch clearance around sides.

2. Combine blueberries and 2 tablespoons of the flour.

3. Mix remaining 1⅞ cups flour, baking powder, sugar, salt, and cinnamon in a large bowl. Add butter and stir. Add lemon zest

Covered tin ice cream mold, early 1900s; *Gateau de Pommes* mold used for steamed chocolate pudding, early 1900s

ALL ABOUT STEAMED PUDDINGS

In the nineteenth century, puddings were often steamed in a pudding cloth, which was a piece of linen spread with a paste of flour and lard so that the actual pudding could be wrapped in the cloth without using a mold. A loop sewn to the cloth allowed the pudding to be suspended inside the pot by means of a string. The pudding never touched the water, and the string was held in place by the pot lid. We don't recommend this practice. We suggest using a covered tin pudding mold or a metal mixing bowl instead.

and lemon oil. Add egg and molasses to milk, add to batter, and stir to combine. Fold in blueberries.

4. Pour batter into pudding mold, making sure that it is no more than two thirds full. Place buttered parchment round on top of mold and add cover. (If mold has no cover, fold 2 sheets of foil over open top and tie securely with kitchen string.)

5. Set filled mold on rack in deep heavy pot. Add water until one third of mold is covered. Remove mold. Cover pot and bring water to a boil. Turn off heat, lift pot cover, and carefully place filled mold on rack. Cover pot. Adjust heat so that water simmers; do not not let water come to boil. Steam pudding 1 hour, checking periodically to make sure that water level remains stable. Do not let the water boil out because a tightly covered mold could explode.

6. Turn off heat. Remove pudding mold carefully from steamer and place on cooling rack. Carefully remove cover (or foil) and parchment from top of mold. Pudding should have risen to top of mold. Allow to cool 10 minutes. Pudding should still be warm and should release easily when mold is inverted. Serve warm in slices with unsweetened whipped cream. Pudding is best served the day it is steamed. Store leftover pudding loosely wrapped in wax paper in refrigerator.

Mary Williams' Coffee Cake with Streusel

1940S

MAKES 16 GENEROUS SLICES

This recipe was given to us by Elinor Jennings in the early 1970s. Several of the recipes she gave to us were from her mother, Daisy Inman, and reflect the cuisine of a southern woman. Mary Williams was a friend of the Inman family. Her coffee cake is rich with butter and nuts.

FOR STREUSEL

½ cup brown sugar

2 tablespoons flour

½ teaspoon cinnamon

2 tablespoons cold butter

½ cup pecans, toasted and coarsely chopped

FOR CAKE

1½ cups flour

3 teaspoons baking powder

¼ teaspoon salt

¾ cup sugar

¼ cup butter

1 egg, beaten

½ cup milk

1 teaspoon vanilla

1. Set the oven rack in the middle position. Preheat the oven to 350°F. Line the bottom and sides of an 8-inch by 8-inch by 2-inch metal pan with foil, shiny side up. Coat with butter or vegetable spray.

2. To make the streusel: Place brown sugar, flour, and cinnamon in a bowl. Work in butter with your fingers (wear disposable gloves if desired) until mixture resembles coarse sand. Add pecans and combine.

3. To make the cake: Sift together flour, baking powder, and salt. Add sugar. Using a pastry blender or two knives, cut butter into dry ingredients. Add egg, milk, and vanilla and combine. Place half of batter in pan. Sprinkle half of streusel on top of batter. Add rest of batter to pan and top with remaining streusel.

4. Bake 35 to 40 minutes, or until tester inserted into cake comes out clean. Cool on rack completely before cutting into squares. Serve plain or with butter. Store loosely wrapped with wax paper at room temperature.

Sweet Tip

Batter for coffee cake may be prepared up to one day ahead and refrigerated.

Classic Bread Pudding

MAKES 20 SERVINGS

FOR BREAD LAYERS

14 to 16 ½-inch slices brioche, trimmed of crusts and cut in half

½ cup plus 2 tablespoons butter, melted

FOR CUSTARD

2 cups milk

2 cups heavy cream

1 cup sugar

1 teaspoon vanilla

½ teaspoon cinnamon

½ teaspoon nutmeg

¼ teaspoon salt

4 eggs, beaten

2 cups raisins, soaked in ½ cup brandy

FOR TOPPING

1 cup brown sugar

4 tablespoons butter, melted

When we read through our many manuscript cookbooks, we found countless recipes for bread puddings that sounded good. It seems that the quintessential bread pudding should include elements from all of them. Although some use only stale bread, milk instead of cream, and a token egg, all of them stay with the original concept of bread, dried fruit, and custard.

1. Set the oven rack in the middle position. Preheat the oven to 350°F. Coat a 9-inch by 13-inch ovenproof glass baking dish with vegetable spray. Set aside a larger metal baking pan and rack for the water bath.

2. To prepare the bread: Brush melted butter on both sides of each brioche slice.

3. To make the custard: Combine milk, heavy cream, sugar, vanilla, cinnamon, nutmeg, and salt in a bowl. Add eggs to custard mixture and combine.

4. Pour small amount of custard in bottom of baking dish. Tilt and swirl dish until bottom is covered. Layer 6 slices of brioche on top of custard. Fill in spaces with extra brioche. Pour half of remaining custard over brioche. Drain brandy from raisins. Sprinkle half of raisins on top of custard. Add remaining brioche to dish. Pour rest of custard over brioche and sprinkle with remaining raisins.

5. To add the topping: Use a knife to cut 8 slits through layered pudding. Cover top of pudding with plastic wrap and press down firmly with your palm until custard rises to the top. (Raisins will sink into pudding.) Let stand 10 minutes, pushing down gently on top of pudding two more times. Remove plastic wrap and cover entire top of pudding with brown sugar. Pour melted butter over brown sugar.

6. Place baking disk on rack in large metal pan. Pour hot water from a glass measuring cup into outer pan until water level rises halfway up sides of glass dish. Place carefully in oven. Bake approximately 1 hour 15 minutes, or until topping puffs up and begins to bubble and a tester inserted into middle comes out

clean. Do not let the water evaporate from the water bath. Check pudding periodically during baking to be sure topping is not burning; cover loosely with foil if topping seems to be drying out.

7. Remove baking dish carefully from oven and water bath. Allow to cool on rack 30 minutes to 1 hour. Serve slightly warm or at room temperature with unsweetened whipped cream. Store covered with a paper towel and plastic wrap in the refrigerator.

LOTTY PECK'S BROWN BREAD

MAKES 14 SLICES   1920S

We found this recipe typed on a lined index card. We don't know much about Lotty, but, we're glad her name was attached to this recipe. We prefer sifting the graham flour before adding it to the all-purpose flour, but if a coarser loaf is desired, this step can be omitted. Lotty Peck's Brown Bread is wonderful spread with whipped cream cheese. It is even better with salted butter and apricot jam.

2 cups graham flour

2 cups flour

2 teaspoons baking soda

1 teaspoon salt

3 tablespoons honey

1 egg, lightly beaten

2 cups milk

3 tablespoons orange zest

1. Set the oven rack in the middle position. Preheat the oven to 350°F. Line the bottom and ends of a 9-inch by 5-inch by 3-inch loaf pan with a single strip of wax paper. Coat the pan and wax paper liner with vegetable spray.

2. Sift together graham flour, flour, baking soda, and salt.

3. Place honey in a large bowl, add egg, and mix well by hand with a wooden spoon. Add sifted dry ingredients alternately with milk, ending with milk. Fold in orange zest.

4. Pour batter into loaf pan. Bake 40 minutes, or until a tester inserted into loaf comes out dry. Let cool completely on rack. Remove from pan and cut into slices. Store loosely wrapped with wax paper at room temperature.

PINEAPPLE RAISIN DESSERT KUGEL

We love kugel, especially sweet dairy kugel made with butter, cheese, sugar, eggs, and sour cream. Some argue that kugel is meant to be served as an accompaniment to a main dish. We disagree. We think kugel can be eaten for breakfast, lunch, and dinner, in between meals, and even as a dessert!

1. Set the oven rack in the middle position. Preheat the oven to 350°F. Coat a 9-inch by 13-inch ovenproof glass baking dish with vegetable spray.
2. To make the kugel: Cook noodles according to package directions and drain thoroughly.
3. Place noodles in a large bowl. Mix in cottage cheese, brown sugar, and sour cream. Add eggs, butter, salt, nutmeg, cinnamon, and vanilla and mix to combine.
4. Roll pineapple in paper towels to remove excess moisture. Chop coarsely and fold into noodle mixture. Fold in raisins.
5. To add the topping: Turn noodle mixture into baking dish. Pour melted butter over top and sprinkle with brown sugar. Bake 50 to 55 minutes, or until kugel bubbles and noodles on top turn golden brown. Place on rack to cool. Serve hot or cold with sour cream. Store covered with wax paper in the refrigerator.

FOR KUGEL

1 12-oz. package wide egg noodles

2 cups cottage cheese

½ cup brown sugar

1 cup sour cream

4 eggs, beaten

½ cup butter, melted

¼ teaspoon salt

¼ teaspoon nutmeg

½ teaspoon cinnamon

1 teaspoon vanilla

1 cup canned pineapple chunks, drained

1 cup raisins

FOR TOPPING

3 tablespoons butter, melted

4 tablespoons brown sugar

Canadian Fruitcake

MAKES 12 SERVINGS

1 cup water

½ cup butter, cut into ½-inch cubes

½ teaspoon nutmeg or mace

½ teaspoon ginger

1 teaspoon cinnamon

1 teaspoon baking soda

1 teaspoon salt

½ teaspoon vanilla

1½ cups mixed candied fruit, coarsely chopped

½ cup plus 1 tablespoon firmly packed brown sugar

½ cup plus 1 tablespoon dark corn syrup

2½ cups flour, sifted

Sweet Tips

- The top of the cake can be brushed with melted honey for added sweetness.
- This cake improves with standing.

We found this recipe in a cookbook inscribed "With love and all good wishes, Christmas/New Years, from Rosamond." The well-used little book contains several wartime recipes, some of them from the BBC. The recipe was written in pounds and ounces, and it took us several tries before we were able to translate the ingredients and determine the correct oven temperature to produce this golden cake studded with candied fruit.

1. Set the oven rack in the middle position. Preheat the oven to 350°F. Coat a 9-inch round cake pan with vegetable spray. Cut a parchment paper or wax paper liner to fit the bottom of the pan. Insert the paper liner and coat pan and liner with vegetable spray. Dust pan with flour and tap out the excess. Set aside a large metal bowl for water bath.

2. Heat water in heavy deep 4-quart saucepan until bubbles form around edge. Do not allow to boil. Shut off heat and remove pan from heat source. Add butter, nutmeg, ginger, cinnamon, baking soda, salt, vanilla, candied fruit, brown sugar, and corn syrup and stir to combine. Cook over medium-low heat, continuing to stir, until mixture comes to a boil; this will take a few minutes. Increase heat slightly if necessary and boil 5 minutes. Mixture will foam up. Be careful not to let mixture boil over.

3. Fill bowl for water bath halfway with ice cubes and cold water. Set saucepan into water bath until mixture is cool. (Alternately, mixture can be carefully transferred to heat-proof bowl and allowed to cool to room temperature.)

4. Transfer mixture to the bowl of a standing mixer fitted with the paddle attachment. Add flour gradually and beat until thoroughly combined.

5. Place batter in cake pan and even top with offset spatula. Bake 40 to 45 minutes, or until tester inserted into cake comes out clean. Cool on rack. Serve cake slightly warm in wedges with whipped cream or serve cooled and cut in thin slices with a glass of port. Store covered with a paper towel and wax paper at room temperature.

MRS. JUSTO'S ORANGE CARROT CAKE

This is one of the best carrot cakes we've ever eaten! A juicy whole orange, peel and all, is added to the crisp grated carrots and the toasted walnuts. This is a very sweet cake with a great texture. We think it really doesn't need embellishment, because it forms its own sugar glaze, but if you like a glaze, try the one for Mrs. Tate's "Old and Tried" Orange Cake (page 93).

1 juice orange, unpeeled

2 cups flour

2 teaspoons baking powder

2 teaspoons baking soda

2 teaspoons cinnamon

2 teaspoons nutmeg

1 teaspoon salt

1½ cups peanut oil

1 cup sugar

1 cup brown sugar

4 eggs

2 cups grated carrots

1 cup chopped toasted walnuts

¼ cup confectioners' sugar

Whipped cream

1. Set the oven rack in the middle position. Preheat the oven to 350°F. Coat a 10-inch tube pan with vegetable spray. Cut a parchment paper or wax paper liner to fit the bottom of the pan. Insert the liner and coat with vegetable spray. Dust pan with flour and tap out the excess.

2. Trim a thin slice from each end of orange. Cut orange in half lengthwise. Make a shallow V-shaped cut to remove center core. Cut into wedges, remove seeds, and cut into 1-inch pieces. Place orange pieces in the bowl of food processor fitted with the metal blade. Pulse three or four times, or until orange turns to "confetti."

3. Sift together flour, baking powder, baking soda, cinnamon, nutmeg, and salt.

4. Combine oil, orange confetti, sugar, and brown sugar in the bowl of a standing mixer fitted with the paddle attachment. Add eggs, one at a time, and combine thoroughly. Add sifted dry ingredients gradually. (Batter will be loose.) Fold in carrots and walnuts.

5. Pour batter into tube pan. Bake 60 minutes, or until a tester inserted into cake comes out clean. Cool in pan on rack 10 to 25 minutes. Run a butter knife gently around edges and invert cake onto a second rack. Turn right side up and allow to cool completely. Dust top of cake with confectioners' sugar and serve with rosette of whipped cream. Store loosely covered with wax paper at room temperature.

Pictured on page 5.

CHAPTER 9

We've noticed in recent years that we've had to redefine what we traditionally think of as summer. When we were growing up, summer began late in June with the

IN THE GOOD OLE SUMMERTIME

closing of school, and ended right after Labor Day when school began again. As we grew older, we began to play with the boundaries, ignoring dates put forth by the weatherman and school schedules and instead allowing ourselves to "summer" whenever the weather is warm and sunny. We celebrate the fruits of June, July, and August, but we do not exclude the bounty that comes to us through September and even into October when the last rays of the sun still warm us as we move toward the winter holidays.

After looking through our collection of handwritten recipes, we concluded that fifty, eighty, even one hundred years ago, special summer desserts made from seasonal ingredients were very much like the ones we enjoy today. For this chapter of *Heirloom Baking*, we found ourselves gravitating to recipes that include fresh blueberries, peaches, nectarines, and strawberries—the fruits of the summer months. The seasons may change, but the recipes of the good ole summertime endure.

We included two lemon desserts in this chapter, for those of you who equate summer with citrus, but we also included a recipe for Caramelized Apple Brioche Bread Pudding and for Esther Pullman's Plum Torte, made with those little soursweet Italian plums that are available only in September and early October.

When we tested the recipe for Double Lemon Shortcake with Lemon Curd (which is really just an excuse for eating the first raspberries or blueberries of the

Recipe for Charles Barker Blueberry Cake, 1890s

HEIRLOOM BAKING

Baking pamphlet, 1930s

season), we found those special summer memories returning, and as we relived the wonderful experiences, we found that the flavor of the shortcakes we were baking seemed to enhance our memories.

In talking with friends, old and young, they told us of their suppers or picnics on the beach with special dessert courses of fruit pies or crumbly betties. They recalled Fourth of July carnivals, attended more than half a century ago, where the mingling smells of barbecue and wonderful berry-filled fried fritters tantalized the appetites of those gathered for a vibrant display of fireworks. We heard stories of trees, both fragrant and fertile, providing enough tart-sweet apples for pies and cobblers for a whole street. Ice cream, hand-churned, dressed with sauces of caramel or chocolate were part of their summers as were afternoons of berry picking ending in soup plates full of rich shortcake stained with mashed strawberries and embellished with puffs of sweetened whipped cream.

We hope some of the recipes we've chosen to share with you—One, Two, Three Open-Faced Blueberry Pie, Mrs. Paul Knight's Bittersweet Chocolate Sauce (perfect over a dish of ice cream), and Double-Crust Pineapple Pie—will encourage you to go into your kitchen and recapture the tastes of your own summertime.

PEACH STREUSEL PIE

MAKES 8 PIECES

FOR STREUSEL

¾ cup brown sugar

3 tablespoons flour

¼ teaspoon salt

¼ teaspoon nutmeg

3 tablespoons cold butter, cut into small dice

¾ cup slivered almonds

FOR PIE

1 tablespoon flour

Unbaked 9-inch pie shell (see Sheila's Pie Crust on page 110)

4 cups "still-firm" peaches, sliced

½ cup sugar

¼ teaspoon salt

2 teaspoons grated lemon zest

¼ teaspoon nutmeg

1 tablespoon lemon juice, divided

3 tablespoons cornstarch

1 teaspoon vanilla

Sweet Tip

We have found that baking fruit pies is very subjective. Much depends on the condition of the fruit. We have always been told to use overripe peaches in pies, but we found they produced too much juice. We feel better using peaches that have a bit of firmness left in them.

Making this pie was a challenge. We found that using overripe peaches just didn't work. Peaches that were still a bit firm helped to control the amount of peach juice in the pie. When this pie comes out of the oven with its crown of crunchy brown sugar and almond streusel, we know it's summertime!

1. To make the streusel: place brown sugar in a medium bowl. Sift together flour, salt, and nutmeg on a sheet of wax paper and add to brown sugar. Mix butter into sifted dry ingredients with your hands (wear disposable gloves if desired) until the texture resembles coarse sand. Add almonds and combine. Chill streusel for 20 minutes.

2. Set the oven rack in the middle position. Preheat the oven to 400°F. Sprinkle flour on bottom of unbaked pie crust.

3. To make the pie: Sprinkle peach slices with sugar, salt, and lemon zest. Mix thoroughly and place in strainer over bowl. Let fruit drain for at least 30 minutes.

4. Remove peaches from strainer and place in a medium bowl. Add nutmeg and ½ tablespoon lemon juice and toss to combine. Measure ½ cup of strained peach juice into small bowl. Whisk in cornstarch until dissolved. Stir in remaining lemon juice and vanilla. Pour cornstarch syrup over peaches and toss until slices are well coated. Gently pour fruit into pie shell. Sprinkle streusel mixture over top.

5. Bake 30 minutes at 400°F. Check pie; if crust is browning too quickly, cover with foil. Continue to bake 20 to 25 minutes, or until crust is browned and fruit bubbles. Remove pie from oven and place on rack. Allow to cool 3 hours before cutting. Serve with vanilla ice cream. Store pie covered with a paper towel and plastic wrap in the refrigerator.

EVALYN'S LIGHTLY LEMON CAKE

We found this recipe in a green metal binder full of recipes spanning the 1890s to the 1940s. Evalyn's name appeared with this spelling on the handwritten recipe we found for simple lemon cake. Nothing fancy here, it's just an old-fashioned light cake, good with a little sweetened whipped cream.

1. Set the oven rack in the middle position. Preheat the oven to 350°F. Coat a 9-inch cake pan or springform pan with butter or vegetable spray. Cut a wax paper or parchment paper liner to fit the bottom of pan. Insert the liner and coat with butter or vegetable spray. Dust pan with flour and tap out the excess.

2. To make the cake: Sift together flour, salt, and baking powder into a medium bowl.

3. Beat eggs in the bowl of a standing mixer fitted with the paddle attachment. Gradually beat in sugar. Add butter and combine.

4. Add vanilla and lemon oil to milk. Add sifted dry ingredients alternately with liquid ingredients to egg mixture, ending with sifted dry ingredients. Pour batter into cake pan or springform pan.

5. Bake 35 minutes, or until a tester inserted into middle comes out clean. Cover loosely with foil if top of cake browns too quickly. Place on rack to cool for 20 minutes. Run a knife around the edges of pan to loosen cake, flip it onto a second rack or flat plate, and remove paper lining. Flip cake back onto first rack and allow to cool completely.

6. To make the lemon glaze: Mix together confectioners' sugar, salt, lemon juice, and lemon zest. Slip a sheet of wax paper under rack to catch drips. Drizzle glaze from a teaspoon or fork over top of cake and allow to set before cutting. Store completely cooled cake loosely covered with wax paper at room temperature.

FOR CAKE

2¼ cups flour

½ teaspoon salt

2 teaspoons baking powder

2 eggs, beaten

1½ cups sugar

½ cup butter, melted

1 teaspoon vanilla

½ teaspoon lemon oil or
   1 teaspoon lemon extract

1 cup milk

FOR GLAZE

1 cup confectioners' sugar

Pinch of salt

2 tablespoons lemon juice

2 teaspoons grated lemon zest

Sweet Tips

- If you don't have time to glaze the cake, sprinkle with confectioners' sugar.
- This cake is best served the day it is baked.

One, Two, Three Open-Faced Blueberry Pie

1930S

MAKES 10 SLICES

FOR GLAZE

2 oz. seedless raspberry jam

FOR CRUST

Prebaked pie shell (see Sheila's Pie Crust on page 110)

FOR FILLING

4 cups blueberries, divided

½ cup plus 2½ tablespoons water, divided

2½ tablespoons cornstarch

½ cup sugar

1 teaspoon lemon juice

2 teaspoons grated lemon zest

1 teaspoon vanilla

½ teaspoon cinnamon

⅛ teaspoon salt

Whipped cream

We wish we could tell you this pie is as easy as one, two, three. It's named as such because there are three stages to its construction—baking the pie shell, glazing the pie, and preparing the filling. The results are outstanding. We found the recipe handwritten in a copy of *Laboratory Recipes* owned by Rachel W. Banks.

1. To make the glaze: Cook raspberry jam in metal saucepan on low heat until bubbles form around the edges or heat jam in glass bowl in the microwave for 25 seconds on low. Brush bottom and sides of cooled pie shell with glaze and let cool.

2. To make the filling: Place 1 cup of the blueberries and ½ cup of the water in metal saucepan. Bring to a boil over medium heat. Boil gently 3 to 4 minutes and remove from heat. Add cornstarch to remaining 2½ tablespoons water and whisk to dissolve. Add cornstarch mixture, sugar, lemon juice, lemon zest, vanilla, cinnamon, and salt to cooked blueberries. Bring to a boil over low heat, and stir for about 1 minute, or until blueberries have the consistency of jam.

3. Transfer cooked blueberry mixture to a medium bowl. Fold in remaining 3 cups of blueberries. Add filling to pie shell and let cool for at least 2 hours. Just before serving, pipe whipped cream around edge of pie. This pie is best served the day it is made, but it will still be good the next day if loosely wrapped in wax paper or placed in a covered container and refrigerated.

Mrs. Charles Barker's Blue Ribbon Blueberry Cake

MAKES 16 SQUARES

1½ cups sifted cake flour

1 teaspoon cream of tartar

½ teaspoon baking soda

½ cup milk

¼ cup butter

¾ cup sugar, sifted, plus 2 tablespoons for topping

1 teaspoon vanilla

1 egg, beaten

1 pint fresh blueberries, washed and dried

This recipe was called Mrs. Charles Barker's Blueberry Cake in the manuscript cookbook in which it was recorded. Our documentation is at least the third recorded version of this recipe. The second was attributed to Miss Elizabeth G. Barker in 1933. She referred to it as Mrs. Charles Barker's "rule."

1. Set the oven rack in the middle position. Preheat the oven to 350°F. Line the bottom and sides of an 8-inch by 8-inch by 2-inch pan with foil, shiny side up, and coat with vegetable spray.

2. Combine flour and cream of tartar in a small bowl. Dissolve baking soda in milk.

3. Cream butter, ¾ cup of the sugar, and vanilla in the bowl of a standing mixer fitted with the paddle attachment. Add egg and combine.

4. Add sifted dry ingredients to mixer in thirds, alternating with milk and beat until blended. Fold in half of blueberries. Spoon half of batter into pan. Level top with a spatula. Sprinkle remaining blueberries on top of batter. Spoon remaining batter over blueberries and smooth. Dust top with remaining 2 tablespoons sugar. Bake 35 minutes, or until tester inserted into middle comes out clean. Cool on rack. Remove from pan and cut into 2-inch squares. Serve with vanilla ice cream. Store under cake dome or loosely covered with wax paper at room temperature.

Sweet Tip

Do not roll the blueberries in flour before adding them to batter if you want to create the blue ribbon effect.

Mrs. Paul Knight's Bittersweet Chocolate Sauce

MAKES I ½ CUPS

You may wonder why we've included a chocolate sauce in a summer-time chapter laden with seasonal fruit recipes. We had to because summer wouldn't be summer to us unless we had a special chocolate sauce to ladle over our ice cream! We wish we knew Mrs. Knight's first name so we could thank her for her delicious chocolate sauce.

1 egg
1 cup sugar
¼ teaspoon salt
1 teaspoon vanilla
6 tablespoons heavy cream
2 tablespoons butter
4 oz. bitter chocolate, melted

1. Beat egg in a small mixing bowl. Add sugar, salt, and vanilla and combine. Set aside.
2. Heat heavy cream and butter in a heavy saucepan over medium heat, stirring occasionally with a wooden spoon until bubbles form around the edges. Remove from heat and add chocolate. Add egg mixture and stir until combined.
3. Return pan to stove over medium heat, stirring until mixture once again starts to bubble around the edges. Remove from heat and pour into glass jars. Cool completely and store in the refrigerator.

Sweet Tip

We like to store this sauce in inexpensive French preserve jars that come with matching plastic covers. We find that they fit in the refrigerator nicely and are easy to microwave for heating.

Green glazed pottery bowl with blueberries, early 1900s

Nectarine Betty

MAKES 9 GENEROUS SERVINGS

FOR BETTY

6 ripe, but still a bit firm, nectarines, cut in slices (5 to 6 cups)

3 tablespoons lemon juice

2 teaspoons grated lemon zest

1½ cups graham cracker crumbs

4 tablespoons butter, melted

¼ cup sugar

1 cup brown sugar

½ teaspoon cinnamon

¼ teaspoon ginger

¼ teaspoon nutmeg

Pinch of cloves

⅛ teaspoon salt

FOR TOPPING

½ cup brown sugar

3 teaspoons butter

Betties differ from crumbles and cobblers because they are usually made with buttered cubes of bread or bread crumbs. This betty appealed to us because it was different from all the others we found in our collection—it is made with buttered, spiced graham cracker crumbs. The layers of fruit and crumbs are further enhanced by a crispy topping of brown sugar and yet more butter.

1. Set the oven rack in the middle position. Preheat the oven to 375°F. Coat a 9-inch by 9-inch by 2-inch baking pan with vegetable spray. Line a 14-inch by 16-inch baking sheet with foil.

2. To make the betty: Place nectarines in a large bowl and sprinkle with lemon juice.

3. Place lemon zest and graham cracker crumbs in another bowl. Add butter and mix thoroughly with your hands (wear disposable gloves if desired) until texture is sandy. Add sugar, brown sugar, cinnamon, ginger, nutmeg, cloves, and salt and mix in.

4. To add the topping: Layer half of crumbs on bottom of pan. Layer sliced nectarines on top of crumbs. Sprinkle remaining crumbs over fruit. Distribute brown sugar evenly over crumb topping and dot with butter.

5. Place pan on baking sheet in oven. Bake 30 to 35 minutes, or until topping is browned. If topping appears to be browning too quickly, cover loosely with foil. Let cool on rack until pleasantly warm. Serve warm with whipped cream or vanilla ice cream. Store covered with wax paper in the refrigerator. Leftover betty may be reheated in 300°F oven for 10 minutes.

Sweet Tip

- A betty is different from a crisp because of the layer of crumbs on the bottom. Don't be surprised if these bottom crumbs are a little juicy—the fruit just melts into them.
- Sometimes the betty falls in a bit if it sits around waiting to be served, but don't fret—the dessert loses none of its flavor or appeal.

Caramelized Apple Bread Pudding

FOR CARAMELIZED APPLES

½ cup butter

8 Granny Smith apples,
   peeled, cored, and cut into
   wedges (8 per apple)

3 tablespoons lemon juice

2 teaspoons grated lemon zest

¼ cup plus 2 tablespoons sugar

1½ teaspoons cinnamon

1½ teaspoons nutmeg

¼ teaspoon salt

FOR BREAD LAYERS

14 to 16 ½-inch slices of brioche
   or firm white bread, trimmed of
   crusts and cut in half

½ cup plus 2 tablespoons butter,
   melted

FOR CUSTARD

2 cups milk

2 cups heavy cream

1 cup plus 2 tablespoons sugar,
   divided

1 teaspoon vanilla

½ teaspoon cinnamon

½ teaspoon nutmeg

½ teaspoon salt

4 eggs, beaten

We found a recipe for bread pudding in almost every manuscript cookbook we read. Because these puddings use not only bits and pieces of leftover bread and fruit, but the staples of the larder—eggs, sugar, butter, and milk—they could be put together on the spur of the moment.

1. Set the oven rack in the middle position. Preheat the oven to 350°F. Coat a 3-quart ovenproof glass baking dish with vegetable spray. Set aside a larger metal baking pan and rack for the water bath.

2. To make the caramelized apples: Melt butter in large heavy frying pan. Fry apples in two batches, turning several times with a wooden spoon, until light golden in color. Return all apples to pan. Add lemon juice, lemon zest, and sugar and continue cooking, turning occasionally, until apples are cooked but still a little firm, 7 to 10 minutes. Add cinnamon, nutmeg, and salt. Bring apples to a boil and cook until the liquid starts to thicken and caramelize, 1 to 2 minutes. Remove from heat.

3. To prepare the bread: Brush brioche slices on both sides with butter.

4. To make the custard: Combine milk, heavy cream, 1 cup of the sugar, vanilla, cinnamon, nutmeg, and salt in a large bowl. Add eggs and whisk to combine.

5. Place ½ cup of the custard on bottom of baking dish. Tilt and swirl dish until bottom is completely covered with a thin layer of custard. Layer 6 slices of brioche on top of custard. Fill in spaces with extra brioche. Layer on half of caramelized apples. Pour half of remaining custard over apples. Add remaining brioche, apples, and custard in layers.

6. Use a knife to cut 8 slits through layered pudding. Cover top of pudding with plastic wrap and press down gently with your palm. Let stand 10 minutes. Remove plastic wrap and sprinkle remaining 2 tablespoons sugar over top.

- Each apple should be cut into at least eight wedges.
- It is easier to fry apples in two batches. You can also use two pans to fry apples; just be sure to divide the other ingredients equally between the two pans.
- Caramelized apples can be made the day before and refrigerated.
- Challah or good-quality sourdough or white bread can be used instead of brioche.

7. Place baking dish on rack in large metal pan. Pour hot water from a glass measuring cup into outer pan until water level rises halfway up sides of baking dish. Place carefully in oven. Bake approximately 1 hour and 15 minutes, or until top is nicely browned and batter and apples have risen to top. Check pudding occasionally during baking and cover loosely with foil if topping seems to be drying out. Do not let water bath evaporate.

8. Carefully remove baking dish from oven and water bath. Allow to cool on rack 1 hour. Serve pudding warm or cold with unsweetened whipped cream or vanilla ice cream. Store covered with a paper towel and plastic wrap in the refrigerator.

SWEET TOUCH   This dessert can be served with Soft Caramel Sauce (page 193).

LEMON CHEESECAKE WITH LEMON CURD TOPPING

1 9 3 0 S

MAKES 16 SLICES

FOR CRUST

13 graham crackers, 2½ inches
by 5 inches each (1 sleeve from
a 3-sleeve box)

¼ cup butter, melted

½ cup sugar

FOR CHEESECAKE

2 8-oz. packages cream cheese, at
room temperature

1½ cups sugar

½ teaspoon vanilla

3 tablespoons lemon juice

2 teaspoons grated lemon zest

1½ cups heavy cream

6 eggs

¼ cup plus 2 tablespoons flour

⅛ teaspoon salt

FOR TOPPING

1 egg

4 egg yolks

¾ cup sugar

Pinch of salt

2 teaspoons grated lemon zest

½ cup lemon juice

¼ cup butter, cut into large dice

This recipe came from a well-loved manuscript cookbook with a very Austrian flavor. Most of the wonderful desserts in this collection were for tortes, tarts, and delectable flaky cookies. The woman who wrote these recipes used loads of cream, butter, and sugar in her sweets. There is evidence that someone annotated these recipes at some later date, slightly modifying ingredients and instructions.

1. Set the oven rack in the middle position. Preheat the oven to 350°F. Coat the bottom and sides of a 9-inch springform pan with vegetable spray. Cut a wax paper liner to fit the bottom of the pan. Insert the liner and coat with vegetable spray.

2. To make the crust: Place graham crackers in the bowl of a food processor fitted with the metal blade. Pulse to make crumbs the size of cornmeal (about 1½ cups). Add butter and sugar and pulse to combine. Press crumbs on bottom and 2 inches up sides of pan. Wrap outside bottom of pan with foil.

3. To make the cheesecake: Place cream cheese in the bowl of a standing mixer fitted with the paddle attachment and beat until smooth. Add sugar and mix well. Add vanilla, lemon juice, and lemon zest. Add heavy cream and mix in. Add eggs two at a time, mixing well after each addition. Add flour and salt and combine.

4. Pour batter into springform pan. Bake 1 hour 15 minutes. Turn off oven and leave door ajar by inserting a wooden spoon between oven and door. Remove cheesecake from oven after 45 minutes and allow to cool thoroughly on rack. Cover baking pan with plastic wrap and refrigerate overnight.

5. To make the topping: Whisk egg and yolks in heavy-bottomed saucepan. Add sugar, salt, and lemon zest and whisk to combine. Whisk in lemon juice. Add butter and whisk over medium heat until butter is melted. Continue to whisk until curd thickens, about 5 minutes. If you prefer smooth curd, strain to remove lemon rind. Let curd cool completely. Remove cheesecake from

refrigerator. Spoon lemon curd gently onto top of cheesecake. Allow 15 minutes for lemon curd to set. Refrigerate until ready to serve. Remove cheesecake from refrigerator 10 minutes before serving. Run a butter knife around edges and remove sides. To store leftover cheesecake, place sides back on pan, cover with plastic wrap, and refrigerate.

SWEET TOUCH   You can use 1½ cups of cookie crumbs instead of graham cracker crumbs for the crust.

Sweet Tip

We also made the cheesecake with artisanal or loose ricotta cheese purchased at an Italian grocery. If you have access to handmade ricotta, you can substitute 18 ounces for the cream cheese. The flavor will be slightly more tangy. Commercial ricotta also works well, but the texture will be lighter.

233

FAMOUS STRAWBERRY FRITTERS

MAKES 12 TO 14 FRITTERS

1 quart strawberries

2 eggs

¾ cup milk

1 tablespoon plus 1 teaspoon butter, melted and cooled to room temperature

2 teaspoons vanilla

3 tablespoons confectioners' sugar

¼ teaspoon salt

1½ teaspoons baking powder

1 cup flour

Sugar

We found this recipe in a manuscript cookbook owned by an artist living in Cambridge, Massachusetts. We don't know just why these fritters were famous, but we do know that in the 1930s they were selling for 3 cents apiece at local strawberry festivals and church fairs. We like them with confectioners' sugar, but granulated sugar is really nice with them, too.

1. Wash strawberries and dry thoroughly on paper towels. Hull and quarter strawberries and place on a dry paper towel.
2. Whisk eggs, milk, butter, and vanilla in bowl. Add confectioners' sugar, salt, and baking powder and combine. Add flour and mix to make a smooth batter. Let stand at least 30 minutes. Mix strawberries into batter.
3. Cover a rack with 3 layers of paper towels. Heat 1 inch of oil to 375°F in a deep flat-bottomed heavy pan (or follow manufacturer's instructions if using an electric fryer).
4. Dip a heaping tablespoon of batter carefully into hot fat. Fat may foam or bubble. Do not fry more than 4 fritters at a time. Fry approximately 1½ minutes on each side, turning with a slotted spoon. Remove fritters when golden brown and place on prepared rack to drain. Cover tops of fritters with additional paper towels. Let cool 5 minutes and roll in granulated sugar. Serve 3 or 4 fritters on a plate. Fritters are best when eaten within 30 minutes. If you wait too long to eat them, the batter becomes soggy.

SWEET TOUCH Dust fritters with sifted confectioners' sugar just before serving and garnish with a whole strawberry.

STRAWBERRY RHUBARB PIE

We found this recipe handwritten on an index card with no directions, so we tested and tested and tested. It's a very delicate pie that should be made only when strawberries and rhubarb are in season. This pie is best served the day it is made. Although strawberry rhubarb pies are often baked with a lattice crust, we like the double-crust version.

1. Set the oven rack in the middle position. Preheat the oven to 400°F. Coat a 9-inch ovenproof glass pie plate with vegetable spray. Cover a 14-inch by 16-inch baking pan with foil, shiny side up. Coat the foil with vegetable spray or use a silicone liner.

2. To make the crust: Roll out pastry dough. Fit half of dough into bottom of pie plate and trim off excess. Chill in the refrigerator. (For detailed instructions, see "To make a double-crust pie," steps 2 and 3, page 110.)

3. To make the filling: Mix rhubarb, sugar, and flour in a large bowl. Set aside 1 hour.

4. Put rhubarb in a strainer. Collect drained juice, pour into a saucepan, and add nutmeg and salt. Cook over medium heat, stirring with a wooden spoon, until juice thickens. Cool 10 minutes. Place rhubarb, strawberries, and juice in a large bowl and toss to combine.

5. Add rhubarb mixture to pie shell. Dot with butter. Add top crust, seal and crimp edges, and cut decorative slits. Brush top crust and edges with beaten egg. (For detailed instructions, see "To make a double-crust pie," step 4, page 110.)

6. Place pie on baking sheet. Bake 30 minutes and check crust for browning. If crust is browning too quickly, cover loosely with foil. Bake another 15 to 20 minutes, or until top crust is evenly browned. Bottom crust should be light brown when completely baked. Cool pie on rack at least 2 hours before serving. Store pie loosely covered with wax paper at room temperature.

FOR CRUST

Pastry for double-crust pie, divided in half and chilled (see Sheila's Pie Crust on page 110)

1 egg, beaten

FOR FILLING

4 to 5 stalks rhubarb, trimmed and cut into ½-inch pieces (about 4 cups)

1½ cups sugar

¼ cup flour

¼ teaspoon nutmeg

Pinch of salt

1 pint strawberries, washed, hulled, sliced, and drained on paper towels

2 tablespoons cold butter, cut into large dice

Dorothy Brass' Pineapple Pie

MAKES 10 GENEROUS SLICES

This is the pie Mama made during those sunny summer months when our entire family ate communally at the kitchen table. Mama always used canned pineapple and glazed the top crust with a beaten whole egg to give it a shine. She always made a daisy design on the top crust with her favorite tool, her pie crimper. We still have her crimper and use it when we bake pies.

1. Set the oven rack in the middle position. Preheat the oven to 400°F. Coat a 9-inch ovenproof glass pie plate with vegetable spray. Cover a 14-inch by 16-inch baking sheet with foil, shiny side up. Coat the foil with vegetable spray or use a silicone liner.

2. To make the crust: Roll out pastry dough. Fit half of dough into bottom of pie plate and trim off excess. Sprinkle bottom of pastry with flour. Chill in the refrigerator. (For detailed instructions, see "To make a double-crust pie," steps 2 and 3, page 110.)

3. To make the filling: Place pineapple in a sieve set over a bowl. Drain 30 minutes, pressing gently with the palm of your hand to remove as much of juice as possible. Reserve and measure juice.

4. Place 2½ tablespoons of the reserved pineapple juice in a large bowl. Whisk in cornstarch until dissolved. Add remaining ½ cup pineapple juice, sugar, lemon zest, lemon juice, vanilla, and salt. Whisk until thoroughly combined. Add pineapple and stir until evenly coated.

5. Add pineapple mixture to pie shell. Add top crust, seal and crimp edges, and cut decorative slits. Brush top crust and edges with beaten egg. (For detailed instructions, see "To make a double-crust pie," step 4.)

6. Place pie on baking sheet. Bake 30 minutes and check crust for browning. If crust is browning too quickly, cover loosely with foil. Bake another 15 minutes, or until top crust is evenly browned. Bottom crust should be light brown when completely baked. Cool pie on rack at least 2 hours before serving. Store pie loosely covered with wax paper at room temperature.

FOR CRUST

Pastry for double-crust pie, divided in half and chilled (see Sheila's Pie Crust on page 110)

1 tablespoon flour

1 egg, beaten

FOR FILLING

2 20-oz. cans unsweetened crushed pineapple

2½ tablespoons cornstarch

½ cups plus 2½ tablespoons juice from canned pineapple

¾ cup sugar

2 teaspoons grated lemon zest

1 tablespoon lemon juice

1 teaspoon vanilla

⅛ teaspoon salt

Sweet Tip

Make your decorations on the top pie crust after rolling it out and before placing it over the pie filling.

DOUBLE LEMON SHORTCAKE

MAKES 15 SHORTCAKES

FOR SHORTCAKE

2 cups flour

2½ teaspoons baking powder

⅛ teaspoon salt

¼ cup sugar

¼ cup cold butter, cut into small dice

2 teaspoons grated lemon zest

½ teaspoon lemon oil or lemon extract

¾ cup heavy cream

1 egg, beaten

2 tablespoons clear sanding sugar

FOR LEMON CURD

1 egg

4 egg yolks

¾ cup sugar

Pinch of salt

2 teaspoons grated lemon zest

½ cup lemon juice

¼ cup butter, cut into small dice

1 cup heavy cream, whipped

Raspberries or blueberries for garnish

This is a very unusual shortcake recipe because there is no fruit involved other than a garnish of summer berries. The shortcake is just what it is—a little cake that is very short and flaky with the richness of its butter and cream. This is not a biscuit masquerading as a shortcake.

1. Set the oven rack in the middle position. Preheat the oven to 450°F. Cover a 14-inch by 16-inch baking sheet with foil, shiny side up. Coat the foil with vegetable spray or use a silicone liner.

2. To make the shortcake: Place flour, baking powder, salt, and sugar in the bowl of a food processor fitted with the metal blade. Pulse three times. Add butter and pulse three more times. Add lemon zest, lemon oil, and heavy cream and pulse until dough forms.

3. Place dough on a lightly floured sheet of wax paper or parchment paper. Roll out or pat to ½-inch thickness. Cut 2-inch circles using a biscuit cutter dipped in flour. Press cutter straight down and up when cutting; do not twist cutter in dough or shortcakes will not rise. Use a spatula to lift and transfer dough to baking sheet. Gather up scraps and reroll to cut more shortcakes. Shortcakes made from scraps may not be as tender, but they will still be good. Brush shortcakes with beaten egg. Sprinkle with sanding sugar. Bake 12 minutes, or until tops are lightly browned. Place on rack to cool.

4. To make the lemon curd: Whisk egg and yolks in heavy-bottomed saucepan. Add sugar, salt, and lemon zest to mixture and combine. Whisk in lemon juice. Add butter and whisk over medium heat until butter is melted. Continue to whisk until curd thickens, about 5 minutes. If you prefer smooth curd, strain to remove lemon rind. Let curd cool completely. Refrigerate until ready to serve.

5. To serve, cut shortcakes in half. Place bottom half on a plate, spoon a generous amount of lemon curd on top, and add the top half. Add a dollop of whipped cream alongside. Garnish with fresh raspberries or blueberries. Store unused shortcakes in a sealed plastic bag in the refrigerator.

Sweet Tips

- Do not handle dough too much or shortcakes will be tough.
- Brushing unbaked shortcakes with beaten egg gives them a brown color.

BAVARIAN FIG TART

This was the tart of choice for us in the 1960s when we were just earning our reputations as sweet young things who baked. Made with sliced apples, sliced pears, or even blueberries, this browned-butter tart is easy to put together. It makes a lovely presentation, too.

1. Set the oven rack in the middle position. Preheat the oven to 375°F. Coat an 8-inch or 9-inch tart pan (with removable bottom) with vegetable spray.

2. To make the crust: Add flour, sugar, and salt to the bowl of a food processor fitted with metal blade. Pulse twice to combine. Add butter and pulse until mixture resembles coarse meal. Add 2 tablespoons ice water. Process just until the mixture comes together in large clumps; add remaining tablespoon water if necessary. Turn dough onto plastic wrap and gather into a ball. Wrap and chill 30 minutes or overnight.

3. To make the filling: Heat butter in a 9-inch or 10-inch frying pan over medium heat about 2 minutes or until butter is bubbly and foamy. Continue to move butter around by swirling pan until butter is golden brown. Do not allow butter to darken or burn. Strain browned butter into a glass bowl (there may be some brown spots left in the butter, but this will improve the flavor). Whisk together sugar, flour, eggs, and vanilla in a bowl. Slowly add browned butter, whisking to combine.

4. Roll out dough on a lightly floured surface to a ⅛-inch thickness. Use the rolling pin to carefully lift and transfer dough to tart pan. If crust breaks or tears, just press it together with your fingers. Press dough into bottom and sides of tart pan. Cut off excess dough with a sharp knife or run your rolling pin over the top edge.

5. Arrange figs, cut side up, in a pattern on top of dough. Pour filling over figs. Bake 1 hour, or until tart filling is brown and bubbly; check for doneness after 45 minutes and in 5-minute increments thereafter. Serve warm or at room temperature. Sprinkle the top with confectioners' sugar before serving. Store loosely wrapped in wax paper on a plate in the refrigerator.

FOR CRUST

1½ cups flour

⅓ cup sugar

⅛ teaspoon salt

½ cup cold butter, cut into large dice

2 to 3 tablespoons ice water

FOR FILLING

½ cup butter

1 cup sugar

¼ cup flour

2 eggs

1½ teaspoons vanilla

6 fresh figs, cut in half, stems removed

Confectioners' sugar (optional)

ESTHER PULLMAN'S PLUM TORTE

MAKES 8 TO 10 SLICES

1 cup flour

1 teaspoon baking powder

⅛ teaspoon salt

½ cup butter

1⅓ cups sugar, divided

2 eggs

1 teaspoon vanilla

12 Italian plums, pitted and halved or 3 large plums, pitted and cut in eighths

2 tablespoons lemon juice

¼ teaspoon cinnamon

Whipped cream (optional)

This is a versatile recipe that our friend Esther Pullman, a talented baker and artist, has been making since she began exchanging recipes in the 1960s. Esther included her version of this torte in an elegant little book of recipes she and her husband, Chris, designed and illustrated in the 1970s. A gift to family and friends at the holidays, this personal collection of living recipes continues to be cherished by its recipients.

1. Set the oven rack in the middle position. Preheat the oven to 350°F. Coat a 9-inch-diameter springform pan with vegetable spray and dust with flour. Cut a parchment paper or wax paper liner to fit the bottom of pan. Insert the liner and coat with vegetable spray. Dust pan with flour and tap out the excess.

2. Sift together flour, baking powder, and salt into a mixing bowl..

3. Cream butter and 1 cup of the sugar in the bowl of a standing mixer fitted with the paddle attachment. Beat in eggs. Add sifted dry ingredients. Add vanilla.

4. Pour batter into springform pan and smooth top with offset spatula. Arrange plums, skin side down, on top of batter, leaving a ½-inch border around edge of pastry. Sprinkle top with lemon juice. Combine cinnamon and remaining ⅓ cup of sugar in a small bowl and sprinkle over top. Bake 55 to 60 minutes, or until fruit bubbles and tester inserted into cake areas of torte comes out clean. Cool on rack for 15 minutes. Run a butter knife around edges while torte is still warm to loosen. Serve slightly warm with a puff of whipped cream. Store when completely cool under cake dome or loosely covered with wax paper, at room temperature.

SWEET TOUCH   A little whipped cream is very good with this torte, but a little whipped cream flavored with brandy is even better!

CHAPTER 10

There is no more wonderful feeling than baking with someone you love or admire. When we began reading through our collection of living recipes and

BAKING WITH MAMA

sweet-talking with family and friends, we discovered that the dynamic of baking with someone you love was not confined to mothers and daughters or even to grandmothers and granddaughters: it's a universal experience. We found that our friend, David Lima, treasured the time he spent assisting his mother, Virginia, when she baked her loaves of Portuguese Sweet Bread in their Providence, Rhode Island, kitchen. He tells us that the smell of yeast and the sweetness of the dough permeated the house. Even better was the smell of the bread baking. Mrs. Lima kept some of the loaves, but she always gave some to family and friends for the souls of departed relatives as an act of love and remembrance.

Esther Pullman told us that she remembers fondly Mary Brinkman, a talented baker, who befriended her as a teenager and taught her to bake her Irish Sponge Cake. Whenever Esther bakes this light cake with its crunchy sugar crust, she is reminded of Mary, who baked this cake for the families of Purchase, New York, where Esther grew up.

The delectable Canadian Butter Tarts come with a story about Greta Leonard, the grandmother of Valerie Lewis. Greta was born in Canada in the early 1890s and died at the age of 94. The mother of six children, she was married to the manager of the Royal Bank of Canada. Because her husband was also the conductor of the Toronto Symphony Orchestra, his constant traveling left her with the responsibility for raising their six children in a snow-covered and sometimes wild country. Valerie

Manuscript cookbook, contains several recipes from World War II, such as this recipe for Brandy Snaps, English, 1940s

tells us that Greta probably learned to bake from her own grandmother who was from the original pioneering stock who emigrated from Ireland to Canada. According to Valerie, baking Canadian Butter Tarts with her grandmother Greta was worth traveling long distances.

We discovered so many different culinary pairings. Yvette Gooding, a wonderful baker herself, learned her culinary skills from her beloved maternal grandmother, Lannie Waters Edmondson, when she was just seven years old. Baking with Grandma Lannie meant learning how to make Grandma's Secret Warm Banana Meringue Pudding, as good today as it was when Lannie and Yvette baked it years ago. A member of St. John's Missionary Baptist Church in Roxbury, Massachusetts, for many years, the late Mrs. Edmondson is also remembered for her coconut cake, biscuits, sweet potato pie, and cornbread.

Every time we bake these treasured recipes, we experience the wisdom and love these baking companions bequeathed to us all. A great part of our culinary legacy, we hope that whenever you bake them, you will become a part of passing down these living recipes.

MAMA'S APRICOT STRUDEL WITH CREAM CHEESE CRUST

MAKES 40 SLICES

FOR APRICOT FILLING

8 ounces dried apricots

1 tablespoon lemon juice

⅓ cup sugar

15 soda crackers, broken into crumbs

1 cup pistachio nuts, toasted

FOR DOUGH

½ cup butter

4 ounces cream cheese

1⅔ cups flour

¼ teaspoon salt

¼ cup cold milk

¼ cup butter, melted

Sweet Tip

Serve this strudel dusted with confectioners' sugar. It is best when eaten within 2 days.

This was one of the recipes we loved baking with our mother. It was a tradition to bake this when summer was just a memory, and we were turning to winter's offerings of dried, candied, and preserved fruit.

1. Set the oven rack in the middle position. Preheat the oven to 400°F. Cover a 14-inch by 16-inch baking sheet with foil, shiny side up. Coat the foil with vegetable spray or use a silicone liner.

2. To make the filling: Place apricots in a saucepan, cover with water, and bring to a boil over medium heat. Cover and simmer about 15 minutes, or until apricots form a soft paste. Check on fruit periodically to see that it does not burn, especially toward end of cooking time. Transfer apricot paste to a bowl and add lemon juice and sugar. Allow to cool.

3. To make the dough: Place butter and cream cheese in the bowl of a standing mixer fitted with the paddle attachment. Cream until soft and fluffy. Add flour and salt and mix to combine. Add milk to form a soft dough. Wrap dough in plastic wrap and chill in the refrigerator until firm enough to roll out.

4. Remove dough from refrigerator and divide into 4 sections. Roll out one section of dough on floured wax paper or parchment paper to a ¹⁄₁₆-inch thick rectangle. Brush surface with melted butter. Place one fourth of the apricot filling at top of dough leaving a 1-inch edge. Sprinkle one fourth of nuts and soda cracker crumbs on top of filling. Roll strudel lengthwise from top to bottom, like a jelly roll, using paper as an aid. Place strudel on baking sheet, seam side down. Repeat with remaining dough and filling.

5. Brush each strudel with melted butter. Bake 20 minutes at 400°F. Turn oven temperature down to 350°F and bake 10 to 12 minutes more. Brush once during baking with melted butter. Remove pan from oven and place on rack. Cool for 10 minutes. While still on pan, cut strudel diagonally into 1-inch slices. Continue to cool. Store between sheets of wax paper in a covered tin.

Grandma's Secret Warm Banana Meringue Pudding

FOR CUSTARD

1¼ cups sugar

1 cup flour

¼ teaspoon salt

4 cups milk

1 cup heavy cream

8 egg yolks

2 teaspoons vanilla

10 ounces vanilla wafers

6 to 8 ripe bananas, sliced
    crosswise

FOR MERINGUE

8 egg whites

¼ teaspoon cream of tartar

½ cup plus 1 tablespoon sugar

Yvette Gooding learned to make this pudding when baking in the kitchen with her grandmother Lannie. When we tried this pudding, we doubled the recipe, and were rewarded with a dessert that tastes—and looks—spectacular. Guess the secret is out!

1. Set the oven rack in the middle position. Preheat the oven to 350°F. Coat a 9-inch by 13-inch ovenproof glass baking dish with vegetable spray.

2. To make the custard: Sift sugar, flour, and salt into a large heavy pan. Add milk and heavy cream and mix thoroughly. Add egg yolks one at a time, blending well after each. Cook mixture over medium to medium-high heat, stirring constantly with wooden spoon, for about 10 minutes, or until thickened. Remove from heat and strain through sieve. Add vanilla to cooked custard.

3. Spread a small amount of custard on bottom of baking dish. Swirl to cover evenly. Cover with half of vanilla wafers. Cover wafers with half of bananas and press down gently with your palm.

4. Pour a generous layer of custard on top of wafers. Add remaining wafers and bananas in two layers. Pour remaining custard on top, smoothing with spatula so that all wafers and bananas are covered. Press down again gently with the palm of your hand. Bake pudding in oven for 10 minutes.

5. To make the meringue: Add egg whites and cream of tartar to bowl of standing mixer fitted with the whisk attachment. Whip on low speed. Gradually increase speed to medium until soft peaks form. Add sugar in thirds while increasing speed of mixer to high. Beat until stiff peaks are formed. Meringue should not be dry.

6. Remove pudding from oven and mound meringue on top, spreading until entire surface is covered. (Be sure to seal edges.) Return pudding to oven for about 20 minutes, checking every 5 minutes to be sure it does not burn. Remove from oven and place on rack to cool. Serve when slightly warm. Store leftover pudding in the refrigerator.

GRANDMOTHER'S BISCUITS

MAKES 72 2-INCH BISCUITS

1 8 7 5

When we looked through the prolific collection of recipes from Marion A. Carter, we were happy to find one for biscuits. The recipe is very old and the original includes words like "basin" for bowl and "paste" for dough. We are instructed to "pound loaf sugar." After some deciphering, we realized that what we were looking at was a recipe for sugar cookies. We love these "biscuits," or cookies, because they are crisp, sweet, and buttery.

1. Set the oven rack in the middle position. Preheat the oven to 375°F. Cover a 14-inch by 16-inch baking sheet with foil, shiny side up. Coat the foil with vegetable spray or use a silicone liner.
2. Sift together flour and salt .
3. Cream butter and sugar in the bowl of a standing mixer fitted with the paddle attachment. Add egg and vanilla and combine. Add the sifted dry ingredients, a third at a time, to make a soft dough. Wrap dough in plastic wrap and chill in the refrigerator 1 hour, or until firm enough to roll out.
4. Remove dough from refrigerator, divide in half, and return half to refrigerator. Place remaining dough between two generously floured sheets of wax paper or parchment paper and roll out to a 3/16-inch thickness. Remove the top sheet, sprinkle more flour on dough, and replace sheet. Turn the packet over and flour the other side in the same way.
5. Using cutters dipped in flour to cut out biscuits in desired shapes. Reroll scraps to cut more biscuits. Use a spatula dipped in flour to transfer biscuits to baking sheet. Remove rest of dough from refrigerator and repeat.
6. Sprinkle unbaked biscuits with sanding sugar. Bake 12 to 13 minutes, or until edges are lightly browned. Cool on rack. Biscuits will firm up as they cool. Store biscuits between sheets of parchment paper or wax paper in a covered tin.

2¼ cups flour

½ teaspoon salt

1 cup butter

1 cup sugar

1 egg

1 teaspoon vanilla

½ cup clear sanding sugar (optional)

Sweet Tip

If the dough becomes too soft to handle, place it in the refrigerator for a few minutes.

Esther Pullman and Mary Brinkman's Irish Sponge Cake

MAKES 10 SLICES   1950S

The recipe for this Irish Sponge Cake came from Esther Pullman who grew up in Purchase, New York. It was given to her by Mary Brinkman, an inspired Irish baker who made special cakes for family parties. The sublime sugar crust makes this sponge cake extraordinary.

1¼ cups sugar, divided

4 eggs, separated

1 teaspoon vanilla

1 cup cake flour

1. Set the oven rack in the middle position. Preheat the oven to 350°F. Coat an 8-inch Bundt pan with vegetable spray. Dust the sides and bottom of pan with 3 tablespoons of the sugar.

2. Beat egg yolks in the bowl of a standing mixer fitted with the paddle attachment. Add ½ cup of the sugar and beat until thick, about 5 minutes.

3. Place egg whites in another bowl of a standing mixer fitted with the whisk attachment. Beat until stiff. Add ½ cup of the sugar and beat again until sugar is incorporated

4. Add egg yolks to egg whites. Add vanilla and continue beating with paddle attachment at medium speed until combined. Fold in cake flour.

5. Pour batter into Bundt pan. Sprinkle remaining tablespoon sugar on top of batter. Bake 30 minutes, or until tester inserted in middle comes out clean. Cake should have a nice yellow color. Place on rack to cool. When completely cool, invert cake onto plate. Slice with sawing motion. Store under cake dome or loosely wrapped in wax paper at room temperature.

Mrs. Marasi's Butterballs

MAKES 50 COOKIES

2 cups butter

4 tablespoons superfine sugar

2 cups sifted flour

⅛ teaspoon salt

1 teaspoon vanilla

1 cup toasted pecans, chopped fairly fine in a food processor

1 cup superfine sugar (for rolling cookies)

When we learned of Mrs. Melania Marasi, an Italian lady who enjoyed baking for her family and friends, we were thrilled to receive a handwritten recipe for her Butterballs. But even after reading Mrs. Marasi's recipe several times, we never imagined how meltingly good they would be—something like shortbread, but better. Mrs. Marasi and her friend Mary Moretti were collaborators on this recipe.

1. Set the oven rack in the middle position. Preheat the oven to 375°F. Cover a 14-inch by 16-inch baking sheet with foil, shiny side up. Coat the foil with vegetable spray or use a silicone liner.

2. Cream butter and sugar in the bowl of a standing mixer fitted with the paddle attachment.

3. Sift together flour and salt into a medium bowl. Add sifted dry ingredients to creamed ingredients in thirds and mix until smooth. Add vanilla and mix in. Fold in pecans.

4. Wrap dough in plastic wrap and chill in the refrigerator 1 hour, or until firm enough to handle. With floured hands or wearing disposable gloves, roll dough into 1-inch-diameter balls. Place balls 2 inches apart on baking sheet (they will not spread during baking).

5. Bake 16 minutes, until cookies are a light golden brown. Cool on baking sheet on rack. While still warm, roll in superfine sugar. Store between sheets of parchment paper or wax paper in a covered tin.

Sweet Tip

Keep rolled butterballs in the refrigerator until you are ready to bake them. If the dough you are working with starts to soften, put it back in the refrigerator to chill.

HOW TO USE SUPERFINE SUGAR

The recipe for Mrs. Marasi's Butterballs calls for superfine sugar. This sugar is traditionally used to sweeten cold beverages. It is sometimes referred to as "bar sugar" or, in Canada, "berry" or "fruit" sugar. It is also sold as caster sugar. It's not an ingredient easily found in the average pantry. To make your own, place regular granulated sugar in the bowl of a food processor fitted with the metal blade and process it for at least 30 seconds to turn it into a finer-grained sugar. Measure the sugar after it's been processed.

Auntie Dot's Fruited Tea Bread

MAKES 12 SLICES   1 9 5 0 S

This was the cake we baked every Christmas and Chanukah. Years later, our kitchen smells the same when we bake it. Our mother baked more than a dozen cakes every year and festively wrapped and tied them with either a red or a blue ribbon and presented them as gifts to family, friends, and business associates of our father. This is actually the racier version because we mellowed it in brandy.

1. Set the oven rack in the middle position. Preheat the oven to 350°F. Line the bottom and ends of a 9-inch by 5-inch by 3-inch loaf pan with a single strip of wax paper. Coat the pan and wax paper liner with vegetable spray. Dust pan with flour and tap out the excess.

2. Place walnuts and glazed fruit in bowl. Add ¼ cup of the flour and mix until coated.

3. Sift together the remaining 1¾ cups flour, cinnamon, nutmeg, cloves, allspice, and baking soda.

4. Place butter and sugar in the bowl of a standing mixer fitted with the paddle attachment. Cream until soft and fluffy. Add egg and vanilla and mix well. Add sifted dry ingredients alternately with sour cream. Fold in floured nuts and fruit.

5. Pour batter into loaf pan. Bake approximately 1 hour, or until tester inserted into middle comes out dry. Place pan on rack and cool for 20 minutes. Remove bread from pan onto another rack to continue cooling.

6. If you wish, brush a skewer with brandy and poke it into the bread. Repeat 5 or 6 times. Soak kitchen cheesecloth in brandy, wrap it around the bread, and store in the refrigerator. Refresh the cheesecloth with brandy from time to time. Serve this mellowed fruit bread in small pieces. Store loosely covered with wax paper in the refrigerator.

½ cup coarsely chopped walnuts

½ cup coarsely chopped mixture of glazed apricots, pineapple, and cherries

2 cups flour, divided

1 teaspoon cinnamon

1 teaspoon nutmeg

1 teaspoon cloves

1 teaspoon allspice

1 teaspoon baking soda

½ cup butter

1 cup sugar

1 egg

1 teaspoon vanilla

1 cup sour cream

Brandy (optional)

Sweet Tip

Fifty years ago, you wouldn't be able to easily find the variety of glazed fruit now available. We suggest that you try variations, such as candied orange and lemon peel and citron, too.

253

AUNTIE IDA'S PECAN RING

These were the pecan rings our Auntie Ida made on her pink Formica table in Brookline, Massachusetts. Well into her nineties, Ida was still available for tea, sympathy, and some honest criticism—and she was never without a Pecan Ring in her postage stamp–sized freezer.

1. Set the oven rack in the middle position. Preheat the oven to 350°F. Cover a 14-inch by 16-inch baking pan with foil, shiny side up. Coat the foil with vegetable spray or use a silicone liner.

2. To make the dough: Dissolve yeast in warm water. Add 1 tablespoon of the sugar. Set in a warm place to proof, about 10 minutes. Mixture will bubble when yeast is proofed.

3. Cream butter, eggs, remaining 3 tablespoons sugar, and salt in the bowl of a standing mixer fitted with the paddle attachment. Add proofed yeast and combine. Remove paddle attachment and attach dough hook. Add 3 cups of the flour, 1 cup at a time, and knead about 5 minutes, or until dough holds together. Add remaining ½ cup of flour if necessary. Place dough in an oiled bowl and turn so entire dough is coated with oil. Cover with a towel and refrigerate 4 hours or overnight.

4. To add the filling: Combine cinnamon, sugar, and brown sugar in a bowl. Remove dough from refrigerator and allow it to sit in a warm place for 30 minutes. Divide dough in half. Place half of dough between two pieces of wax paper or parchment paper sprinkled with flour and roll out into a rectangle ¼-inch thick. Brush surface of dough with melted butter. Scatter half of pecans and half of sugar mixture over dough, allowing a 1-inch margin on all sides. Roll up dough from top to bottom, jelly roll–style, using the paper as an aid. Place roll on baking sheet and join ends to form ring. Use scissors or knife to make 16 cuts in ring. Let rise for 20 minutes in a warm place. Repeat with remaining dough.

5. Brush tops of rings with melted butter. Bake 30 to 33 minutes, or until golden brown. Remove from oven and cool on rack. Store loosely wrapped in wax paper at room temperature.

FOR DOUGH

- 1 package (2¼ teaspoons) active dry yeast
- ½ cup water, warmed to 110°F
- ¼ cup sugar, divided
- 1 cup butter
- 3 eggs
- 1 teaspoon salt
- 3½ cups flour, divided

FOR FILLING

- 1 teaspoon cinnamon
- ½ cup sugar
- ½ cup brown sugar
- ½ cup butter, melted
- 1 cup toasted pecans, coarsely chopped

DADDY'S FUDGE

MAKES 36 PIECES

- 1 14-oz. can sweetened condensed milk
- 1 2-lb. package confectioners' sugar, sifted
- ⅛ teaspoon salt
- 1 tablespoon vanilla
- 3 ounces bitter chocolate, melted
- 3 tablespoons butter, melted
- 1 cup toasted pecans, chopped

This is the fudge that our father made after he married our mother. When we searched for this recipe, all we could find was a tattered scrap of paper with some handwritten notes on a memo form from Daddy's tenure at the Beth Israel Hospital. The ingredients were still there, but the amounts were missing. After much trial and error, we think we have rediscovered the magic of Daddy's Fudge.

1. Cover an 8-inch by 8-inch by 2-inch pan with foil, shiny side up. Butter the bottom and sides of the pan generously.

2. Add condensed milk to heavy saucepan. Add sifted confectioners' sugar and salt to pan in thirds, whisking vigorously after each addition until thoroughly mixed. Whisk in vanilla. Heat over low to medium heat 5 to 7 minutes, stirring continuously with a wooden spoon until tiny bubbles form at the edges.

3. Remove saucepan from heat and add chocolate, beating quickly. Stir in butter. Fold in pecans.

4. Pour fudge into pan. Chill in the refrigerator 6 hours or overnight. Remove foil-lined package of fudge from pan and place on a cutting board. Remove fudge from the foil and cut into squares using a wide-bladed knife; wipe knife blade clean on a paper towel as necessary. Store in layers between sheets of wax paper in a covered tin in the refrigerator.

HOW TO MELT CHOCOLATE IN A MICROWAVE

We like to take a twenty-first-century approach to melting chocolate. We chop the chocolate, place it in a glass bowl, and put it into the microwave. We microwave on low at 30-second intervals, stirring between each one, until the chocolate is fully melted.

Aunt Liz O'Neill's Shortbread

MAKES 32 I-INCH BY 2-INCH PIECES

1 cup butter
½ cup sugar
⅛ teaspoon salt
2⅓ cups sifted flour

Danese and Barbara Carey still talk about their great-aunt Liz O'Neill, who was married to their great-uncle Mike. A native of Glasgow and a superb shortbread maker, she emigrated to the United States as a young woman. The Carey sisters remember sitting at Aunt Liz's table taking notes while watching her bake. Although shortbread is traditionally made by hand, we have interpreted this recipe using a standing mixer.

1. Set the oven rack in the middle position. Preheat the oven to 350°F. Line the bottom and sides of a 9-inch by 9-inch by 2-inch pan with foil. Grease the foil with butter or coat with vegetable spray.

2. Cream butter, sugar, and salt in the bowl of a standing mixer fitted with the paddle attachment. Add flour ½ cup at a time, beating just until flour is completely absorbed and dough comes together. Do not overbeat or shortbread will be tough.

3. Gently pat dough into pan. Do not press too hard or shortbread will be tough, not crumbly, after baking. Press down edges of dough with tines of fork. Prick top of dough evenly about 25 times.

4. Bake 35 minutes, or until shortbread is a light brown. Cover loosely with foil if surface browns too quickly. Cool on rack 20 to 25 minutes, or until slightly warm. Score shortbread with a knife into 1-inch by 2-inch pieces, but do not cut through entirely. When completely cool, cut into pieces along scored lines. The texture should be sandy and crumbly.

Sweet Tip

If you don't use all the flour in the shortbread, save it; it can be reused.

257

GRETA LEONARD'S CANADIAN BUTTER TARTS

1860s

MAKES 28 TARTS

FOR DOUGH

1 tablespoon cider vinegar

1 egg

Ice water

3 cups flour

⅓ cup sugar

1 cup cold butter or lard

3 walnut halves, broken or
  2 teaspoons dry raisins per tart

FOR FILLING

¼ cup butter

½ cup brown sugar

¼ teaspoon salt

1 teaspoon vanilla

1 tablespoon cider vinegar

¾ cup maple syrup or cane syrup

1 egg

Valerie Lewis was born in Canada, and these are the tarts her grandmother, Greta Leonard, from Point Clarke, Ontario, made for her. The recipe was handed down to Valerie's mother, Florence, and then to Valerie. She now makes these tarts for her family for Thanksgiving and has taught her two daughters how to make their great-grandmother's Butter Tarts so the recipe will be carried on in the family.

1. Set the oven rack in the middle position. Preheat the oven to 375°F. Coat the cups and top surface of five 6-cup muffin pans (or the equivalent) with vegetable spray.

2. To make the dough: Whisk together cider vinegar and egg in a 1-cup glass measuring cup. Add enough ice water to make ⅓ cup liquid.

3. Add flour and sugar to the bowl of a food processor fitted with a metal blade. Place both sticks of butter side by side on a sheet of wax paper, cut into sixteen slices, and add to food processor. Pulse several times to form a sandy mixture. Add liquid ingredients and process until dough comes together. Remove dough from processor and knead briefly to combine. Wrap dough in plastic wrap and chill in the refrigerator 1 hour, or until firm enough to roll.

4. Divide dough in half. Return unused half to the refrigerator until needed. Roll out half of the dough on a floured sheet of wax

SWEET TOUCH ♥ We prefer using walnuts in our filling, rather than raisins, but both are delicious. If you use raisins, fill the tarts a little more than half-full because the dry raisins will absorb some of the fluid in the filling.

paper or parchment paper to a ³⁄₁₆-inch thickness. Cut 3¼-inch circles using a cookie cutter or a glass dipped in flour. Place each circle of dough in a muffin cup and top with 3 broken walnut halves or 2 teaspoons raisins. Place muffin pans in the refrigerator. Repeat with remaining dough.

5. To make the filling: Place butter in a glass bowl and microwave for 60 seconds on low until melted. Remove butter from microwave (bowl should not be hot). Add brown sugar, salt, vanilla, cider vinegar, and maple syrup and mix thoroughly. Whisk in egg.

6. Pour filling into muffin cups until they are half-full. Bake 20 minutes, or until filling bubbles and is golden. (We found we could bake one 6-cup pan and one 12-cup pan on the middle shelf of our oven at one time.) Remove muffin pans from oven. Cool 15 minutes. Run sharp knife around edges of tarts and invert onto rack while still a little warm. (Tarts release from pans more easily than muffins.) Place tarts right side up on racks and allow to continue cooling. Store loosely covered with wax paper at room temperature.

Sweet Tip

Although we used the lard called for in the dough, Valerie confided that she often substitutes vegetable shortening. We also tried it with butter. We found that the lard gave an old-world grainy texture to the pastry, but the butter, although giving an equally rich feel and taste, lent a lightness to the tarts.

THE DIFFERENCE BETWEEN CANE SYRUP AND CORN SYRUP

Cane syrup is made from sugarcane and is not the same as corn syrup. Cane syrup is not available everywhere, although it is readily found in the southern United States. Lyle's Golden Syrup is an English product you can use—if you can find it. If you can't find cane syrup, combine 2 parts corn syrup to 1 part molasses, or 1 part corn syrup to 1 part honey as a substitute.

VIRGINIA P. LIMA'S
PORTUGUESE SWEET BREAD

This living recipe is from David Lima, who often assisted his mother when she made her signature Portuguese Sweet Bread for Christmas, for Easter, and as holiday gifts for family and friends. David recalls his mother tying a large washbasin to a stool so that she could mix the dough. It was a tradition to put two shots of whiskey in the dough, pour a shot of whiskey for the baker, and make the sign of the cross over the bread.

1 cup milk

2 packages (4½ teaspoons) quick-rising yeast

½ cup water, warmed to 110°F

1 cup plus 1 tablespoon sugar, divided

5½ to 6 cups flour

½ cup butter

2 teaspoons salt

3 eggs, beaten

2 tablespoons whiskey or 1 teaspoon lemon extract

1 egg, beaten, for glaze

1. Set the oven rack in the middle position. Preheat the oven to 350°F. Coat two 9-inch cake pans with vegetable spray or butter.

2. Warm milk in microwave for 40 seconds at low. Set aside.

3. Dissolve yeast in warm water. Add 1 tablespoon of the sugar. Set in a warm place to proof, about 10 minutes. Mixture will bubble when yeast is proofed.

4. Mix 5½ cups of the flour, butter, salt, and 1 cup of the sugar in the bowl of a standing mixer fitted with the paddle attachment. Add eggs. Add yeast mixture and whiskey or lemon extract. Add up to ¾ cup milk gradually, continuing to work the dough. If dough continues to be sticky, add remaining ½ cup flour until dough firms up. Change to the dough hook and continue to knead for 5 minutes at medium speed.

5. Butter a large bowl. Place dough in bowl and turn dough so that all surfaces have a film of butter. Put in a warm place and allow to rise until double in size, about 1 hour. Punch down dough and divide in half. Shape into 2 rounds, using a little flour if necessary. Place in cake pans and let rise for 30 minutes. Make slit on top. Brush with beaten egg. Bake 40 to 45 minutes, or until crust is golden brown. Cool on rack. Slice bread with a serrated knife. Store in a plastic bag when completely cool.

Sweet Tip

To make mini-loaves (as pictured), divide dough in half and then form into six round portions each. Fit six rounds into two 9-inch prepared cake pans and bake as for loaves.

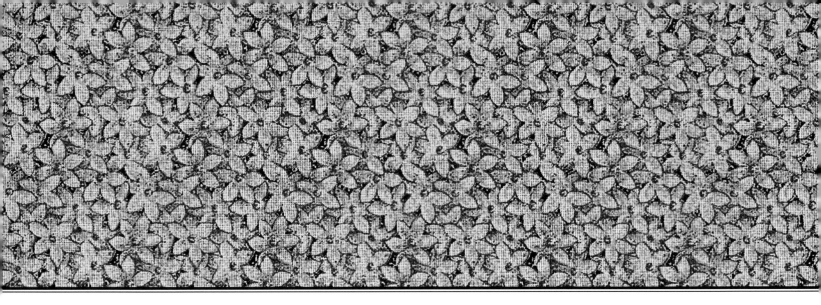

CHAPTER II

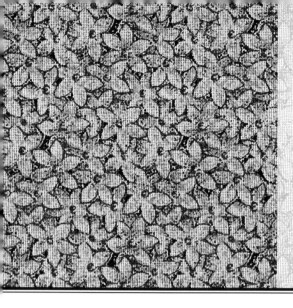

We don't really consider chocolate an indulgence. We think of it as one of life's necessities. We are quick to acknowledge the long and loving relationship we all

FOR THE LOVE OF CHOCOLATE

have with chocolate. Everyone has a chocolate history, even those who can't or won't eat it. Remembering our earliest chocolate experience, we learn that the story of chocolate is really our own personal story, whether it's our first baby bites of a bar of Hershey's Milk Chocolate or an Oreo pulled apart so we could lick the filling before munching the chocolate cookie. Because we grew up in

Massachusetts, a state with a history of candy-making, we, like so many others who were raised here, are heirs to an impeccable chocolate heritage—from the opening of the first chocolate mill in Milton, to the invention of the Toll House Cookie by Ruth Wakefield, in Whitman.

In sifting through collections of living recipes, we've found that chocolate has long been the personal language into which women have translated their best recipes. We shouldn't forget that for many years chocolate was a once-in-a-while luxury for home cooks and was used only for special occasions. Not so long ago, chocolate was simple; we used a few terms like bitter, sweet, or milk to describe the chocolate with which we baked. Now chocolate has even more nuances and is more readily available for those of us who continue to want to explore its mysteries and who want to revisit the recipes of the past. It may go by exotic foreign names or puzzle us with its percentages of cocoa butter or chocolate liquor, but in the end, it is simply chocolate.

In this chapter we pay tribute to the bakers who provided us with our early chocolate experiences. For the Katziff cousins, it was their mother Ida's Spice Cake with an unlikely, but delicious, mocha frosting. For Rachel Banks, it was the recipe for

Chocolates & Bon-bons candy book, 1924; Chocolate Candies, Walter Baker & Co., Inc. pamphlet, 1936

Handwritten recipes for Divinity Fudge and Egg Nog, 1920s

Chocolate Peanut Butter Cake, a trufflelike confection, carefully handwritten in her copy of *Laboratory Recipes*, the text she used when taking a cooking course in the early part of the twentieth century. A recipe for chocolate-covered matzo inspired the nondenominational confection Chocolate Graham Toffee Fingers, which utilized the humble graham cracker and lifted it to new heights of chocolate splendor. For Karen Johnson, it was Brown Sugar Brownies that turned her into a local celebrity; and for us, it was Mama's Chocolate Velvet Cake, served with a cold glass of milk, which resonates with our own personal chocolate memories.

Whether it's fancy or whether it's plain, there is nothing like chocolate in a cake, a cookie, a pudding, a candy, or a sauce. We don't hesitate to add cinnamon to our Mexican Devil's Food Cake, and we continue to celebrate the fraternization of chocolate with coffee, coconut, or citrus. We acknowledge chocolate has always been a good team player. As Americans, we are quick to reassure you that we revere apple pie, but we still pledge culinary allegiance to Chocolate Coconut Bread Pudding, Chocolate Graham Toffee Fingers, and Mocha Ricotta Cake with Ganache Topping.

CHOCOLATE COCONUT BREAD PUDDING

1 9 3 0 S

MAKES 20 SERVINGS

FOR CHOCOLATE GANACHE

2 cups heavy cream

16 oz. bittersweet chocolate, chopped

1 teaspoon vanilla

⅛ teaspoon salt

FOR BREAD

14 to 16 ½-inch slices brioche or white bread, trimmed of crusts and cut in half

10 tablespoons butter, melted

FOR CUSTARD

2 cups milk

2 cups heavy cream

6 eggs, beaten

1 teaspoon coconut extract

1 teaspoon vanilla

¼ teaspoon salt

1 cup sugar

7 oz. sweetened shredded coconut

This recipe reminds us of those delectable candy bars we used to purchase as young girls when we went to the movies. Clutching our candy money inside our mittens, we enjoyed our favorite chocolate-covered coconut treat while watching the big screen.

1. Set the oven rack in the middle position. Preheat the oven to 350°F. Coat a 9-inch by 13-inch ovenproof glass baking dish with vegetable spray. Set aside a larger metal baking pan and rack for the water bath.

2. To make the chocolate ganache: Heat heavy cream in heavy saucepan over medium heat, stirring with a wooden spoon until little bubbles form around the edges. Remove from heat. Add chocolate to cream, let sit 3 minutes, and then stir to combine. Add vanilla and salt and stir again. Ganache should be thick but spreadable; if it starts to harden, warm it in a glass bowl in the microwave for 30 seconds on low.

3. To prepare the bread: Brush brioche slices on both sides with melted butter.

4. To make the custard: Combine milk, heavy cream, eggs, coconut extract, vanilla, salt, and sugar in a large bowl.

5. Layer 6 slices of brioche on bottom of baking dish. Fill in spaces with extra brioche. Pour half of chocolate ganache on top of brioche layer and smooth with an offset spatula. Pour half of custard over chocolate. Sprinkle half of shredded coconut over custard. Add remaining brioche, chocolate ganache, and custard in layers, smoothing with a spatula as needed.

6. Use a knife to cut 8 slits through pudding. Cover top of pudding with plastic wrap and press down gently. Let stand 10 minutes. Remove plastic wrap and sprinkle remaining coconut on top.

7. Place baking disk on rack in large metal pan. Pour hot water from a glass measuring cup into outer pan until water level rises halfway up sides of baking dish. Place carefully in oven. Bake

approximately 65 minutes. Check water bath occasionally and add more water as needed. Do not let the water evaporate from the water bath. Cover pudding loosely with foil when the coconut starts to brown. Remove foil from pudding after 50 minutes and bake 5 minutes longer to allow coconut to crisp. Pudding is done when it looks solidified, coconut is a warm brown (do not allow coconut to burn), and tester inserted comes out clean.

8. Carefully remove baking dish from oven and water bath. Allow to cool on rack at least 1 hour. Serve pudding warm or at room temperature with slightly sweetened whipped cream. Cover cooled pudding with a paper towel and plastic wrap and store in the refrigerator.

Sweet Tips

- We baked our pudding for about 18 minutes before covering it loosely with foil because the coconut was beginning to brown.
- Pudding baking times vary because everyone's oven is different.
- Pudding should look firm on sides when done.

French Chocolate Cake with Mocha Frosting

MAKES 12 SLICES

FOR CAKE

2 oz. bitter chocolate

½ cup boiling water

2½ cups flour

1 teaspoon baking soda

1 cup butter

2 cups brown sugar

2 eggs

1½ teaspoons vanilla

½ cup buttermilk

FOR MOCHA FROSTING

1½ cups heavy cream

2 tablespoons instant coffee or espresso powder

12 oz. bittersweet or semisweet chocolate, chopped

Sweet Tip

We decorated the finished cake with coarsely chopped pecans while the frosting was still soft.

Often when browsing through our collection of living recipes, we discovered that the names of certain straightforward desserts were amended with references to foreign countries. Many recipes have the prefix of French, German, or Swiss in front of their names. Often, they are the same dessert, or a close cousin. We added mocha frosting to this cake; you can use your favorite.

1. Set the oven rack in the middle position. Preheat the oven to 350°F. Coat two 9-inch or three 7-inch metal cake pans with vegetable spray. Cut a parchment paper or wax paper liner for the bottom of each pan. Insert the liners and coat with vegetable spray. Dust pans with flour and tap out the excess.

2. To make the cake: Dissolve chocolate in boiling water and let cool.

3. Sift together flour and baking soda in a bowl.

4. Cream butter and brown sugar in the bowl of a standing mixer fitted with the paddle attachment. While the mixer is running, add eggs, one at a time, and blend in. Add chocolate mixture to batter. Add vanilla to buttermilk and combine with batter. Add sifted dry ingredients and mix well.

5. Pour batter into cake pans. Bake 40 minutes (for 3 cakes) or 50 minutes (for 2 cakes), or until a tested inserted into middle comes out clean. Set on racks and allow to cool completely.

6. To make the mocha frosting: Heat heavy cream and coffee in a saucepan on medium heat, stirring with a wooden spoon, until bubbles form around edges. Remove from heat. Pour mixture over chocolate, let sit 5 minutes, and stir to combine. Chill frosting in the refrigerator 30 minutes, stirring every 5 minutes, until it is thick enough to spread. Assemble the cake layers, spreading frosting between the layers and on the top and sides. Store loosely wrapped in wax paper in the refrigerator. Bring to room temperature half an hour before serving.

HOT FUDGE SAUCE

MAKES 2 CUPS

This Hot Fudge Sauce is easy to make and inexpensive, and it can be refrigerated and reheated in the microwave. We used this as a launching sauce for the Chocolate Fudge Pie, Chocolate Bread Pudding, and Brown Sugar Brownies with outstanding results. We also find that pooling this sauce on a plate before serving a vanilla, citrus, or coffee dessert enhances their flavors.

1 14-oz. can (1¼ cups) sweetened condensed milk

6 tablespoons butter, cut into ½-inch pieces

¼ cup heavy cream

⅛ teaspoon salt

1 teaspoon vanilla

1 oz. bitter chocolate, chopped

5 oz. semisweet baking chocolate, chopped

1. Prepare two 8-oz. glass jars with matching plastic lids.
2. Combine sweetened condensed milk, butter, heavy cream, salt, and vanilla in a heavy-bottom saucepan. Heat on medium, stirring constantly with a wooden spoon until little bubbles form around the edges.
3. Remove from heat, add bitter chocolate and semisweet chocolate, and stir until smooth.
4. Pour hot fudge sauce into glass jars and let cool. Cover with plastic lids and store in the refrigerator. Before serving, warm in microwave at 30-second intervals on low until sauce is warm enough to pour. Serve over ice cream or with cake, pie, or pudding.

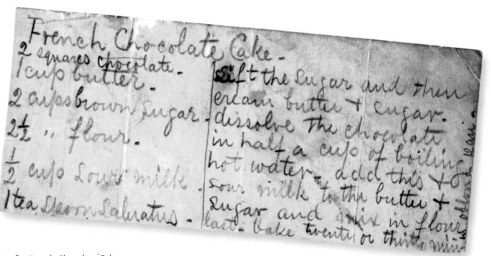

Handwritten recipe for French Chocolate Cake, 1920s

Chocolate Peanut Butter Cake

This chocolate cake comes from Rachel Bank's copy of *Laboratory Recipes*. Rachel's handwritten recipes show a strong French-Canadian influence, and we suspect that she may have traveled from her home in Maine to attend the cooking school run by the Boston YWCA. As for this cake, it reminds us of a giant chocolate–peanut butter truffle.

1. Set the oven rack in the middle position. Preheat the oven to 350°F. Cut a wax paper liner to fit the bottom of an 8-inch cake pan. Coat the pan and liner with vegetable spray. Dust pan with flour and tap out the excess.
2. To make the cake: Sift together cake flour, baking powder, and salt.
3. Cream butter, peanut butter, and sugar in the bowl of a standing mixer fitted with the paddle attachment. Add chocolate and mix well. Add sifted dry ingredients alternately with milk and vanilla and beat vigorously.
4. Pour batter into cake pan. Bake 45 minutes, or until a tester inserted into cake comes out clean. Cool on a rack.
5. To add frosting: Frost completely cooled cake with Brown Sugar Chocolate Frosting. Press peanuts into frosting on top of cake. Store loosely covered with wax paper at room temperature.

FOR CAKE

1¾ cups cake flour

1 teaspoon baking powder

¼ teaspoon salt

4 tablespoons butter

¼ cup chunky peanut butter

1 cup sugar

2 oz. bitter chocolate, melted

1 cup milk

1 teaspoon vanilla

FOR FROSTING

Brown Sugar Chocolate Frosting (see Marshmallow Fudge Brownies on page 62)

¾ cup salted peanuts

SWEET TOUCH   This cake is delicious served with whipped cream and a cup of strong black coffee.

BROWN SUGAR BROWNIES

MAKES 40 TO 50 1-INCH SQUARES

1 cup cake flour

½ teaspoon salt

1 cup cocoa (American, not Dutch-processed)

1½ cups butter

10 oz. bittersweet chocolate, chopped

2 oz. bitter chocolate, chopped

2 cups sugar, sifted

1 cup brown sugar

6 eggs

2 teaspoons vanilla

These are just one of the brownies we grew up baking and eating. We find that combining the bitter and bittersweet chocolate provides these brownies with complexity and the brown sugar helps to make them moist. We sometimes serve them as tea brownies in fluted paper cups.

1. Set the oven rack in the middle position. Heat oven to 350°F. Cover the bottom and sides of a 9-inch by 13-inch by 2-inch metal pan with foil, shiny side up. Coat the foil with butter or vegetable spray.

2. Sift together cake flour, salt, and cocoa.

3. Melt butter, bittersweet chocolate, and bitter chocolate in a large metal bowl set over a saucepan of slightly simmering water, stirring occasionally until smooth. Remove bowl from pan. Sift in sugar, add brown sugar, and whisk to combine. Blend in eggs one at a time. Stir sifted dry ingredients into batter. Add vanilla.

4. Pour batter into pan. Bake approximately 40 minutes, or until top seems firm and a tester inserted into middle comes out fairly clean. There may be a few cracks on top. Do not overbake. Cool in pan on rack to room temperature. Place pan in the refrigerator for 3 hours or overnight to chill, for easier cutting. Remove cake from pan and foil and place on a cutting surface. If you prefer, trim the edges using a wide knife or a cleaver (reserve the scraps). Cut into 1-inch squares, wiping knife or cleaver clean as needed. Store brownies in layers between sheets of wax paper in a covered tin.

SWEET TOUCH The reserved edges of brownies are wonderful mixed in with ice cream or for snacking.

MAMA'S CHOCOLATE VELVET CAKE

This was our mother's signature cake. A passionate baker, Mama was well-known for her wonderful cakes. The recipe was featured in the "Hash 'n' Homecraft" column in the Winthrop Transcript in the 1950s. Chocolate Velvet refers to the cake's delicate smooth crumb. Equally delicious with a dusting of confectioners' sugar or a generous frosting of your favorite chocolate icing, this cake is unbelievable with a glass of cold milk.

1 tablespoon lemon juice

1 cup milk

¼ teaspoon baking soda

3 oz. bitter chocolate, melted

2 tablespoons hot water

2¼ cups sifted cake flour

2½ teaspoons baking powder

1 teaspoon salt

½ cup butter

1½ cups sugar

2 eggs

1 teaspoon vanilla

Confectioners' sugar (optional)

1. Set the oven rack in the middle position. Preheat the oven to 350°F. Coat a 10-inch springform pan with vegetable spray. Cut a parchment paper or wax paper liner to fit the bottom of the pan. Insert the liner and coat with vegetable spray. Dust pan with flour and tap out the excess. (This cake can also be baked in an 8-cup Bundt pan.)

2. Add lemon juice to milk, stir, and set aside to sour, about 15 minutes.

3. Combine baking soda, chocolate, and hot water in a small bowl, stirring briskly. Let cool slightly. (The mixture will become very stiff but will combine with batter.)

4. Sift together cake flour, baking powder, and salt into a medium bowl.

5. Cream butter and sugar in the bowl of a standing mixer fitted with the paddle attachment until soft and fluffy. Add eggs, one at a time, and blend in. Add chocolate mixture and combine. Add vanilla to soured milk. Add sifted dry ingredients alternately with milk to batter.

6. Place batter in springform pan. Bake 35 minutes (45 minutes for Bundt pan), or until tester inserted into cake comes out dry. The top of cake may be slightly cracked. Place pan on rack and allow to cool 30 minutes. Run a butter knife gently around edges and remove sides of pan. When completely cool, run butter knife around bottom of pan, invert cake, and remove the wax paper liner. Place the cake on a serving plate and dust with confectioners' sugar, if desired. Store cake loosely wrapped in wax paper at room temperature.

Sweet Tip

This cake cuts easily when cooled to room temperature. Do not attempt to cut it while it is still warm, though—it will crumble.

Chocolate Lemon Cream Cheese Pound Cake

MAKES 2 LOAVES

3 tablespoons lemon juice

2 teaspoons grated lemon zest

½ teaspoon lemon oil or lemon extract

3 cups flour

1½ teaspoons salt

1½ cups butter

1 8-oz. package cream cheese

1 cup brown sugar

2 cups sugar

6 eggs, beaten

1 oz. bitter chocolate, melted and cooled

½ teaspoon vanilla

There is something very satisfying about a slice of dense rich pound cake, especially if it's flavored with chocolate and lemon. In looking through our manuscript cookbooks, we found that almost every home cook had a recipe variation for an old-fashioned pound cake because the basic ingredients—butter, sugar, and eggs—were so readily available. This recipe is special because it has the added richness of cream cheese and it produces not one, but two loaf cakes.

1. Set the oven rack in the middle position. Preheat the oven to 325°F. Prepare two 9-inch by 5-inch by 3-inch loaf pans. Cover the bottom and ends of each pan with a single strip of wax paper. Coat the pans and wax paper liners with vegetable spray.

2. Combine lemon juice, zest, and oil or extract in a small bowl.

3. Sift together flour and salt.

4. Cream butter, cream cheese, brown sugar, and sugar in the bowl of a standing mixer fitted with the paddle attachment. While the mixer is running, add eggs. Add sifted dry ingredients and combine. Transfer one fourth of the batter to another bowl and stir in chocolate and vanilla. Add the lemon mixture to the batter in the mixer bowl and beat thoroughly.

5. Fill loaf pans, starting and ending with a layer of lemon batter and alternating with heaping tablespoons of chocolate batter. Swirl a butter knife gently through the batter to form a marble effect.

6. Bake loaves approximately 1 hour 10 minutes, or until a tester inserted into middle comes out clean. Cool cakes on rack 30 minutes before removing from pans. Continue to cool completely. Cut cake with a serrated knife, using a sawing motion for about ⅛ inch and then cutting straight down. Serve dusted with confectioners' sugar or with a small scoop of vanilla ice cream. Store cakes covered with a paper towel and plastic wrap in the refrigerator.

Chocolate Tangerine Sugar Cookies

MAKES 48 SMALL COOKIES

FOR COOKIES

1¾ cups flour

½ cup cocoa

4 teaspoons baking powder

⅛ teaspoon salt

½ cup butter

1 cup sugar

1 egg

1 teaspoon tangerine oil

¼ cup orange juice

FOR TOPPING

¾ cup sugar

This recipe was originally for orange cookies. We discovered it in a manuscript cookbook purchased in western Massachusetts, near Stockbridge. We liked it so much as an orange cookie, we decided to try it with chocolate and tangerine oil to see what it would be like. Simple, unpretentious and light, this is a very smart little cookie, and the combination of chocolate and tangerine enhances it.

1. Set the oven rack in the middle position. Preheat the oven to 350°F. Cover a 14-inch by 16-inch baking sheet with foil, shiny side up. Coat the foil with vegetable spray or use silicone liner.

2. To make the cookies: Sift together flour, cocoa, baking powder, and salt.

3. Cream butter and sugar in the bowl of a standing mixer fitted with the paddle attachment. Add egg and tangerine oil and blend in. Add sifted dry ingredients alternately with orange juice.

4. Line a 1-quart bowl with plastic wrap and turn the dough into it. Chill dough for at least 2 hours, or until firm enough to form into small balls. With floured hands or wearing disposable gloves, roll teaspoons of dough into balls.

5. To add the topping: Dip bottom of a drinking glass in sugar, flatten several balls, and sprinkle additional sugar on top. Continue until all balls have been flattened and have a light coating of sugar. Place cookies on baking sheet. Bake 10 minutes, or until the bottoms of cookies are firm. Remove cookies from baking sheet and cool on rack. When completely cool, store between sheets of wax paper in a covered tin.

Sweet Tip

If you are using two baking sheets at a time, switch the top and bottom sheets in the oven, and from front to back, after the first 5 minutes to allow for even baking.

Chocolate Walnut Icebox Cookies

We found this recipe written on a sheet of notepaper pasted onto a page in a copy of *Laboratory Recipes*, owned by Rachel W. Banks. Rachel loved to write recipes on the end sheets of chapters. The address on the personalized notepaper is Grove Street in Augusta, Maine, so we have a lady on Grove Street to thank for this rich little cookie.

1. Set the oven rack in the middle position. Preheat the oven to 350°F. Cover a 14-inch by 16-inch baking sheet with foil, shiny side up. Coat the foil with vegetable spray or use a silicone liner.

2. Sift together flour, baking soda, salt, and cocoa.

3. Cream butter and brown sugar in the bowl of a standing mixer fitted with the paddle attachment. Add eggs and vanilla. Add sifted dry ingredients. Remove bowl from mixer stand and fold in walnuts. Chill dough 1 hour, or until firm enough to form rolls.

4. Remove dough from refrigerator and divide into thirds. Working on wax paper, use your hands to form each piece into a cylinder 10 inches long by 1½ to 1¾ inches wide. Wrap each cylinder in wax paper. Refrigerate 2 hours, or until firm enough to cut.

5. Cut each cylinder of dough into ¼-inch-thick disks. Set cookies on baking sheets, with no more than 20 cookies per sheet. Bake 15 minutes, or until the bottoms of the cookies are firm. Allow to cool on rack. Store between sheets of wax paper in a tin container.

3 cups sifted flour

1 teaspoon baking soda

½ teaspoon salt

¾ cup cocoa

1 cup butter, melted

2 cups brown sugar

2 eggs, beaten

1 teaspoon vanilla

1 cup walnuts, finely chopped

CHOCOLATE GRAHAM TOFFEE FINGERS

1 9 9 0 S

MAKES 40 PIECE

13 or 14 chocolate or plain graham crackers, each broken into 4 sections

1 cup butter, melted

1 cup brown sugar

8 oz. semisweet chocolate, coarsely chopped or 8 oz. semisweet chocolate chips

½ cup walnuts or pecans, toasted and coarsely chopped

2 oz. white chocolate, melted (optional)

Several years ago, Cynthia Broner gave us a recipe for chocolate-covered matzo. It was an instant success. We began experimenting with different kinds of chocolate—dark, milk, and white. We added coconut and chopped walnuts and pecans to this seasonal treat. We threw caution to the winds, and our adaptation morphed into an everyday treat: Chocolate Graham Toffee Fingers.

1. Set the oven rack in the middle position. Preheat the oven to 375°F. Cover a 9-inch by 13-inch by 1-inch jelly roll pan with foil, shiny side up, and coat with vegetable spray. Line the bottom of pan evenly with graham crackers.

2. Heat butter and brown sugar in a heavy-bottomed saucepan over medium heat, stirring constantly with a wooden spoon until mixture comes to a boil. Cook 3 more minutes, stirring constantly.

3. Pour butter mixture over graham crackers in jelly roll pan, spreading evenly with an offset spatula. Place pan in oven and bake 7 to 8 minutes, or until surface is bubbling and golden brown. Check every few minutes to make sure mixture is not burning or browning too quickly.

4. Remove pan from oven and place on rack. Sprinkle chocolate across top, let sit 5 minutes, and then spread melted chocolate with an offset spatula. Sprinkle toasted nuts across top. Drizzle white chocolate from a pastry bag over the surface. Cut into sections while still slightly warm, following the outline of the crackers. Chill in the refrigerator until set. Store between sheets of wax paper in a covered tin in refrigerator.

Sweet Tip

When doubling recipe, bake one tray at a time to avoid burning.

Mocha Ricotta Cake with Ganache Topping

1 9 3 0 S

MAKES 16 SLICES

FOR CRUST

13 graham crackers, 2½ inches by 5 inches each

¼ cup butter, melted

½ cup sugar

FOR FILLING

18 oz. full-cream artisanal or commercial ricotta cheese

1½ cups sugar

12 oz. bittersweet or semisweet chocolate, melted and cooled

4 tablespoons instant espresso powder, dissolved in 2 tablespoons hot water

1 teaspoon vanilla

1½ cups heavy cream

6 eggs

¼ cup plus 2 tablespoons flour

¼ teaspoon salt

FOR TOPPING

¾ cup heavy cream

4 teaspoons instant coffee or espresso

6 oz. bittersweet or semisweet chocolate, chopped

Pinch of salt

½ teaspoon vanilla

This recipe is an adaptation of the Lemon Cheesecake on page 232, but it's made with full-cream ricotta and espresso powder. Who would have thought that a dessert that came from a manuscript cookbook containing mostly Austrian recipes could result in a cheesecake with an Italian flavor? This gives real meaning to the term "melting pot."

1. Set the oven rack in the middle position. Preheat the oven to 350°F. Coat sides and bottom of a 9-inch springform pan with vegetable spray. Cut a parchment paper liner to fit the bottom of the pan. Add the liner and coat with vegetable spray.

2. To make the crust: Place graham crackers in the bowl of a food processor fitted with a metal blade. Pulse to make crumbs the size of cornmeal (about 1½ cups). Add butter and sugar and pulse to combine. Press crumbs on bottom and 2 inches up sides of pan. Wrap outside bottom of pan with foil.

3. To make the filling: Beat cheese in the bowl of a standing mixer fitted with the paddle attachment until smooth. Add sugar and mix well. Add chocolate and espresso mixture. Add vanilla and heavy cream. Add eggs, two at a time. Add flour and salt and combine.

4. Pour batter into springform pan. Bake 1 hour 15 minutes. Turn off oven and leave door ajar by inserting a wooden spoon between oven and door. Remove cheesecake from the oven after 45 minutes and allow to cool thoroughly on rack. Cover pan with plastic wrap and refrigerate overnight.

5. To make the topping: Heat heavy cream and coffee in a heavy saucepan over medium heat until bubbles form around the edges. Remove from heat, add chocolate, and let sit 5 minutes. Stir with a wooden spoon to combine. Stir in salt and vanilla. Cool ganache slightly and pour gently over top of cake. Store cake in the refrigerator. About 10 minutes before serving, remove cake from refrigerator, go around edge of pan with butter knife, and remove sides. Cut into serving slices.

Pictured on page 13.

MOCHA ROUNDS

MAKES 48 COOKIES

1920S

We found this recipe tucked into a manuscript cookbook full of recipes spanning the first six decades of the twentieth century. The recipes we've selected for this book were all handwritten gems, but we decided to include Mocha Rounds despite it being printed on a yellowed slip of newsprint, Regardless of its source, it represents a recipe that the owner of this collection of living recipes would have baked often until it became part of her own baking repertoire.

1. Set the oven rack in the middle position. Preheat the oven to 350°F. Cover a 14-inch by 16-inch baking sheet with foil, shiny side up. Coat the foil with vegetable spray or use silicone liner.

2. To make the cookies: Sift together flour, baking powder, and salt.

3. Cream butter and sugar in the bowl of a standing mixer fitted with the paddle attachment. Add egg and vanilla and beat well. Add coffee and chocolate. Add sifted dry ingredients and combine until dough begins to form. Turn dough onto sheet of plastic wrap. Wrap tightly and chill 1 hour, or until firm enough to roll out.

4. Place dough between 2 sheets of parchment paper or wax paper. Roll out to ⅜-inch to ¼-inch thick. Cut 1¾-inch circles using a round biscuit cutter dipped in flour. Transfer to baking sheet using a floured spatula. Combine and reroll scraps of dough to make additional cookies.

5. To add the topping: Sprinkle unbaked cookies with clear sanding sugar. Bake 12 minutes, or until the bottoms of cookies are firm. Cool in pan on a rack. Store between sheets of wax paper in a covered tin. The coffee flavor intensifies after being stored this way.

FOR COOKIES

- 1¾ cups flour
- 2 teaspoons baking powder
- ¼ teaspoon salt
- ½ cup butter
- 1 cup sugar
- 1 egg
- 1 teaspoon vanilla
- 2 tablespoons cold strong coffee
- 1½ oz. baking chocolate, melted and slightly cooled

FOR TOPPING

- ½ cup clear sanding sugar

Sweet Tip

For an even stronger coffee flavor, dissolve 2 tablespoons instant espresso in 2½ tablespoons boiling water. Cool the mixture in the refrigerator before adding it to the dough.

Milk Chocolate Sauce

MAKES APPROXIMATELY 2 CUPS

1 cup milk

1 teaspoon vanilla

1 tablespoon butter

1 teaspoon flour

½ cup sugar

⅛ teaspoon salt

2 oz. milk chocolate, melted

¼ cup heavy cream

This unassuming little sauce is another of those anonymous treasures we found while hunting for heirloom recipes. Most of the chocolate sauces we discovered were served either thick and hot or dark and syrupy. The light color and taste of this sauce is what makes it stand out among its more assertive cousins.

1. Set aside two 8-oz. glass jars with matching plastic lids.
2. Heat milk, vanilla, and butter in a heavy saucepan over medium heat, stirring with a wooden spoon. When butter is melted, add flour, sugar, salt, and chocolate. Continue stirring until mixture comes to a boil. Add heavy cream and continue to boil for 1 minute, stirring constantly. Sauce will begin to thicken, but will still be liquid.
3. Remove sauce from heat and pour into glass jars. Let cool completely. This is a thin, light sauce that will thicken slightly upon cooling. Store in the refrigerator.

SWEET TOUCH   Although this milky sauce is wonderful over a scoop of ice cream, it can also be spooned onto a plate as a base for other desserts. Heat in microwave on low in 30-second intervals, stirring between each one, to achieve the desired consistency.

IDA'S SPICE CAKE

This is the spice cake our cousins grew up eating. Into adulthood, they still talk lovingly about this modest confection. Our aunt once confided in us that she often "threw in" a tablespoon of whatever jam she had sitting in her pink refrigerator. We baked the cake from ingredients and instructions as dictated to us by Joanie Katziff Kline, Ida's daughter.

1. Set the oven rack in the middle position. Preheat the oven to 350°F. Cover the bottom and ends of a 9-inch by 5-inch by 3-inch loaf pan with a single strip of wax paper. Coat the pan and wax paper liner with vegetable spray.

2. To make the cake: Combine walnuts, raisins, cherries, and ¼ cup of the flour in a mixing bowl.

3. Sift together remaining 1¾ cups flour, baking soda, cinnamon, cloves, and salt in another mixing bowl.

4. Cream butter, sugar, and brown sugar in the bowl of a standing mixer fitted with the paddle attachment until fluffy. Add eggs, one at a time, and blend in. Add vanilla and reserved cherry juice. Add sour cream, jam, and mashed banana. Add sifted dry ingredients gradually and mix well. Fold in floured fruit and nuts.

5. Pour batter into loaf pan. Bake 1 hour, or until tester inserted into center of cake comes out clean. Cool on rack for 20 minutes and remove from pan.

6. To make the mocha frosting: Sift confectioners' sugar, cocoa, and salt into the bowl of a standing mixer fitted with the paddle attachment. Add butter and beat until smooth. Add vanilla and coffee mixture and beat until proper spreading consistency. If frosting is too stiff, add up to 2 tablespoons water as needed.

7. Frost the cake and let it rest until frosting sets. Store loosely wrapped in wax paper at room temperature.

FOR CAKE

1 cup walnuts, chopped

½ cup raisins

½ cup maraschino cherries, drained and chopped (reserve 2 tablespoons juice)

2 cups flour, divided

1 teaspoon baking soda

1 teaspoon cinnamon

½ teaspoon cloves

1 teaspoon salt

½ cup butter

½ cup sugar

½ cup brown sugar

2 eggs

1 teaspoon vanilla

½ cup sour cream

1 tablespoon apricot or ginger jam (optional)

1 ripe banana, mashed

FOR MOCHA FROSTING

3 cups confectioners' sugar

¼ cup cocoa

Pinch of salt

½ cup butter

1 teaspoon vanilla

2 tablespoons instant coffee dissolved in 2 tablespoons water

2 tablespoons water (as needed)

Sources

INGREDIENTS AND EQUIPMENT

Bob's Red Mill
Bob's Red Mill Natural Foods
Tel: 800-349-2173
Fax: 503-653-1339
www.bobsredmill.com
Flours, grains

Christina's Homemade Ice Cream, Spice & Specialty Foods
1255 Cambridge Street
Cambridge, MA 02139
Tel: 617-492-7021
Fax: 617-576-0922
Spices, extracts, flours, chocolate

Dairy Fresh Candies
57 Salem Street
Boston, MA 02113
Tel: 800-336-5536
Fax: 617-742-9828
sales@dairyfreshcandies.com
Baking supplies

Formaggio Kitchen
244 Huron Avenue
Cambridge, MA 02138
Tel: 888-212-3224
Specialty foods, baking supplies

Nordic Ware
Tel: 800-328-4310
www.nordicware.com
Baking equipment

Penzeys Spices
Tel: 800-741-7787
www.penzeys.com
Spices, extracts

Sur la Table
Tel: 800-243-0852
www.surlatable.com
Baking supplies, equipment

The Baker's Catalogue
Tel: 800-827-6836
www.bakerscatalogue.com
Grains, ingredients, equipment

Williams-Sonoma
Tel: 800-541-2233
www.williams-sonoma.com
Baking supplies, equipment

BOOK DEALERS SPECIALIZING IN COOKBOOKS AND MANUSCRIPT COOKBOOKS

Cooks Books
T & M McKirdy
34 Marine Drive
Rottingdean
Sussex BN2 7HQ UK
Tel: 44 (0)1273-302707
Fax: 44 (0)1273-301651

The Reynolds
352 Front Street
Bath, ME 04530-2749
Tel: 203-443-8812
Fax: 203-443-2638
oldeport@TTLC.net

Liz Seeber
The Old Vicarage
3 College Road
Brighton BN2 1JA UK
Tel: 44 (0)1273-684949
seeber.books@virgin.net
www.lizseeberbooks.co.uk

Bonnie Slotnick Cookbooks
163 West Tenth Street
New York, NY 10014-3116
Tel: 212-989-8962
bonnieslotnickbooks
@earthlink.net

BIBLIOGRAPHY

Kimball, Christopher. *The Best Recipe by the Editors of Cook's Illustrated Magazine.*
    Brookline: Boston Common Press, 1999.

King, Caroline. *Victorian Cakes.* Berkeley: Harris Publishing Company, Inc., 1986.

Malgieri, Nick. *Chocolate.* New York: HarperCollins Publishers, Inc., 1998.

Malgieri, Nick. *Cookies Unlimited.* New York: HarperCollins Publishers, Inc., 2000.

Nathan, Joan. *Jewish Cooking in America.* New York: Alfred A. Knopf, 1994.

Oliver, Sandra. *Saltwater Foodways: New Englanders and Their Food, at Sea and Ashore, in*
    the Nineteenth Century. Mystic: Mystic Seaport Museum, Inc., 1995.

Patten, Marguerite. *We'll Eat Again, A Collection of Recipes from the War Years.* London:
    Hamlyn Food & Drink Series, 2004.

Rodgers, Rick. *Kaffeehaus.* New York: Clarkson Potter/Publishers, 2002.

Rombauer, Irma S., and Marion Rombauer Becker. *Joy of Cooking.* Indianapolis: The
    Bobbs-Merrill Company, Inc., 1967.

Rombauer, Irma S., Marion Rombauer Becker and Ethan Becker. *The All New All*
    Purpose Joy of Cooking. New York: Scribner, 1997.

Sax, Richard. *Classic Home Desserts: A Treasury of Heirloom and Contemporary Recipes*
    From Around the World. Shelbourne: Chapters Publishing Ltd., 1994.

Tighe, Eileen, ed. *Woman's Day Encyclopedia of Cookery.* New York: Fawcett
    Publications, Inc., 1966.

ACKNOWLEDGMENTS

Writing *Heirloom Baking with the Brass Sisters* has been both a challenge and a joy, but first we had to find people who shared our vision of preserving the best recipes from America's home kitchens.

We were fortunate that J.P. Leventhal, of Black Dog & Leventhal, understood us and what we wanted to create. His knowledge and encouragement continue to be invaluable. Laura Ross and the BD&L team always made us feel found when we were lost, and Judy Pray, our editor, provided the good culinary and editorial nurturing that first-time cookbook authors always need. Susi Oberhelman, our book designer, and Andy Ryan, our photographer, have become members of our extended family. Andy always knows where the scissors are kept, and Susi knows that there is always a cup of coffee and a slice of Lemon Poppy Seed Cake waiting for her. Our copy editor, Candie Frankel, brought a fresh approach to what we wrote and helped to make it clearer and more complete. We are ever grateful for the optimism and professionalism of our publicist, Lisa Sweet.

Karen Johnson and Steve Axlerod, our agents, had the courage and foresight to recognize that two sixtyish ladies could write a cookbook that would be fun to read and use in a home kitchen. Their wisdom and guidance kept us on an even keel when the USS *Heirloom Baking* ventured onto literary seas.

Barbara, Danese, and Dan Carey and the entire Carey and McCoy Families opened their homes to us. They tasted and lovingly criticized, and adopted us. We could never have done this without sitting around their kitchen tables sharing ideas and cups of tea. They helped us view each new adventure with humor and great expectations. Special thanks to Joan Katziff Kline, whose love and long-distance advice helped to make this book what it is.

Finally, our friend, Nick Malgieri, master baker, cookbook author, and gracious host, set our culinary standard. Although classically trained, he inspired two home cooks to ask the questions, test the recipes, and write the stories that are *Heirloom Baking with the Brass Sisters*.

The following people generously gave us the encouragement and support, personal, as well as professional, that made it possible for us to write *Heirloom Baking*: Jon Abbott, Naushab Ahmed, Bonnie Asslein, Richard Band, Henry Becton, Harry Brass, Sadie Martha Brass, Kristine Cataneo, Lynn Chase, Cheever Cressy, Laurie Donnelly, Margaret Drain, Michael Enwright, Edward Ferrin, Jane Fineberg, Mandy and Fran Finizio, Ihsan and Valerie Gurdel, Barbara Haber, Jason Hinds, Anne Hosmer, Michael Jenike, Lee Joseph, Sherri and Jerry Kaplow, Kathleen our Chocolate Angel, Neal Kline, Jim Levine, Valerie Lewis, Scott Limanek, Graziella Macchetta, Liza Maugham, Larry McCargar, Jack Milan, Alexandra Myles, Dennis O'Reilly, our friends on the "L" and the WGBH Educational Foundation, Fred Prickett, Pamela Rajpal, Bev and Phil Reynolds, Leah Brass Rosenblatt, Judy Scott, Susan Sherman, Ken Shulman, Bonnie Slotnick, Michelle Tennen, Rick Tompkins, Rachel Tortorici, Kathy Walsh, Barbara Wheaton, Mary Beth Williams.

Conversion Charts

(METRIC AMOUNTS ARE THE NEAREST EQUIVALENTS)

WEIGHT

1 ounce	28 grams
¼ pound	114 grams
1 pound	454 grams
2.2 pounds	1 kilogram

VOLUME

1 teaspoon	5 milliliters
1 tablespoon	15 milliliters
⅛ cup	30 milliliters
¼ cup	60 milliliters
½ cup	120 milliliters
1 cup	240 milliliters (¼ liter)
1 pint	480 milliliters
1 quart	1 liter
1 gallon	3¾ liters

LENGTH

1 inch	2½ centimeters (25 millimeters)
12 inches	30 centimeters

OVEN TEMPERATURE

FAHRENHEIT	CENTIGRADE
212°F	100°C
225°F	107°C
250°F	121°C
275°F	135°C
300°F	149°C
325°F	163°C
350°F	177°C
375°F	191°C
400°F	204°C
425°F	218°C
450°F	232°C
475°F	246°C
500°F	260°C
525°F	274°C
550°F	288°C

SELECTED CONVERSIONS

BUTTER

1 teaspoon	5 grams
1 tablespoon	15 grams
½ cup (1 stick)	115 grams
1 cup (2 sticks)	230 grams
2 cups (4 sticks)	454 grams

FLOUR

1 teaspoon	3 grams
1 tablespoon	9 grams
1 cup	120 grams

NUTS (CHOPPED)

1 cup	155 grams

SUGAR (REGULAR GRANULATED)

1 teaspoon	5 grams
1 tablespoon	15 grams
1 cup	185 grams

CONFECTIONERS' SUGAR

1 teaspoon	4 grams
1 tablespoon	9 grams
1 cup	100 grams

INDEX

PUDDINGS AND PASTRY

Foolish Pie (Sad C...)

... sugar + 1/3 teaspoo...
... egg white. Beat...
... sugar - beat to sti...
... well buttered...
... over. Cool in...
... berries an...
2 eggs, small...

Raised Doughnuts
...solve 1 cake yeast...
...in 1 1/4 cups...
...has been...
1/2 cu...

A good Cake

Take 2 pounds of fine Flour & put into it 1 1/4
pound of white Sugar and Nutmeg six Cloves, as
much Cinnamon as will lye on a Shilling & a little
Salt, put into it also the Yolks of 10 & 7 or 8
well with a little Flower then put a pint of Ale Yest
boil, so beat them very well together, then boil a pint
of Cream & put in a pound of butter when ye Cream is
cold or bloodwarm put into it a 1/4 of a pt. 1/4 of Rose
water then mix all your Flower, & put in all
your things together, then make a hole in your Flower, & put
over with a warm dish & cover it with flower, cover it
first to rise a quarter of an hour, ye Shril very quick the
to corrupt & lay it on, you may also make it heavy, ye work it as
little as you can for fear of making it heavy, ye work it as
& put in 3 pounds of Currants well dry'd, 1 pd Raysons stand
& shred, to mix in a 1/4 of fruit very quick in ye fruit
quick Oven, & giving it liberty enough. then draw it and to its
then put it in your oven again for almost a quarter of an
hour there

... 3 cups pale rais...
1 cup cream
1 cup walnuts
Boil all quickly 3/4 of an hou...

apple fritters
...but apple into thick rings - scrap out c...
...then dip in batter & fry.

Amber Cream
3 eggs   1/4 gill cold water
1/2 oz. instantaneous gelatine   2 oz castor sugar
1/2 lemon   1 1/2 gills orange j: 1 gill milk
measure milk & sugar : sep: eggs & beat &
add yolks. stir till thick (doth saucepan good)
Dissolve gel: in the water. Stir in and the
orange & lemon juice - Beat whites to froth.
fold in & pour in glass dish & serve.

With love and all good wishes
for Christmas & New Year
from Rosamond.

apricot Cream
tin apricots   gill cream   small tin unsweet
1/2 oz. gelatine powdered -   condensed milk
apricots through sieve. Whip cond: milk &   2 tablespoon water
cream & stir into fruit. Dissolve gel: in
water over gentle heat & stir in well. Put
in mould to set.

apple delight.
4 baking apple   4 oz sugar . lemon rind
2 egg whites   3 tablespoons water.
peel, core, slice & stew apples sugar & rind
... core rind & beat till smooth
... little apple del.....

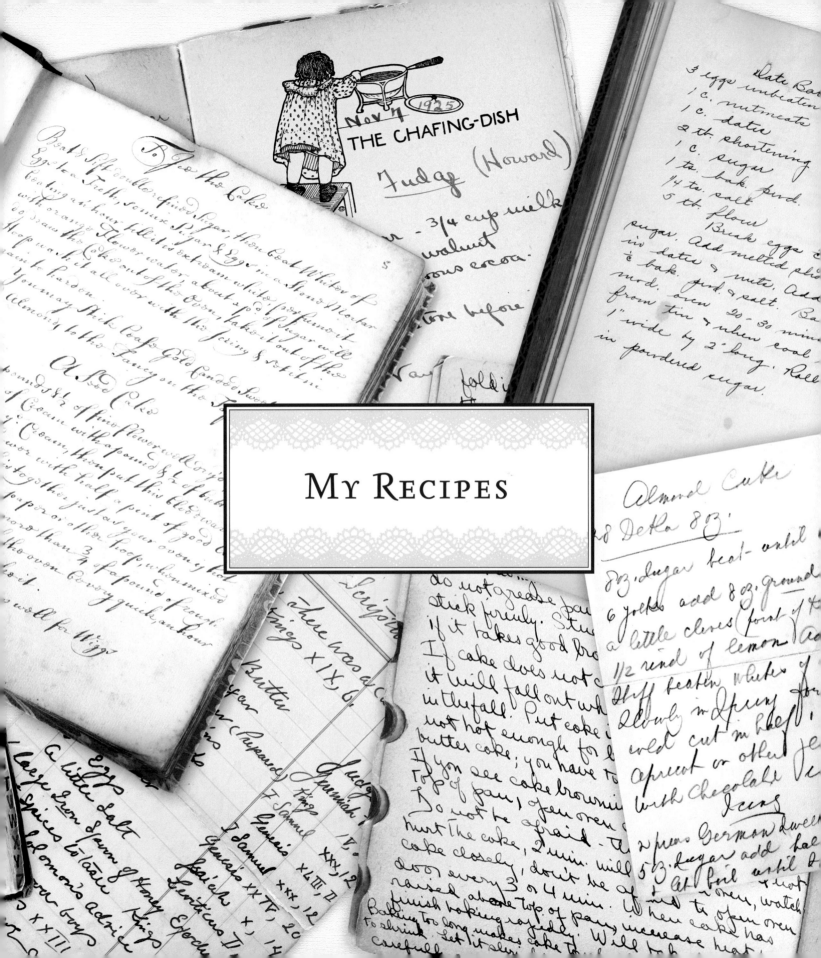

MY RECIPES

A NOTE FROM THE AUTHORS

We hope you've enjoyed reading *Heirloom Baking with the Brass Sisters* and trying the living recipes we selected from our collection of manuscript cookbooks. It's been a joy to share them with you and to share the stories we discovered when writing the book. We ask that you share with us the handwritten or oral recipes from family and friends that you've managed to preserve. We are always interested in trying new "old" recipes and learning about the people who created them. There are usually interesting stories connected to these scraps of paper and much-loved notebooks. We hope you will contact us at www.thebrasssisters.com. We'd love to hear from you.

MARILYNN BRASS AND SHEILA BRASS

— pour in mixture
or 3 hrs.
It is nicer
quite a

Stuffed Artichokes

Soak in salted water
Boil 15 min — remove and drain — set into a measuring
cup. Spread leaves apart and put about a t. of dressing.
Put on rack in a deep dish and steam about 20 min. Serve and ds.
of melted butter.

dressing

3 stalks celery
1 sm. onion
piece green pepper
1/2 clove garlic
piece of strong cheese

chop all together —
bread and soak in cold water and squeeze
1 lg T. butter } let melt together and a
1 T. water } salt + pepper and sugar. Pour hot
water and butter on and stir together.
Stuff chokes.

Take 3 slices

Irish Bread   (Mrs Powell's Irish maid, Mrs Scituate)

3 cups flour
2 cups milk
5 t Bak. pow.
1/2 cup raisins
1/2 cup currants
1 T. caraway seed
2 eggs
1 tab. Crisco

mix together and bake in 350°
oven about 1 hr. or until a
silver knife comes out clean
when you put it through the
bread.

Irish Bread

Lemon Cake Pudding

1 cup milk
1 cup sugar
tablespoon flour — or
table cake flour
and grated rind
and fold in egg
uncooked pie shell
pudding. Slow

mother

Bran Bread.

2 cup sugar.
1 " sour milk
1 teaspoon soda
1 1/2 cups m
1/2 " bran
1/2 " cor
3 teas
salt.

Dissol
sugar in
which ha
add 1 1/2
Cover + set
for 1 hour
add to
which has been
1/4 teaspoon
3 cups flour
moderately
Knead lightly
bowl. Cover +
warm place for
light, turn on flour
about one thin
Cut with small
cover + let rise
until a
Drop lighter in
which has been
rope begins to rise
hot temp. to fry

Alabama Icebox Rolls

Good

1/2 cup shortening
1/4 cup sugar
3/4 Tsp. salt
1/2 cup boiling water

1 egg, beaten
1 cake compressed yeast
1/2 cup cold water
3-3 1/2 cups flour (not sifted)

Place shortening, sugar + salt in bowl,
mix + pour over them the boiling water.
Stir until well mixed + cool. Add yeast
to cold water + dissolve. Add egg + yeast
mixture to shortening mix. Add flour
+ beat until well mixed. Turn into greased
bowl, + place in refrig. for overnight or longer,
let rise in warm place. Bake in hot oven
400° about 10 or 15 minutes.

Good

Steamed Brown Bread (Aunt Hanna)

3 cups graham flour — 1 cup sour milk
1 cup molasses — 2 eggs
2 level teaspoon soda
salt

— 3 cups
Tablespoons

add sour milk
melted shorten

vanil)

until like
enough
set 3 hours.
Grease pan

1/2 tsp sugar)

PUDDINGS AND PASTRY

Foolish Pie (Sad C...)

...ugar + 1/3 teaspoo...
...egg white. Beat...
...ugar - beat To st...
well buttered...
over. Cool in...
...d berries an...
2 eggs, small...

Doughnuts

...e Yeast

...ve and all good wishes
...Christmas & New Year
from Rosamond.

...Cream

...icols   gill cream   small tin unsweet...
...latine powdered - 2 tablespoon water   condensed milk
...ls through sieve. Whip cond: milk &
...stir into fruit. Dissolve gel: in
...over gentle heat & stir in well. Put
...mould to set.

...le delight.

...baking apple   ...op sugar - lemon rind
...egg whites   3 tablespoons water.
...core, slice & stew apples sugar & rind
...lemon rind & beat till smooth.
...little apple ...

A good Cake

Take 4 pounds of fine Flour & put into it 1½
pound of white Sugar and Nutmeg, or Cloves, as
much Cinnamon as will by on a Shilling, & a little
Salt, put into it also the Yolks of 10 Eggs Beaten very
well with a little Flower, then put a pint of Ale Yeast
to it, So beat them very well together, then boil a pint
of Cream & put in a pound of butter, when ye Cream is
cold or bloodwarm put into it a ½ pt of ap: & ½ pt of Rose
water, then make a hole in your flower, & put in all
your things together & cover it with flower, & let it stand against the
fire to rise a quarter of an hour, ye 3th it very quick, the
over with a warm dish & cloth, & let it stand against the
& put in 3 pounds of Currants well dry'd, 1 pd Raysons stoned
& shred, So mix in all ye ingredients, & when it has
little as you can for fear of making it heavy, yn work it as
paper & lay it on, you may also make a Border of paper
to compass it, giving it liberty enough, then have a
quick oven, & bake it one hour, then draw it and do it's
then put it in your oven again for almost a quarter of an
hour there

almond...

Amer...

3 cups pale nois...
1 cup cream   1 teasp...
1 cup walnuts
Boil all quickly ¾ of an ho...

Apple fritters

...but apple into thick rings - scoop out c...
...ripp dip in batter & fry.

Amber Cream

3 eggs   ¼ gill cold water
½ z. instantaneous gelatine   2z. castor sugar
½ lemon   1½ gills orange j: 1 gill milk
measure milk & sugar : cep: eggs & beat &
add yolks. stir till thick (double saucepan good)
Dissolve gel: in the water. Stir in and the
orange & lemon juice - Beat whites to path.
fold in & pour in glass dish & serve.

...

Take 3 pounds &...
...it a pint of Cream...
...molted my: Cream...
...into the flower with...
...Yest, mix this together...
...& hoop it with a paper or a...
...put into it the more than...
Carraway Comfits, if the...
...and half will bake it.
This way does well for...

...

Beat...
Eggs to...
beating a...
with an or...
do draw the...
Hoop it...
again to har...
You may...
and almond...

Take 3 pounds & ...

FORST
...UVWXY